1000 GREAT
rail-trails
A Comprehensive Directory

Help Us Keep This Directory Up to Date

Every effort has been made by the authors and editors to make this directory as accurate and useful as possible. However, many things can change after a directory is published—organizations close, phone numbers change, and so on.

We would love to hear from you concerning your experiences with this directory and how you feel it could be made better and kept up to date. While we may not be able to respond to all comments and suggestions, we'll take them to heart and share them with the authors. Please send your comments and suggestions to the following address:

The Globe Pequot Press
Reader Response/Editorial Department
P.O. Box 480
Guilford, CT 06437

Or you may e-mail us at:

editorial@GlobePequot.com

Thanks for your input.

1000 GREAT
rail-trails
A Comprehensive Directory

The Official Rails-to-Trails Conservancy Directory

Third Edition

The Globe Pequot Press

GUILFORD, CONNECTICUT

Text design by Lisa Reneson

ISBN 0–7627–2819–1

Manufactured in the United States of America
Third Edition/Second Printing

RAILS
- to -
TRAILS
CONSERVANCY

Dear Trail Enthusiast,

Welcome to a world of trails! Since 1986 the nonprofit Rails-to-Trails Conservancy (RTC) has been effectively advocating for trail-friendly policy, assisting communities with technical information and providing public education to develop former rail lines as trails.

With this third edition of *1,000 Great Rail-Trails,* Rails-to-Trails Conservancy proudly offers you a glimpse at the best in a nationwide network of more than 12,500 rail-trail miles. Trails are now open in all fifty states and, thanks to thousands of volunteers and professionals throughout America, approximately 1,200 additional trail projects are under way.

If you are looking for maps, photos and detailed narratives to guide you along the top rail-trails, visit our Web site at www.railtrails.org. While there you can become a member of Rails-to-Trails Conservancy and receive immediate benefits such as a subscription to RTC's quarterly membership magazine and discounts on guidebooks and apparel. And by supporting trails and greenways, you are helping to create healthy people and communities by making it easy and fun to get outside for exercise, transportation, and recreation.

Whether you walk, use a wheelchair, bike, skate, ride horses, or cross-country ski, enjoy the trails in our new directory.

Yours sincerely,

Keith Laughlin

Keith Laughlin
President
Rails-to-Trails Conservancy

1100 Seventeenth Street, NW
10th Floor
Washington, DC 20036
202-331-9696
Fax: 202-331-9680
www.railtrails.org

With Field Offices in California,
Florida, Michigan, Ohio,
Pennsylvania & a Northeast
Regional Office

100% Recycled Paper

1996 Recipient of Presidential Award
for Sustainable Development

Member of

Earth Share.

Rails-to-Trails Conservancy would like to thank Kara Pessoa, Ginger Smith, and Sarah Steers for their assistance in compiling the information in this book.

Contents

The Rail-Trails

Introduction

Across America there are more than 1,000 rail-trails now open for public use. With the help of this directory, you can embark upon 1,000 diverse and exciting trail adventures, such as hiking the recently completed Lake Wobegon Trail in Minnesota, bicycling through nearly a dozen tunnels on West Virginia's 60-mile North Bend Rail-Trail, hiking along the spectacular Katy Trail State Park that parallels the Missouri River and the Lewis and Clark expedition route, or riding horseback through the Badlands and rugged canyons of the Caprock Canyons Trailway in Texas.

Explore the remains of once-thriving coal mining communities by visiting the Ghost Town Trail in Pennsylvania. Trace history along the Minuteman Bikeway outside of Boston, following the route marched by British soldiers in 1776. Discover the scenic beauty of the Black Hills along South Dakota's George S. Mickelson Trails. Wander along the sparkling Susan River against a backdrop of jagged canyon cliffs on Northern California's Bizz Johnson Trail. To learn more about these trails and the others in this directory, visit www.traillink.com, Rails-to-Trails Conservancy's on-line trail directory. Whether you walk, use a wheelchair, bike, skate, ride a horse, or cross-country ski, rail-trails are for you!

Because they are built on abandoned railroad corridors, rail-trails offer gentle grades and easy access for all types of recreation enthusiasts. Reflecting the booming railroad system of yesteryear, rail-trails connect urban hubs with sprawling suburbs, traverse small towns, and stretch through state and national forests.

In 1916 the United States boasted the largest rail system in the world, with nearly 300,000 miles of steel connecting every large city and small town in a massive transportation network. Today that impressive system has shrunk to less than 145,000 miles, taking a back seat to cars, trucks, and airplanes. As more than 2,000 miles of track are abandoned each year, unused corridors (with tracks and ties removed) offer a perfect backbone for another type of transportation network and a new recreation system—rail-trails.

The rail-trail movement began in the Midwest in the mid-1960s. In 1963 the late Chicago naturalist May Theilgaard Watts wrote a letter to the editor of the *Chicago Tribune* proposing the constructive reuse of an abandoned right-of-way outside of Chicago.

"We are human beings," she wrote. "We are able to walk upright on two feet. We need a footpath. Right now, there is a chance for Chicago and its suburbs to have a footpath—a long one." She evoked images of a trail rich in maple trees with stretches of prairie open to walkers and bicyclists. This practical letter inspired thousands of citizens to undertake the twenty-year creation of the 55-mile Illinois Prairie Path, complete with hand-built bridges, prairie remnants, and wildlife-rich wetlands.

The idea spread slowly, with some of today's most well-used trails serving as cornerstones for the new movement. Wisconsin opened the Elroy Sparta Trail in 1967. Seattle cut the ribbon on the Burke-Gilman Trail in 1978. The first half of Virginia's Washington and Old Dominion Trail became available in 1981. In 1986, when the Rails-to-Trails Conservancy opened its doors and began helping communities see their dreams become reality, we knew of only one hundred open rail-trails and another ninety projects in the works. Today, 1,000 trails in all fifty states serve the public, and nearly 1,200 additional projects are under way. When completed, these rail-trails will cover 38,000 miles, or almost 90 percent of the current 43,000 miles of interstate highway.

While the Rails-to-Trails Conservancy does not promote the curtailment of railroad service or the abandonment of tracks, we work to keep abandoned rights-of-way in public ownership as trails. Also, rail-trails provide a means of preserving our nation's valuable corridor system for possible future rail use.

The invaluable benefits of rail-trails speak for themselves. When the Little Miami Scenic Trail opened in southern Ohio, wheelchair-bound Sandy Stonerock traveled to a local department store on her own for the first time ever. An Iowa couple initially opposed a trail project that spanned the length of their farm but completely changed their outlook after the trail was built. They even opened a bed-and-breakfast for trail users. An abandoned corridor between Baltimore and Annapolis was notorious for its vandals and open-air drug market until the B&A Trail turned the route into the pride of the community and the most popular park in the county's system—not to mention a model rail-trail for the rest of the nation.

The success of our movement depends on thousands of volunteers and professionals across the United States. So whatever your time allows, get involved by joining the Rails-to-Trails Conservancy. Together we will make our dream of a coast-to-coast system of rail-trails a reality.

How to Use Rail-Trails

By design, rail-trails accommodate a variety of trail users. While this is generally one of the many benefits of rail-trails, it can also lead to occasional conflict among trail users. Everyone should take responsibility to ensure trail safety and harmony by following a few simple trail etiquette guidelines.

One of the most basic rules of etiquette is, "Wheels yield to heels." Bicyclists (and in-line skaters) yield to other users; pedestrians yield to equestrians.

Generally, this means that you need to warn other users (to whom you are yielding) of your presence. If, as a bicyclist, you fail to warn a walker that you are about to pass, the walker could step in front of you, causing an accident that could have been prevented. Similarly, it is best to slow down and warn an equestrian of your presence. A horse can be startled by a bicycle, so make verbal contact with the rider and be sure it is safe to pass.

Here are some other guidelines you should follow to promote trail safety:

- Obey all trail-use rules posted at trailheads.
- Stay to the right except when passing.
- Pass slower traffic on the left. Yield to oncoming traffic when passing.
- Give a clear warning signal when passing. For example, call out, "Passing on your left."
- Always look ahead and behind when passing.
- Travel at a reasonable speed.
- Keep pets on a leash.
- Do not trespass on private property.
- Move off the trail surface when stopped to allow others to pass.
- Yield to other trail users when entering and crossing the trail.
- Do not disturb any wildlife.

How to Use This Book

At the beginning of each state, you will find a map showing the general location of each rail-trail listed in that state. The description of every rail-trail begins with the following information:

Trail name: The official name of the rail-trail is stated here.

Endpoints: This heading lists the endpoints for the entire trail, usually identified by a municipality or a nearby geographical point.

Mileage: This heading lists the total trail mileage (including mileage that is not on former railroad right-of-way).

Surface: The materials that make up the surface of the rail-trail vary from trail to trail. This heading describes the surface or surfaces you will find, ranging from asphalt to crushed stone to the significantly more rugged original railroad ballast.

Location: The county or counties through which the trail passes are stated here.

Contact: The name, address, telephone number, and e-mail and Web site address (when available) are listed here. The selected contacts are generally responsible for managing the trail and can provide additional information about the trail and its condition.

Many trail managers have maps or other descriptive brochures available free or for a small fee. Managers can answer specific questions about their trails. If a trail is not yet fully developed, the manager can provide information about which sections are presently open and usable.

Legend: Every trail also has a series of icons depicting the activities allowed on the trail.

walking, hiking, running		access to fishing	
bicycling		cross-country skiing	
mountain biking		snowmobiling	
horseback riding		wheelchair access	
in-line or roller skating			

the

rail-trails

ALABAMA

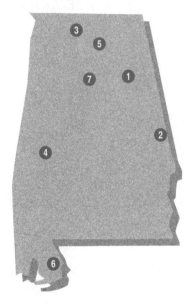

1 Chief Ladiga Trail

Endpoints: Anniston, Cleburne/Calhoun county line
Mileage: 33
Surface: asphalt, gravel

Location: Calhoun; Cleburne
Contact: Tommy Allison
Trail Manager
City of Piedmont
109 North Center Avenue
P.O. Box 112
Piedmont, AL 36272-2013
(256) 447–9007
www.calhounconews.com

2 CVR Trail

Endpoints: Shawmut, Riverview
Mileage: 7.5
Surface: asphalt

Location: Chambers
Contact: Sue Ellen Snowden
Director
City of Valley Parks and
Recreation
P.O. Box 186
Valley, AL 36854
(334) 756–5290
valpkrec@mindspring.com

3 Limestone Trails

Endpoints: Athens, Alabama state line
Mileage: 3.3
Surface: crushed stone

Location: Limestone
Contact: Richard Martin
Coordinator for Rail-Trails
Limestone County Parks and
Recreation Board
Athens Road Runners
P.O. Box 945
310 West Washington Street
Athens, AL 35612-0945
(256) 732–3379

4 Marion Walking Trail

Endpoints: Marion
Mileage: 1
Surface: asphalt

Location: Perry
Contact: Carolyn Thomas
City Clerk, City of Marion
P.O. Box 959
Marion, AL 36756-0959
(334) 683–6545

5 Monte Sano Railway Trail

Endpoints: Monte Sano, Huntsville
Mileage: 2
Surface: ballast

Location: Madison
Contact: Jill Gardner
Executive Director
Huntsville Land Trust
P.O. Box 43
Huntsville, AL 35804-0043
(205) 534–5263
www.landtrust-hsv.org
hsvland@landtrust-hsv.org

6 Robertsdale Trail

Endpoints: Robertsdale
Mileage: 2.1
Surface: concrete

Location: Baldwin
Contact: Jackie Lipscomb
City of Robertsdale
P.O. Box 429
Robertsdale, AL 36567-0429
(334) 947-7354

7 Vulcan Rail-Trail

Endpoints: Birmingham
Mileage: 2
Surface: asphalt

Location: Jefferson
Contact: William Gilchrist
City of Birmingham
2nd Floor, City Hall
710 North 20th Street
Birmingham, AL 35203-2216
(205) 254–2336

ALASKA

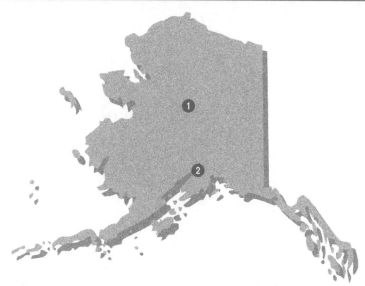

1 Chase Trail

Endpoints: Talkeetna, Clear Creek
Mileage: 14
Surface: gravel, dirt

Other use: ATVs, dog mushing
Location: Matanuska Susitna Borough
Contact: Chase Trail Service Area c/o Matanuska Susitna Borough
350 E. Dahlia Avenue
Palmer, AK 99645
(907) 745–4801

2 Tony Knowles Coastal Bicycle Trail

Endpoints: Anchorage (2nd Avenue and H Street downtown), Kincaid Park (Point Campbell)
Mileage: 11
Surface: asphalt

Location: Anchorage
Contact: Dave Gardner
Municipality of Anchorage
Department of Culture and Recreation
Parks and Beautification Division
P.O. Box 196650
Anchorage, AK 99519-6650
(907) 343–4474

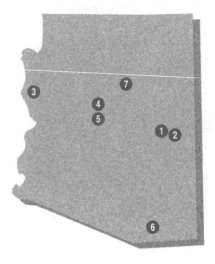

1 Apache Railroad Multi-Use Trail

Endpoints: Apache Reservation/National Forest boundary, Big Lake
Mileage: 21
Surface: crushed stone

Location: Apache
Contact: Kathy Moore
U.S. Forest Service
Springerville Ranger District
P.O. Box 760
Springerville, AZ 85938-0760
(520) 333–4372

2 Indian Springs Trail

Endpoints: Apache Sitgreaves National Forest, Springerville
Mileage: 7.5
Surface: gravel

Location: Apache
Contact: Barbara Romero
Recreation/Lands Assistant
U.S. Forest Service
Springerville Ranger District
P.O. Box 760
Springerville, AZ 85938-0760
(520) 333–4372
bromero/r3_apachesitgreaves@
fs.fed.us

3 Mohave and Milltown Railroad Trails

Endpoints: Oatman (near), Mohave Valley (near)
Mileage: 7
Surface: ballast

Other use: ATVs
Location: Mohave
Contact: Bruce Asbjorn
Outdoor Recreation Planner
BLM, Kingman Field Office
2475 Beverly Avenue
Kingman, AZ 86401
(520) 692–4400
basbjorn@az.blm.gov

4 Peavine Trails

Endpoints: Peavine Park
Mileage: 5.7
Surface: ballast, cinder

Location: Yavapai
Contact: Ron Grittman
Director, Chino Valley
Department of Public Works
P.O. Box 406
Chino Valley, AZ 86323-0406
(520) 636–2646

5 Prescott Peavine Trail

Endpoints: Highway 89A, Prescott
Mileage: 5.5
Surface: crushed stone, dirt

Location: Yavapai
Contact: Eric Smith
Trails and Open Space
City of Prescott
Prescott, AZ 86302
(520) 445–5880
esmith@ci.prescott.az.us

6 Railroad Trail

Endpoints: Patagonia/Sonoita Creek Preserve
Mileage: 1
Surface: dirt

Location: Santa Cruz
Contact: Edward Wilk
Preserve Assistant
The Nature Conservancy
P.O. Box 815
Patagonia, AZ 85624-0815
(520) 394–2400

7 University Heights to Fort Tuthill Trail

Endpoints: University Heights, Fort Tuthill (Flagstaff)
Mileage: 3
Surface: crushed stone

Location: Coconino
Contact: Paul Jones
City of Flagstaff
211 W. Aspen Avenue
Flagstaff, AZ 86001
(520) 779–7632

ARKANSAS

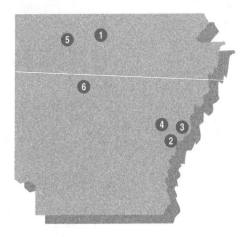

1 Big Spring Nature Trail

Endpoints: Cotter
Mileage: 2.5
Surface: crushed stone, ballast

Location: Baxter
Contact: Town of Cotter
P.O. Box 9
Cotter, AR 72626
(870) 435–6325

2 Delta Heritage Trail

Endpoints: Helena Junction
(1 mile south of Lexa), Barton (at
Lick Creek)
Mileage: 4
Surface: crushed stone

Location: Phillips
Contact: Park Superintendent
P.O. Box 193
Watson, AR 71674
(870) 644-3474
deltaheritagetrail@arkansas.com

3 Levee Walking Trail

Endpoints: Ohio Street, Missouri
Street (Helena)
Mileage: 4.7
Surface: asphalt

Location: Phillips
Contact: Sandi Ramsey
Mayor's Assistant, City of Helena
226 Perry Street
Helena, AR 72342-3338
(501) 338–9831

4 Marvell Bike Trail

Endpoints: Marvell
Mileage: 1.3
Surface: asphalt

Location: Phillips
Contact: Barbie Washburn
Administrative Assistant
City of Marvell
City Hall
P. O. Box 837
Marvell, AR 72366-0837
(501) 829–2573
Marvell@nnb.com

5 Old Railroad Trail

Endpoints: Gilbert (Buffalo
National River)
Mileage: 1.7
Surface: ballast, grass, dirt

Location: Searcy
Contact: Lowell Butts
Chief of Maintenance
Buffalo National River
P.O. Box 1173
Harrison, AR 72602-1173
(870) 741–5444
Lowell_Butts@nps.gov

6 Ozark Highlands Trail

Endpoints: Lake Fort Smith Park
across Ozark Forest, Buffalo
National River
Mileage: 174 (2.7 are rail-trail)
Surface: ballast

Location: Franklin; Johnson;
Newton; Searcy; Crawford
Contact: Joe Wallace
Recreation Staff Officer
Ozark–St. Francis N.F.
Russellville, AR 72801
(501) 968–2354

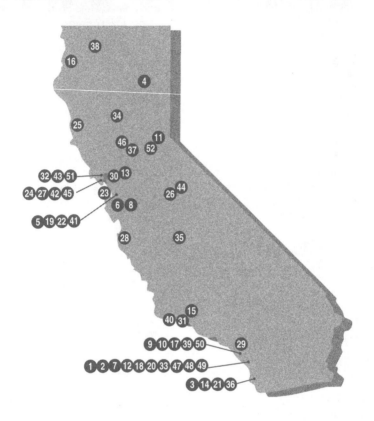

1 Alton to Bristol Bike Trail

Endpoints: Santa Ana
Mileage: 1.8
Surface: asphalt

Location: Orange
Contact: Paul Johnson
Senior Parks Supervisor
City of Santa Ana Recreation and
Community Services Agency
P.O. Box 1988 M-23

Santa Ana, CA 92702-1988
(714) 571–4211

2 Atchison, Topeka and Santa Fe Trail

Endpoints: Harvard Avenue,
Sand Canyon Avenue (Irvine)
Mileage: 3
Surface: asphalt

Location: Orange

Contact: Katie Berg
Associate Transportation Analyst
City of Irvine Department of
Public Works
P.O. Box 19575
Irvine, CA 92623-9575
(949) 724–7347

3 Bayshore Bikeway

Endpoints: Coronado, Imperial
Beach
Mileage: 9
Surface: asphalt

Location: San Diego
Contact: Joel Rizzo
Bicycle Coordinator
City of San Diego
1010 Second Avenue, Suite 800
San Diego, CA 92101
(619) 533–3110
r8h@sddpc.sannet.gov

4 Bizz Johnson Trail

Endpoints: Susanville, Westwood
Mileage: 30
Surface: gravel, ballast

Location: Lassen
Contact: Stan Bales
Outdoor Recreation Planner
Bureau of Land Management
Eagle Lake Resource Area Office
2950 Riverside Drive
Susanville, CA 96130
(530) 257–0456
sbales@ca.blm.gov
www.ca.blm.gov/eaglelake

5 Black Diamond Mines Regional Preserve RR Bed Trail

Endpoints: Black Diamond
Mines Regional Preserve
Mileage: 1
Surface: dirt

Location: Contra Costa
Contact: Steve Fiala
Trails Specialist
East Bay Regional Park District
2950 Peralta Oaks Court
P.O. Box 5381
Oakland, CA 94605-5381
(510) 544–2602, ext. 2602

6 Bol Park Bike Path

Endpoints: Palo Alto
Mileage: 1.25
Surface: asphalt

Location: Santa Clara
Contact: Gayle Likens
Senior Planner
City of Palo Alto
Transportation Division
P.O. Box 10250
Palo Alto, CA 94303-0250
(650) 329–2520
gaylelikens@city.palo-alto.ca.us

7 Bud Turner Trail

Endpoints: Laguna Lake Park at
Hermosa Drive, Euclid Street,
and Valencia Mesa Drive
(Fullerton)
Mileage: 1.84

Surface: wood chips, dirt

Location: Orange
Contact: Greg Meek
Engineering Department
303 West Commonwealth
Avenue
Fullerton, CA 92632-1710
(714) 738–6590

8 Creek Trail

Endpoints: San Jose
Mileage: 2.4
Surface: asphalt, dirt

Location: Santa Clara
Contact: Mike Will
Park Ranger
Alum Rock Park
16240 Alum Rock Avenue
San Jose, CA 95127-1307
(408) 259–5477

9 Culver City Median Bikeway

Endpoints: Culver City, Los
Angeles
Mileage: 1.4
Surface: asphalt

Location: Los Angeles
Contact: Pam Keyes
Deputy Public Works
Director/Engineer
Public Works Dept.
P.O. Box 507
Culver City, CA 90232-0507
(310) 253–6420

10 Duarte Bike Trail

Endpoints: Duarte
Mileage: 1.6
Surface: asphalt, dirt

Location: Los Angeles
Contact: Donna Georgino
Director
Duarte Parks and Recreation
1600 E. Huntington Drive
Duarte, CA 91010-2592
(626) 357–7931

11 El Dorado Trail

Endpoints: Camino, Placerville
Mileage: 4
Surface: asphalt

Location: El Dorado
Contact: John Segerdell
Chief Executive Officer
Sacramento-Placerville
Transportation Corridor
Joint Powers Authority
c/o Sacramento Regional Transit
2811 O Street
Sacramento, CA 95816

12 Electric Avenue Median Park

Endpoints: Seal Beach
Mileage: 0.5
Surface: concrete, grass

Location: Orange
Contact: Barry Curtis
Planning Assistant
City of Seal Beach
211 Eighth Street
Seal Beach, CA 90740-6305
(562) 431–2527

13 Fairfield Linear Park

Endpoints: Fairfield
Mileage: 4
Surface: asphalt, concrete

Location: Solano
Contact: Sandra Reece-Martens
Assistant Comm. Services
Director
City of Fairfield
1000 Webster Street
Fairfield, CA 94533-4883
(707) 428–7420

14 Fay Avenue Bike Path

Endpoints: San Diego, La Jolla
Mileage: 0.8
Surface: asphalt

Location: San Diego
Contact: Joel Rizzo
Bicycle Coordinator
City of San Diego
1010 Second Avenue, Suite 800
San Diego, CA 92101-4101
(619) 533–3110
r8h@sddpc.sannet.gov

15 Fillmore Trail

Endpoints: Fillmore
Mileage: 2
Surface: asphalt

Location: Ventura
Contact: Bert Rapp
City Engineer
The City of Fillmore
250 Central Avenue
Fillmore, CA 93015-1907
(805) 524–3701

16 Hammond Trail

Endpoints: McKinleyville
Mileage: 3
Surface: asphalt, crushed stone

Location: Humboldt
Contact: Bob Walsh
Parks Supervisor
Humbolt County Department of
Public Works
1106 Second Street
Eureka, CA 95501-0531
(707) 445–7652

17 Hermosa Valley Greenbelt

Endpoints: Hermosa Beach,
Manhattan Beach
Mileage: 3.7
Surface: wood chips

Location: Los Angeles
Contact: Mike Flaherty
Public Works Superintendent
City of Hermosa Beach
1315 Valley Drive
Hermosa Beach, CA 90254-3884
(310) 318–0214

18 Hoover Street Trail

Endpoints: Westminster
Mileage: 2
Surface: asphalt

Location: Orange
Contact: Dennis Koenig
Engineering Technician
City Hall–Engineering
Department
8200 Westminster Boulevard
Westminster, CA 92683-3395
(714) 898–3311

19 Iron Horse Regional Trail

Endpoints: Concord (Monument
Boulevard), Dublin/Pleasanton
BART Station
Mileage: 23.14
Surface: asphalt, concrete

Location: Alameda; Contra Costa
Contact: Steve Fiala
Trails Specialist
East Bay Regional Park District
2950 Peralta Oaks Court
P.O. Box 5381
Oakland, CA 94605-5381
(510) 544–2602, ext. 2602
www.ebparks.org

20 Juanita Cooke Greenbelt

Endpoints: Fullerton
Mileage: 3.5
Surface: wood chips, dirt

Location: Orange
Contact: Greg Meek
Engineering Department
303 West Commonwealth
Avenue
Fullerton, CA 92632-1710
(714) 738–6590

21 King Promenade Trail

Endpoints: San Diego (South
Harbor Drive)
Mileage: 1.5
Surface: asphalt

Location: San Diego
Contact: Paul Fiske
Planning and Development
City of San Diego
202 C Street, M.S. 4A
San Diego, CA 92101-4806
(619) 533–7125

22 Lafayette/Moraga Regional Trail

Endpoints: Lafayette, Moraga
Mileage: 7.6
Surface: asphalt, concrete

Location: Contra Costa
Contact: Lane Powell
Publication Coordinator
East Bay Regional Park District
2950 Peralta Oaks Court
Oakland, CA 94605
(510) 635–0135

23 Lands End Trail

Endpoints: San Francisco
Mileage: 2
Surface: crushed stone

Location: San Francisco
Contact: Don Giovanetti
Golden Gate National Recreation
Area
Fort Mason Building 201
San Francisco, CA 94123
(415) 561–4511

24 Larkspur Path

Endpoints: Corte Madera,
Larkspur
Mileage: 1
Surface: asphalt

Location: Marin
Contact: Ben Berto
Associate Planner
Town of Corte Madera
300 Tamalpais Drive
Corte Madera, CA 94925-1417
(415) 927–5064

25 MacKerricher Haul Road Trail

Endpoints: Fort Bragg, Ten Mile
River
Mileage: 7
Surface: asphalt

Location: Mendocino
Contact: Greg Picard
Superintendent
California Department of
Parks and Recreation
P.O. Box 440
Mendocino, CA 95460
(707) 937–5804
gpica@parks.ca.gov
www.mcn.org/1/10milecoastal-
trail/

26 Merced River Trail

Endpoints: Briceburg
Mileage: 8
Surface: ballast, dirt

Location: Mariposa
Contact: Jeff Horn
Outdoor Recreation Planner
Department of Interior USDI
Bureau of Land Management
63 Natoma Street
Folsom, CA 95630
(916) 985–4474
jhorn@ca.blm.gov

27 Mill Valley—Sausalito Path

Endpoints: Mill Valley, Sausalito
Mileage: 3.5
Surface: asphalt

Location: Marin
Contact: Don Dimitratos
Director
Parks, Open Space and Cultural
Services Department
Marin County Civic Center
San Rafael, CA 94903
(415) 499–6387

28 Monterey Peninsula Recreational Trail

Endpoints: Pacific Grove,
Seaside
Mileage: 7
Surface: asphalt

Location: Monterey
Contact: Tim Jenson
Program Manager
Monterey Peninsula Regional
Park District
700 West Carmel Valley Road
Carmel Valley, CA 93924-9457
(831) 659–6068
jenson@mprpcl.org
www.mprpd.org

29 Mt. Lowe Railroad Trail

Endpoints: Angeles National
Forest, Echo Mountain to Mt.
Lowe Trail Camp

Mileage: 4
Surface: ballast, dirt

Location: Los Angeles
Contact: Donald Gilliland
Supervisor
Angeles National Forest
Arroyo-Seco District
4600 Oak Grove Drive
Flint Ridge, CA 91011-3757
(818) 790–1151

30 Ohlone Greenway

Endpoints: Berkeley, Richmond
Mileage: 3.8
Surface: asphalt

Location: Alameda; Contra
Costa
Contact: Beth Bartke
Management Assistant
City of El Cerrito
10890 San Pablo Avenue
El Cerrito, CA 94530-2321
(510) 215–4382
BBARTKE@ci.el-cerrito.ca.us

31 Ojai Valley Trail

Endpoints: Libbey Park in Ojai,
Foster Park north of Ventura
Mileage: 9.5
Surface: asphalt, grass, wood
chips

Location: Ventura

Contact: Andrew Oshita
Parks Manager
GSA Parks
800 South Victoria
Ventura, CA 93009-0001
(805) 654–3945

32 Old Railroad Grade

Endpoints: Mill Valley, Mt.
Tamalpais State Park
Mileage: 9
Surface: ballast, dirt

Location: Marin
Contact: Eric McGuire
Environmental Services
Coordinator
Marin Municipal Water District
220 Nellen Avenue
Corte Madera, CA 94925-1105
(415) 924–4600

33 Pacific Electric Bicycle Trail

Endpoints: Santa Ana
Mileage: 2.1
Surface: asphalt

Location: Orange
Contact: Ron Ono
Design Manager
Recreation and Community
Services Agency
P.O. Box 1988
Santa Ana, CA 92702-1988
(714) 571–4200

34 Paradise Memorial Trailway

Endpoints: Paradise

Mileage: 5.5
Surface: asphalt

Location: Butte
Contact: Al McGreehan
Community Development
Director
Town of Paradise
5555 Skyway
Paradise, CA 95969
(916) 872–6291

35 Reedley Rail-Trail Community Parkway

Endpoints: Reedley
Mileage: 1
Surface: asphalt, crushed stone

Location: Fresno
Contact: Andrew Benelli
Public Works Director/City
Engineer
City of Reedley
1733 Ninth Street
Reedley, CA 93654
andrew.benelli@reedley.com
www.reedley.com

36 Rose Canyon Bicycle Path

Endpoints: San Diego
Mileage: 1.3
Surface: asphalt

Location: San Diego

Contact: Joel Rizzo
Bicycle Coordinator
City of San Diego
1010 Second Avenue, Suite 800
San Diego, CA 92101-4101
(619) 533–3110
r8h@sddpc.sannet.gov

37 Sacramento Northern Bike Trail

Endpoints: Sacramento, Rio Linda
Mileage: 8
Surface: asphalt

Location: Sacramento
Contact: Gayle Totton
Landscape Architecture Section
Department of Public Works
1023 J Street, Room 200
Sacramento, CA 95814
(916) 264–5540

38 Sacramento River Rail-Trail

Endpoints: Shasta Dam, near Redding (Keswick Reservoir)
Mileage: 8.2
Surface: crushed stone

Location: Shasta
Contact: Bill Coons
Bureau of Land Management
(530) 224–2157
www.ci.redding.ca.us/comsrv/parktrl/trails2

39 Santa Clara River Trail

Endpoints: Canyon Country, Newhall-Valencia (Santa Clarita)
Mileage: 8
Surface: asphalt

Location: Los Angeles
Contact: Joseph Inch
Project (Trail) Coordinator
City of Santa Clarita
23920 Valencia Boulevard
Santa Clarita, CA 91355
jinch@santa-clarita.com
www.santa-clarita.com

40 Santa Maria Valley Railroad Multi-Purpose Trail

Endpoints: YMCA at Skyway Drive, Santa Maria Country Club
Mileage: 1.2
Surface: asphalt

Location: Santa Barbara
Contact: Kirk Lindsey
Director, Community Development Department
City of Santa Maria
110 East Cook Street
planning@ci.santa-maria.ca.us
www.ci.santa-maria.ca.us

41 Shepherd Canyon Trail

Endpoints: Oakland
Mileage: 3
Surface: asphalt

Location: Alameda
Contact: Martin Matarrese
Parkland Resource Supervisor
Oakland Parks and Recreation
3590 Sanborn Drive
Oakland, CA 94602
(510) 482–7857

42 Sir Francis Drake Bikeway (Cross Marin Bike Trail)

Endpoints: Samuel P. Taylor
State Park, Lagunitas
Mileage: 6
Surface: asphalt, ballast

Location: Marin
Contact: Lanny Waggoner
State Park Ranger
Samuel P. Taylor State Park
P.O. Box 251
Lagunitas, CA 94938-0251
(415) 488–9897

43 Sonoma Bike Path

Endpoints: Sonoma
Mileage: 1.5
Surface: asphalt

Location: Sonoma
Contact: Sandra Cleisz
Assistant Planner
City of Sonoma
No. 1 The Plaza
Sonoma, CA 95476-9000

(707) 938–3794
sandra@sonomacity.org

44 Sugarpine Railway Trail (Westside Trail)

Endpoints: Twain Harte
Mileage: 16.5
Surface: gravel, dirt

Location: Tuolumne
Contact: Mike Cook
Recreation Technician
Mi-Wuk Ranger District
P.O. Box 100
Mi-Wuk Village, CA 95346-0100
(209) 586–3234

45 Tiburon Linear Park

Endpoints: Tiburon
Mileage: 3.7
Surface: asphalt

Location: Marin
Contact: Tony Iacopi
Director
Tiburon Public Works
Department
1155 Tiburon Boulevard
Tiburon, CA 94920-1550
(415) 435–7399

46 Truckee River Bike Trail

Endpoints: Tahoe City, Squaw
Valley
Mileage: 4
Surface: asphalt

Location: Placer
Contact: Cindy Gustafson
Director, Resource Development
Tahoe City P.U.D.
P.O. Box 33
Tahoe City, CA 96145-0033
(916) 538–3796, ext. 19

47 Tustin Branch Trail— Esplanade

Endpoints: Tustin
Mileage: 1
Surface: crushed stone

Location: Orange
Contact: Sherri Miller
Trails Planner
Harbors, Beaches and Parks
EMA/County of Orange
P.O. Box 4048
Santa Ana, CA 92702-4048
(714) 834–3137

48 Tustin Branch Trail— Newport Avenue

Endpoints: Tustin
Mileage: 1
Surface: asphalt

Location: Orange
Contact: Sherri Miller
Trails Planner
Harbors, Beaches and Parks
EMA/County of Orange
P.O. Box 4048
Santa Ana, CA 92702-4048
(714) 834–3137

49 Tustin Branch Trail— Wanda Road

Endpoints: Villa Park
Mileage: 0.5
Surface: asphalt

Location: Orange
Contact: James Konopka
Assoc. Environmental Planner
Caltrans
Lake Forest, CA 92630
(714) 724–2224

50 Watts Towers Crescent Greenway

Endpoints: Los Angeles
Mileage: 0.2
Surface: asphalt, crushed stone, grass, wood chips

Location: Los Angeles
Contact: Dale Royal
Project Manager
Metropolitan Transportation
Authority
P.O. Box 194
Los Angeles, CA 90053-0194
(213) 244–6456

51 West County Trail (Joe Redota Trail)

Endpoints: Sebastopol, Santa Rosa, and Granton
Mileage: 6.5
Surface: asphalt

Location: Sonoma

Contact: Mickey Karagan
Administrative Aide
Sonoma County Regional Parks
2300 County Center Drive
Suite 120-A
Santa Rosa, CA 95403-3013
(707) 527–2041
Trailnet88@aol.com
www.sonoma-county.org

52 Western States Pioneer Express Recreation Trail

Endpoints: Auburn, American River

Mileage: 100 (2.0 are rail-trail)
Surface: gravel, dirt

Location: El Dorado; Placer
Contact: Greg Wells
Trails Coordinator
California Department of Parks and Recreation
P.O. Box 3266
Auburn, CA 95604-3266
(916) 885–4527

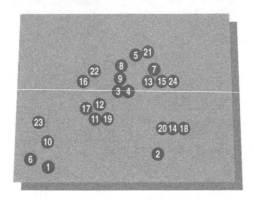

1 Animas River Trail

Endpoints: Durango
Mileage: 3
Surface: asphalt, gravel, concrete

Location: La Plata
Contact: Kathy Metz
Parks and Recreation Director
Durango Parks and Recreation Department
949 East Second Avenue
Durango, CO 81301
(970) 385–2959

2 Arkansas Riverwalk Trail

Endpoints: Cañon City
Mileage: 3.5
Surface: crushed stone

Location: Fremont
Contact: Jeff Friesner
Executive Director
Cañon City Metropolitan
Recreation and Park District
P.O. Box 947
Cañon City, CO 81215
(719) 275–1578

3 Blue River Bikeway

Endpoints: Breckenridge, Dillon Reservoir (Farmer's Corner)
Mileage: 6
Surface: asphalt

Location: Summit
Contact: Summit County
Chamber of Commerce

P.O. Box 215
Frisco, CO 80443
(800) 530–3099
info@summitchamber.org

4 Boreas Pass

Endpoints: Breckenridge, Como
Mileage: 21.7
Surface: crushed stone, gravel

Location: Summit Park
Contact: Scott Hobson
Open Space and Trails Manager
Summit County Community
Development Department
P.O. Box 68
Breckenridge, CO 80424-0068
(970) 547–0681

5 Corridor Trail

Endpoints: Lyons
Mileage: 0.8
Surface: crushed stone, ballast,
concrete

Location: Boulder
Contact: Kurt Carlson
Parks, Recreation and Cultural
Director
Town of Lyons
P.O. Box 49
Lyons, CO 80540-0049
(303) 823–6640

6 East Fork Trail

Endpoints: San Juan National
Forest
Mileage: 7.5
Surface: ballast

Location: Dolores
Contact: John Reidinger
Trails Specialist
San Juan National Forest
Dolores Ranger District
P.O. Box 210
Dolores, CO 81323-0210
(970) 882–7296

7 Fowler Trail

Endpoints: Eldorado Canyon
State Park
Mileage: 0.7
Surface: crushed stone

Location: Boulder
Contact: Tim Metzger
Park Manager
Eldorado Canyon State Park
Box B
Eldorado Springs, CO 80025
(303) 494–3943

8 Fraser River Trail

Endpoints: Fraser, Winter Park
Mileage: 6.3
Surface: asphalt

Location: Grand
Contact: Tom Russell
Director
Public Works Department
Town of Winter Park
P.O. Box 3327
Winter Park, CO 80482
(970) 726–8011

9 Frisco-Farmer's Corner Recreation Trail

Endpoints: Frisco, Dillon
Reservoir
Mileage: 2.5
Surface: asphalt

Location: Summit
Contact: Summit County
Chamber of Commerce
P.O. Box 215
Frisco, CO 80443
(800) 530–3099
info@summitchamber.org

10 Galloping Goose Trail

Endpoints: Telluride, Lizard
Head Pass
Mileage: 15
Surface: gravel, ballast

Location: San Miguel
Contact: Bill Dunkleberger
Recreation Specialist

U.S. Forest Service
Norwood Ranger District
P.O. Box 388
Norwood, CO 81423-0388
(970) 327–4261

11 Midland Bike Trail

Endpoints: Pike and San Isabel
National Forest, Buena Vista to
Trout Creek Pass
Mileage: 12
Surface: dirt

Location: Chaffee
Contact: Jeff Hyatt
Recreation Forester
Salida Ranger District
325 West Rainbow Boulevard
Salida, CO 81201-2233
(719) 539–3591

12 Mineral Belt Trail

Endpoints: Loop through
Leadville
Mileage: 12.5
Surface: asphalt

Location: Lake
Contact: Mineral Belt Trail
Committee
P.O. Box 666
Leadville, CO 80461
(719) 486–4288
www.leadvilleusa.com

13 Narrow Gauge Trail

Endpoints: Pine Valley Ranch Park
Mileage: 2
Surface: crushed stone

Location: Jefferson
Contact: Mark Hearon
Trail Planner
Jefferson County Open Space
700 Jeffco County Parkway
Suite 100
Golden, CO 80401
(303) 271–5925

14 New Santa Fe Regional Trail

Endpoints: Palmer Lake Recreation Area off County Line Road, Colorado Springs
Mileage: 15
Surface: gravel

Location: El Paso
Contact: Susan Johnson
Supervisor of Planning
El Paso County Park
2002 Creek Crossing
Colorado Springs, CO 80118
(719) 520–6992

15 Platte River Trail

Endpoints: Commerce City, Chatfield Reservoir

Mileage: 28.5
Surface: concrete, cinder

Location: Arapahoe; Adams
Contact: Chad Anderson
Trails Coordinator
Denver Parks and Recreation
945 South Huron
Denver, CO 80223-2805
(303) 698–4903

16 Rio Grande Trail

Endpoints: Aspen, Basalt (via Woody Creek)
Mileage: 17.5
Surface: asphalt, gravel

Location: Pitkin
Contact: www.trailcentral.com/
trails/Aspen_Glenwood_Vail/Rio
Grande.shtml

17 Roaring Fork Trail

Endpoints: Basalt, Woody Creek
Mileage: 12
Surface: asphalt, gravel

Other use: llamas, skateboarding
Location: Garfield, Pitkin
Contact: John Kruger
Trails Supervisor
Aspen Parks Department

130 South Galena
Aspen, CO 81611-1902
(970) 920–5120

18 Rock Island Trail

Endpoints: Falcon, Payton
Mileage: 9.5
Surface: crushed stone

Location: El Paso
Contact: Susan Johnson
Superintendent of Planning and
Resource Management
El Paso County Parks
2002 Creek Crossing
Colorado Springs, CO 80118
(719) 520–6992
sue_johnson@co.el-paso.co.us

19 Salida Trail System

Endpoints: Salida
Mileage: 7
Surface: asphalt, concrete

Location: Chaffee
Contact: Donna & John Rhoads
Chairpersons
Salida Trail System
317 West Second
P.O. Box 417
Salida, CO 81201-1613
(719) 539–6738

20 Shooks Run Trail

Endpoints: Colorado Springs
Mileage: 1.8
Surface: asphalt

Location: El Paso
Contact: Fred Mais
Design and Development
Manager
City of Colorado Springs
Parks and Recreation
P.O. Box 1575, Mail Code 1200d
Colorado Springs, CO 80901-
1575
(719) 385–6522

21 Switzerland Trail

Endpoints: Glacier Lake,
Sugarloaf Mountain
Mileage: 5.5
Surface: gravel, dirt

Location: Boulder
Contact: Brent Wheeler
Open Space Ranger
City of Boulder Open Space
66 South Cherryvale Road
Boulder, CO 80303-9717
(303) 441–4495

22 Ten Mile Canyon National Recreation Trail

Endpoints: Frisco, Vail
Mileage: 24
Surface: asphalt

Location: Summit; Eagle
Contact: Summit County
Chamber of Commerce
P.O. Box 215
Frisco, CO 80443
(800) 530–3099
info@summitchamber.org

23 Uncompahgre River Trail Bikepath—Montrose RiverWay

Endpoints: Montrose
Mileage: 4.5
Surface: concrete

Location: Montrose
Contact: Dennis Erickson
Parks Superintendent
City of Montrose
P.O. Box 790
Montrose, CO 81402-0790
(970) 240–1481

24 Union Pacific Trail

Endpoints: Thornton
Mileage: 0.5
Surface: asphalt, concrete

Location: Adams
Contact: Lynn Lathrop
Parks Supervisor
Thornton Parks and Recreation
Department
2211 Eppinger Boulevard
Thornton, CO 80229-7656
(303) 255–7875

CONNECTICUT

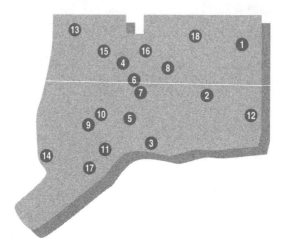

1 Airline North State Park Trail

Endpoints: Windham, Putnam
Mileage: 27
Surface: ballast, dirt

Location: Windham
Contact: John Folsom
Park Supervisor
Mashamoquet Brook State Park
147 Wolfden Drive
Pomfret Center, CT 06259
(860) 928–6121

2 Airline South State Park Trail

Endpoints: East Hampton, Windham
Mileage: 22.7

Surface: crushed stone, gravel, ballast

Location: Hartford; Middlesex; New London; Windham
Contact: William Mattioli
Trails Coordinator
Department of Environmental Protection
79 Elm Street
Hartford, CT 06106-1632
(860) 424–3202

3 Branford Trolley Trail

Endpoints: Pine Orchard, Stony Creek
Mileage: 1
Surface: crushed stone, gravel, concrete

Location: Branford (New Haven County)
Contact: John Moss
Planning and Zoning Department
P.O. Box 150
Town Hall Drive
Branford, CT 06405-0150
(203) 488–1255

4 Farmington Canal Heritage Trail

Endpoints: Avon, Farmington
Mileage: 3.25
Surface: asphalt

Location: Hartford
Contact: John McCahill
Environmental Compliance Officer
Town of Avon—Planning Department
60 West Main Street
Avon, CT 06001-3743
(860) 409–4391

5 Farmington Canal Linear State Park Trail

Endpoints: Cheshire, Hamden
Mileage: 2.9
Surface: asphalt, gravel

Location: New Haven
Contact: Bob Ceccolini
Director of Parks and Recreation

Town of Cheshire
559 South Main Street
Cheshire, CT 06410
(203) 272–2743

6 Farmington River Trail (Farmington River Fishing Access Area)

Endpoints: Farmington to Collinsville, Collinsville to Stratton Brook State Park
Mileage: 7
Surface: asphalt, crushed stone, gravel

Location: Hartford
Contact: Daniel Dickinson
Park and Forest Supervisor
State of Connecticut
Department of Environmental Protection
178 Scott Swamp Road
Farmington, CT 06032
(860) 677–1819

7 Farmington Valley Greenway

Endpoints: Farmington, Suffield
Mileage: 25
Surface: asphalt, gravel

Location: Hartford
Contact: Glenn Marston
Director Parks and Recreation
Town of Avon
60 West Main Street

Avon, CT 06001
(860) 409–4332

8 Hop River State Park Trail

Endpoints: Manchester (Taylor Street), Windham (Cards Mill Road)
Mileage: 20
Surface: ballast

Location: Hartford; Tolland
Contact: Joseph Hickey
Environmentalist
Department of Environmental Protection
79 Elm Street
Hartford, CT 06106-1632
(860) 424–3202
www.ct.gov/dot/cwp/view.asp?a=1380&q=259676

9 Larkin Bridle Trail

Endpoints: Southbury, Naugatuck
Mileage: 10.7
Surface: gravel, ballast, cinder

Location: New Haven
Contact: Tim O'Donoghue
Supervisor
Southford Falls State Park
175 Quaker Farms Road
Southbury, CT 06488-2750
(203) 264–5169

10 Middlebury Greenway

Endpoints: Rose Court, Quassy Amusement Park (Middlebury)
Mileage: 4.3
Surface: asphalt
Location: New Haven

Contact: Edward St. John
Middlebury Public Works Department
1212 Whittemore Road
P.O. Box 392
Middlebury, CT 06762

11 Monroe (Housatonic Rail-Trail)

Endpoints: Newton town line, Purdy Hill Road (Monroe)
Mileage: 4.25
Surface: crushed stone

Location: Fairfield
Contact: Ron Wallisa
Director
Monroe Parks and Recreation Department
7 Fan Hill Road, Room 213
Town Hall
Monroe, CT 06468
(203) 452–5416
www.ct.gov/dot/cup/view.asp?a=1380&q=259676

12 Moosup Valley State Park Trail

Endpoints: Moosup, Rhode Island border
Mileage: 8
Surface: ballast

Location: Windham
Contact: Scott Dawley
Park Supervisor
Pachaug State Forest
Headquarters
P.O. Box 5
Voluntown, CT 06384-0005
(860) 376–4075

13 Railroad Ramble

Endpoints: Salisbury, Lakeville
Mileage: 1
Surface: grass, dirt

Location: Litchfield
Contact: Mary Alice White
President
Salisbury Association
P.O. Box 553
24 Main Street
Salisbury, CT 06068-0553

14 Ridgefield Rail Trail

Endpoints: Ridgefield (Prospect Street), Branchville (Florida Road)
Mileage: 2.3
Surface: cinder

Location: Fairfield
Contact:www.ridgefielddems.org/news000326.html

15 Stillwater Greenway (Winsted Riverfront Recapture)

Endpoints: Winchester, Torrington
Mileage: 5
Surface: gravel

Location: Litchfield
Contact: Art Matiella
Stillwater Greenway
40 Yale Avenue
Torrington, CT 06790

16 Stratton Brook Trail

Endpoints: Simsbury, Stratton Brook State Park
Mileage: 3
Surface: asphalt, gravel, dirt

Location: Hartford
Contact: Gerard Toner
Director
Simsbury Department of Culture, Parks and Recreation
P.O. Box 495
Simsbury, CT 06070-0495
(860) 658–3255
Toner@simsbury.th.ccmail.compuserve.com

17 Trumbull Old Mine Park Trail

Endpoints: Tait Road, near Merritt Parkway (Trumbull)
Mileage: 3
Surface: grass, dirt

Location: Fairfield
Contact: Dmitri Paris
Park Superintendent
Trumbull Parks Department
Town Hall
5866 Main Street
Trumbull, CT 06611
(203) 452–5075

18 Vernon Hop River Rail-Trail

Endpoints: Rockville (Vernon Avenue), Vernon (Church Street)

Mileage: 3.8
Surface: crushed stone

Location: Tolland
Contact: Bruce Dinnie
Director
Vernon Parks and Recreation
120 South Street
Vernon, CT 06066-4404
(860) 870–3520
vernonrecreation@erols.com

DELAWARE

1 Brandywine Park Trail

Endpoints: Wilmington,
Brandywine Park
Mileage: 0.75
Surface: crushed stone

Location: New Castle
Contact: Kyle Gulbronson
Grants and Community Assistance
Delaware Division of
Parks and Recreation
89 Kings Highway
Dover, DE 19901
(302) 739–5285
k.gulbronson@state.de.us

2 Pomeroy Line Trail

Endpoints: Newark
Mileage: 2
Surface: crushed stone

Location: New Castle
Contact: Susan Moerschel
Manager
Park Resource Office
Delaware State Parks
89 Kings Highway
Dover, DE 19901-7305
(302) 739–5285
susan.moerschel@state.de.us

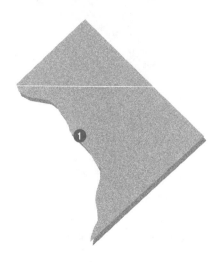

1 Capital Crescent Trail

Endpoints: Silver Spring, MD, Washington, D.C. (Georgetown)
Mileage: 12
Surface: asphalt, crushed stone

Location: Montgomery; District of Columbia
Contact: Gail Tait-Nouri
Montgomery County Bikeways
Coordinator
Department of Public Works and
Transportation
101 Monroe Street, 9th Floor
Rockville, MD 20850
(240) 777–7244
gail.nouri@co.mo.md.us
www.bikeways.info;
www.cctrail.org

FLORIDA

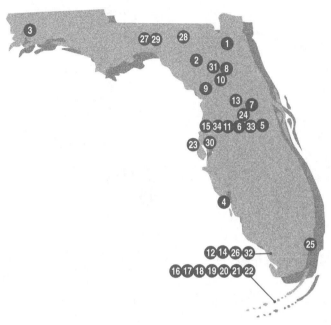

1 Baldwin to Jacksonville Trail

Endpoints: Baldwin, Jacksonville
Mileage: 14.5
Surface: asphalt

Location: Duval
Contact: Louie Jenkins Jr.
Department of Parks and
Recreation
851 North Market Street
Jacksonville, FL 32203
(904) 630–3596

2 Bell Trail

Endpoints: Bell
Mileage: 0.5
Surface: grass, dirt

Location: Gilchrist
Contact: Mark Gluckman
Consultant
Development Advisory Services,
Inc.
P.O. Box 160
Bell, FL 32619-0116
(352) 463–7185

3 Blackwater Heritage State Trail

Endpoints: Milton, Whiting
Mileage: 9
Surface: asphalt

Location: Santa Rosa
Contact: Robert Barlow
Park Manager
Blackwater River State Park
7720 Deaton Bridge Road
Holt, FL 32564-9005
(904) 983–5363
brsp_bob@erec.net
www.bikesplus.com/rails

4 Boca Grande Bike Path

Endpoints: Gasparilla Island
Mileage: 6.5
Surface: asphalt

Location: Lee
Contact: Andy Getch
Bicycle/Pedestrian Coordinator
Lee County Department of
Transportation
15 Monroe Street
Fort Myers, FL 33901-3643
(941) 479–8900
getchan@bocc.co.lee.fl.us

5 Cady Way Trail

Endpoints: Winter Park (Cady
Way Park), Orlando (Fashion
Square Mall Area)
Mileage: 3.5

Surface: asphalt

Location: Orange
Contact: Dan Gallagher
Chief Planner
City of Orlando
400 South Orange Avenue
Orlando, FL 32801-3317
(407) 246–3395
dgallagh@ci.orlando.fl.us
www.ci.orlando.fl.us/
departments/planning_and_
development/rtc.html

6 Clermont Trail

Endpoints: Clermont
Mileage: 1.14
Surface: asphalt, concrete

Location: Lake
Contact: Michael Woods
Alternative Transportation
Planner
Lake County Public Works
123 N. SInclair Avenue
Tavares, FL 32778
(352) 253–4982
mwoods@co.lake.fl.us
www.co.lake.fl.us/public.htm

7 Cross Seminole Trail

Endpoints: Winter Springs,
Oviedo
Mileage: 3.7
Surface: asphalt

Location: Seminole
Contact: Seminole County Public Works
1101 East First Street
Sanford, FL 32771
(407) 665–0311
www.co.seminole.fl.us/trails/
trails_crosssem.asp

8 Depot Avenue Rail-Trail

Endpoints: Gainesville
Mileage: 2
Surface: asphalt

Location: Alachua
Contact: Linda Dixon
Transportation Planning Analyst
City of Gainesville
Public Works Department
P.O. Box 490, MS 58
Gainsville, FL 32602-0490
(352) 334–5074
dixonlb@ci.gainesville.fl.us

9 Dixie-Levy-Gilchrest Greenway (Nature Coast Greenway)

Endpoints: Chiefland, Trenton
Mileage: 4
Surface: asphalt

Location: Dixie; Gilchrest; Levy
Contact: Manatee Springs State Park
11650 NW 115th Street
Chiefland, FL 32626
(352) 493–6738

10 Gainesville-Hawthorne State Trail

Endpoints: Hawthorne, Gainesville (Boulware Springs Park)
Mileage: 16
Surface: asphalt

Location: Alachua
Contact: Tim Vitzenty
Park Ranger
Florida DEP
Route 2, Box 41
Micanopy, FL 32667
(904) 466–3397
geotim1@aol.com

11 General James A. Van Fleet State Trail

Endpoints: Mabel, Polk City
Mileage: 29.2
Surface: asphalt

Location: Lake; Polk; Sumter
Contact: Robert Seifer
Trail Manager
Division of Parks and Recreation
12549 State Park Drive
Clermont, FL 34711-8667
(352) 394–2280
wstvft@juno.com

12 Jones Grade Trail

Endpoints: Fakahatchee Strand State Preserve

Mileage: 6
Surface: grass

Location: Collier
Contact: Mike Hart
Park Ranger
Fakahatchee Strand State
Preserve
P.O. Box 548
Copeland, FL 33926-0548
(941) 695–4593

13 Lake Minneola Scenic Trail

Endpoints: Minneola, Clermont
Mileage: 1.7
Surface: asphalt

Location: Lake
Contact: Michael Woods
Alternative Transportation
Planner
Lake County Public Works
123 N. Sinclair Avenue
Tavares, FL 32778
(352) 253–4962
mwoods@co.lake.fl.us
www.co.lake.fl.us/public.htm

14 Mud Tram Trail

Endpoints: Fakahatchee Strand
State Preserve
Mileage: 1
Surface: grass

Location: Collier
Contact: Mike Hart
Park Ranger

Fakahatchee Strand State
Preserve
P.O. Box 548
Copeland, FL 33926-0548
(941) 695–4593

15 Nature Coast Greenway

Endpoints: Cross City, Cheifland
(Cheifland High School)
Mileage: 23
Surface: asphalt

Location: Dixie; Gilchrist; Levy
Contact: www.xtalwind.net/
~kclamer/ncrec.htm

16 Overseas Heritage Trail— Channel 5 Fishing Bridge/ Pedestrian Path

Endpoints: Fiesta Key, Craig Key
Mileage: 1
Surface: asphalt

Location: Monroe
Contact: Silvia Vargas
Parks and Recreation Planner
Monroe County Planning
Department
2798 Overseas Highway
Suite 410
Marathon, FL 33050-4277
(305) 289–2500

17 Overseas Heritage Trail– Cudjoe Key Pedestrian Path

Endpoints: Cudjoe Key
Mileage: 2
Surface: asphalt, dirt

Location: Monroe
Contact: Silvia Vargas
Parks and Recreation Planner
Monroe County Planning
Department
2798 Overseas Highway
Suite 410
Marathon, FL 33050-4277
(305) 289–2500

18 Overseas Heritage Trail– Long Key to Conch Key

Endpoints: Long Key, Conch Key
Mileage: 2.3
Surface: asphalt

Location: Monroe
Contact: Silvia Vargas
Parks and Recreation Planner
Monroe County Planning
Department
2798 Overseas Highway
Suite 410
Marathon, FL 33050-4277
(305) 289–2500

19 Overseas Heritage Trail– Lower Matecumbe Boardwalk

Endpoints: Lower Matecumbe
Key
Mileage: 4.4

Surface: asphalt

Location: Monroe
Contact: Silvia Vargas
Parks and Recreation Planner
Monroe County Planning
Department
2798 Overseas Highway
Suite 410
Marathon, FL 33050-4277
(305) 289–2500

20 Overseas Heritage Trail– Marathon Key to Pigeon Key Bridge

Endpoints: Marathon Key,
Pigeon Key
Mileage: 2.3
Surface: asphalt

Location: Monroe
Contact: Silvia Vargas
Parks and Recreation Planner
Monroe County Planning
Department
2798 Overseas Highway
Suite 410
Marathon, FL 33050-4277
(305) 289–2500

21 Overseas Heritage Trail– Missouri Key to Ohio Key

Endpoints: Missouri Key, Ohio
Key
Mileage: 0.5
Surface: asphalt

Location: Monroe
Contact: Silvia Vargas

Parks and Recreation Planner
Monroe County Planning
Department
2798 Overseas Highway
Suite 410
Marathon, FL 33050-4277
(305) 289–2500

22 Overseas Heritage Trail– Tom's Harbor Walkway

Endpoints: Grass Key, Walker's Island
Mileage: 5
Surface: asphalt, dirt

Location: Monroe
Contact: Silvia Vargas
Parks and Recreation Planner
Monroe County Planning
Department
2798 Overseas Highway
Suite 410
Marathon, FL 33050-4277
(305) 289–2500

23 Pinellas Trail

Endpoints: St. Petersburg, Tarpon Springs
Mileage: 34
Surface: asphalt

Location: Pinellas
Contact: Brian Smith
Executive Director
Pinellas County Planning
Department
14 South Ft. Harrison Avenue
Clearwater, FL 33756
(813) 464–4751
bsmith@co.pinellas.fl.us
www.co.pinellas.fl.us/mpo

24 Seminole Wekiva Trail

Endpoints: SR 436, SR 434
(Altamonte Springs)
Mileage: 2.2
Surface: asphalt

Location: Seminole
Contact: www.co.seminole.fl.us/
growth/pubwrks/trails/trails_
semwekiva.asp

25 South Dade Trail

Endpoints: South Dade, Kendall
Mileage: 18.4
Surface: asphalt

Location: Miami–Dade
Contact: Jeffrey Hunter
Bicycle/Pedestrian Coordinator
Miami Dade County MPO
111 NW First Street, Suite 910
Miami, FL 33128-1999
(305) 375–1647
jhunter@co.miami-dade.fl.us

26 South Main Trail

Endpoints: Fakahatchee Strand State Preserve
Mileage: 3
Surface: crushed stone, grass

Location: Collier
Contact: Greg Toppin
Fakahatchee Strand State Preserve

P.O. Box 548
Copeland, FL 34137
(941) 694–4593
fssp@mindspring.com
www.floridastatepark

27 Stadium Drive Bikepath

Endpoints: Tallahassee
Mileage: 1.5
Surface: asphalt

Location: Leon
Contact: Gregory Wilson
Bike/Ped Coordinator
Tallahassee Traffic Engineering
Division
City Hall
300 S. Adams Street
Tallahassee, FL 32301-1731
(904) 891–8090
wilsonG@ch.ci.tlh.fl.us

28 Suwannee River Greenway

Endpoints: Branford, Little River
Springs
Mileage: 8
Surface: asphalt, grass, dirt

Location: Suwannee
Contact: Eddy Hillhouse
President
Suwannee County Chamber of
Commerce
P.O. Drawer C
Live Oak, FL 32060
(904) 362–3071

29 Tallahassee–St. Marks Historic Railroad State Trail

Endpoints: Tallahassee, St. Marks
Mileage: 18.5
Surface: asphalt

Location: Wakulla; Leon
Contact: Wes Smith
Park Manager
Division of Parks and Recreation
Florida DNR, Environmental
Protection Department
1022 Desoto Park Drive
Tallahassee, FL 32301-4555
(904) 922–6007
www.dep.state.fl.us:80/parks/big-
bend/stmarks.html

30 Upper Tampa Bay Trail

Endpoints: Citrus Park
Mileage: 4
Surface: asphalt

Location: Hillsborough
Contact: Tina Russo
Senior Park Manager
Hillsborough County Parks and
Recreation Department
7508 Ehrlich Road
Tampa, FL 33625
(813) 264–8511
tarusso@aol.com

31 Waldo Road Trail

Endpoints: Gainesville
Mileage: 3
Surface: asphalt

Location: Alachua
Contact: Linda Dixon
Transportation Planning Analyst
City of Gainesville Department of
Public Works
P.O. Box 490, MS 58
Gainesville, FL 32602-0490
(352) 334–5074
dixonlb@ci.gainsville.fl.us

32 West Main Trail

Endpoints: Fakahatchee Strand
State Preserve
Mileage: 3
Surface: grass

Location: Collier
Contact: Mike Hart
Park Ranger
Fakahatchee Strand State
Preserve
P.O. Box 548
Copeland, FL 33926-0548
(941) 695–4593

33 West Orange Trail

Endpoints: Apopka,
Orange/Lake county line
Mileage: 22
Surface: asphalt, concrete, dirt,
wood chips

Location: Orange
Contact: Tim Bucher
Orange County Parks and
Recreation
501 Crown Point Crossroad
Winter Garden, FL 34787
(407) 654–1108

34 Withlacoochee State Trail

Endpoints: Citrus Springs, Trilby
Mileage: 46
Surface: asphalt

Location: Citrus; Hernando;
Pasco
Contact: Robert Seifer
Trail Manager
Florida Division of
Recreation and Parks
12549 State Park Drive
Clermont, FL 34711-8667
(352) 394–2280

GEORGIA

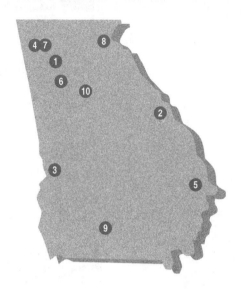

1 Allatoona Pass

Endpoints: Cartersville (Lake Allatoona Area)
Mileage: 2.1
Surface: crushed stone

Location: Bartow
Contact: www.georgiatrails.com/trails/allatoona.html

2 Augusta Canal Trail

Endpoints: Headgates, Turning Basin
Mileage: 7
Surface: dirt

Location: Richmond
Contact: Thomas Robertson
Augusta Canal Authority
P.O. Drawer 2367
Augusta, GA 30903
(706) 722–1071

3 Chattahoochee Trail

Endpoints: Bibb City through downtown Columbus, Ft. Benning
Mileage: 22
Surface: asphalt

Location: Muscogee
Contact: Richard Bishop
Director
Columbus Parks and Recreation
Department

P.O. Box 1340
Columbus, GA 31902-1340
(706) 653–4175
www.visitcolumbusga.com/
see_desc.shtml

4 Heritage Park Trail

Endpoints: Rome
Mileage: 6
Surface: asphalt, grass

Other use: skateboarding
Location: Floyd
Contact: Tim Banks
Assistant Director
Rome-Floyd Parks and
Recreation Authority
300 West Third Street
Rome, GA 30165-2803
(706) 291–0766
rfprp@rfpa.com

5 McQueens's Island Historic Trail (Old Savannah–Tybee Rail-Trail)

Endpoints: Savannah,
McQueen's Island
Mileage: 6
Surface: asphalt

Location: Chatham
Contact: Jim Golden
Director
Chatham County Parks,
Recreation and Cultural Affairs
P.O. Box 1746
Savannah, GA 31402-1746
(912) 652–6785

6 Silver Comet Trail

Endpoints: Smyrna, Rockmart
Mileage: 37
Surface: asphalt, concrete

Location: Cobb; Paulding; Polk
Contact: Shawn Callahan
PATH Foundation
P.O. Box 14327
Atlanta, GA 30324
(404) 875–7284
www.pathfoundation.org

7 Simms Mountain Trail (Pinhoti Trail)

Endpoints: Lavender, Armuchee
Mileage: 4.5
Surface: cinder

Location: Chattooga; Floyd
Contact: Tim Banks
Assistant Director
Rome-Floyd Parks and
Recreation Authority
300 West Third Street
Rome, GA 30165-2803
(706) 291–0766
TBank@fc.peachnet. edu

8 Tallulah Falls Rail-Trail – Short Line Trail

Endpoints: Tallulah Gorge State
Park
Mileage: 3
Surface: asphalt

Location: Habersham, Rabun
Contact: Tallulah Gorge State
Park
P.O. Box 248
Tallulah Falls, GA 30573
(706) 754–7970

9 Tom "Babe" White Linear Park

Endpoints: Lower Meigs Road,
Municipal Airport (Moultrie)
Mileage: 5.2
Surface: asphalt

Location: Colquitt
Contact: Rick Gehle
Director
Moultrie-Colquitt Co. Parks and
Recreation
P.O. Box 3368
Moultrie, GA 31776
(912) 890–5428

10 Trolley Trail

Endpoints: Atlanta (the King
Center downtown), Decatur
(Agnes Scott College)
Mileage: 7
Surface: asphalt, concrete

Location: Dekalb; Fulton
Contact: Alycen Whidden
Assistant
Atlanta City Hall Bureau of
Planning
68 Mitchell Street, SW
Suite 3350
Atlanta, GA 30335
(404) 330–6145

1 Kapa'a Bike Path

Endpoints: Kauai
Mileage: 2
Surface: asphalt

Location: Kauai
Contact: Mel Nishihara
Kauai County Parks and
Recreation
4444 Rice Street, Suite 150
Lihue, HI 96766
(808) 241–6670

2 Pearl Harbor Bike Path

Endpoints: Ewa, Pearl Harbor
Mileage: 10
Surface: asphalt

Location: Honolulu
Contact: Michael Medeiros
Bike/Ped Coordinator
Department of Transportation
HWY-T
601 Kamokila Boulevard,
Room 602
Kapolei, HI 96707
(808) 692–7675

IDAHO

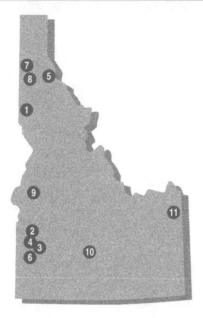

1 Bill Chapman Palouse Trail

Endpoints: Pullman, WA (Bishop Boulevard), Moscow, ID
Mileage: 7.5
Surface: asphalt

Location: Whitman, Latah
Contact: Roger Marcus
Whitman County Parks
310 North Main Street
Colfax, WA 99111
(509) 397–6238
ranger@co.whitman.wa.us
www.whitmancounty.org/parks/
index_pages/the_bcpt.htm

2 Boise River Greenbelt

Endpoints: Boise
Mileage: 12
Surface: asphalt

Location: Ada
Contact: www.ci.boise.id.us/
parks/parks_facilities/greenbelt_
features.shtml

3 Greenbelt Trail

Endpoints: Lucky Peak Reservoir, Boise
Mileage: 12

Surface: asphalt

Location: Ada
Contact: Donna Griffin
Parks & Waterways Director
Ada County Parks and Waterways
4049 South Eckert Road
Boise, ID 83706-5721
(208) 343–1328

4 Indian Creek Pathway

Endpoints: Swam Falls Road,
Sego Prarie Park (Kuna)
Mileage: 3.5
Surface: asphalt, grass

Other use: Skateboard parks
Location: Ada
Contact: Jim Taylor
Supervisor
City of Kuna Public Works
P.O. Box 13
Kuna, ID 83634
(208) 922–3397

5 Mullan Pass—Lookout Pass Loop (Route of the Hiawatha)

Endpoints: Lookout Pass, Mullan
Mileage: 13
Surface: ballast

Other use: ATVs
Location: Shoshone
Contact: Jaime Schmidt
Idaho Panhandle National Forest
Avery Ranger Station
HC Box 1
Avery, ID 83802
(208) 245–4517

6 Nampa to Stoddard Trail

Endpoints: Nampa, Stoddard
Mileage: 1.5
Surface: gravel

Location: Ada; Canyon
Contact: Alan Caba
Parks and Recreation Director
411 Third Street South
Nampa, ID 83651-3721
(208) 465–2220

7 North Idaho Centennial Trail

Endpoints: Coeur d'Alene, Idaho
state line
Mileage: 18
Surface: asphalt

Location: Kootenai
Contact: Sheryl Ward
Administrative Supervisor
Kootenai County Commissioner
P.O. Box 9000
Coeur d'Alene, ID 83816-9000
(208) 769–4450
kcbbcc@kootenai.co.id.us

8 Trail of the Coeur d'Alenes

Endpoints: Plummer, Mullan (via Harrison and Wallace)
Mileage: 72
Surface: asphalt

Location: Benewah; Kootenai; Shoshone
Contact: Jack Gunderman
Trail Manager
Coeur d'Alene Tribe
(208) 686–1118
wallace-id.com/CdA_trail/

9 Weiser River Trail

Endpoints: Weiser, Mesa Siding (near Council)
Mileage: 60
Surface: gravel, ballast

Location: Adams; Washington
Contact: Dick Pugh
Friends of the Weiser River Trail
2165 Seid Creek Road
Cambridge, ID 83610-5019
pugh@cyberhighway.com
weiserrivertrail.org

10 Wood River Trails

Endpoints: Ketchum, Bellevue
Mileage: 22
Surface: asphalt

Location: Blaine
Contact: Mary Austin Crofts
Director
Blaine County Recreation District
308 North Main Street
Hailey, ID 83333
(208) 788–2117
www.bcrd.org

11 Yellowstone Branch Line Trail

Endpoints: Warm River, Montana state line
Mileage: 34
Surface: ballast

Location: Fremont
Contact: Bart Andreasen
Landscape Architect
420 North Bridge Street
P.O. Box 208
St. Anthony, ID 83445-1425
(208) 624–3151

ILLINOIS

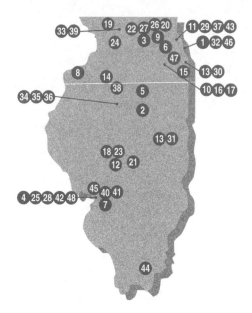

1 Burnham Greenway

Endpoints: 106th Street, William Powers Conservation Area; 142nd Street, Little Calumet River
Mileage: 4
Surface: asphalt

Location: Cook
Contact: Calumet-Memorial Park District
P.O. Box 1158
626 Wentworth Avenue
Calumet City, IL 60409
(708) 868–2530

2 Constitution Trail

Endpoints: Bloomington, Normal
Mileage: 13.5
Surface: asphalt

Location: McLean
Contact: Keith Rich
Director
Bloomington Parks and Recreation Department
109 East Olive Street
Bloomington, IL 61701-5219
(309) 823–4260
www.b-n.com/pages/
bsConsttrail.html

3 DeKalb Nature Trail

Endpoints: DeKalb
Mileage: 1.3
Surface: asphalt

Location: DeKalb
Contact: Terry Hannan
Superintendent
DeKalb County Forest Preserve
110 East Sycamore Street
Sycamore, IL 60178-1448
(815) 895–7191

4 Delyte Morris Trail

Endpoints: Edwardsville
(Southern Illinois University),
Madison
Mileage: 2.8
Surface: asphalt

Location: Madison
Contact: Anna Schonlau
Southern Illinois University at
Edwardsville
Recreation Department
P.O. Box 1157
Edwardsville, IL 62026
(618) 650–3235
aschonl@siue.edu
www.mct.org/bikeways/

5 El Paso Walking Trail

Endpoints: El Paso
Mileage: 5
Surface: crushed stone

Location: Woodford
Contact: Ted Gresham
City Administrator
Town of El Paso
475 West Front Street
El Paso, IL 61738-1422
(309) 527–4005
dfever@elpaso.net

6 Fox River Trail

Endpoints: Aurora, Crystal Lake
Mileage: 35
Surface: asphalt

Location: Kane; McHenry
Contact: William Donnell
Landscape Architect
Fox Valley Park District
712 S. River Street
Aurora, IL 60506-5911
(708) 897–0516

7 Glen Carbon Heritage Bike Trail

Endpoints: Meridian and West Main Street, Kuhn Station Road (Glen Carbon)
Mileage: 6.7
Surface: asphalt, gravel

Location: Madison
Contact: Village of Glen Carbon
151 North Main Street
Glen Carbon, IL 62034-0757
(618) 288–1200
www.glen-carbon.il.us/
Recreation/bike.htm

8 Great River Trail

Endpoints: Rock Island, Savanna
Mileage: 28
Surface: asphalt, crushed stone

Location: Rock Island; Whiteside; Carroll
Contact: Patrick Marsh
Bikeway Coordinator
Bi-State Regional Commission
1504 Third Avenue
Rock Island, IL 61201-8646
(309) 793–6300

9 Great Western Trail

Endpoints: St. Charles, Sycamore
Mileage: 17
Surface: asphalt, crushed stone

Location: Kane; DeKalb
Contact: Jon Duerr
Director of Field Services
Kane County Forest Preserve
719 Batavia Avenue
Geneva, IL 60134-3077
(708) 232–5981

10 Great Western Trail (DuPage Parkway Section)

Endpoints: Villa Park, West Chicago
Mileage: 12
Surface: crushed stone

Location: DuPage
Contact: Ruth Krupensky
Principal Planner
DuPage County DOT
130 North County Farm Road
Wheaton, IL 60187-3957
(603) 682–7318

11 Green Bay Trail

Endpoints: Highland Park, Wilmette
Mileage: 9.5
Surface: asphalt, crushed stone

Location: Lake; Cook
Contact: Bill Lambrecht
Superintendent of Parks/Planning
Wilmette Park District
3555 Lake Avenue
Wilmette, IL 60091-1016
(847) 256–6100
blambrecht@wilpark.org

12 Green Diamond Rail Trail

Endpoints: Farmersville, Waggoner
Mileage: 4
Surface: asphalt

Location: Montgomery
Contact: www.montgomeryco.com/outdoors.htm#biketrail

13 Heartland Pathways

Endpoints: Seymour, Clinton and Cisco
Mileage: 33
Surface: ballast

Other use: ATVs

Location: Champaign; De Witt; Piatt
Contact: David Monk
President
Heartland Pathways
115 North Market Street
Champaign, IL 61820-4004

14 Hennepin Canal Parkway

Endpoints: Atkinson, Rock Falls
Mileage: 96
Surface: grass

Location: Bureau; Henry; Lee; Whiteside
Contact: Steve Moser
Site Superintendent
Illinois Department of Natural Resources
Hennepin Canal Parkway
RR 2, Box 201
Sheffield, IL 61361-9571
(815) 454–2328

15 Illinois & Michigan Canal NHC

Endpoints: Joliet, La Salle
Mileage: 68.5
Surface: asphalt, gravel

Location: DuPage; Grundy; La Salle; Will
Contact: Vincent Michael
Associate Director
Canal Corridor Association
220 South State Street
Suite 1880
Chicago, IL 60604-2001
(312) 427–3688

16 Illinois Prairie Path

Endpoints: Maywood to Wheaton, spurs to Aurora, Batavia, Elgin, and Geneva
Mileage: 55
Surface: crushed stone, dirt

Location: Cook; DuPage; Kane
Contact: Ruth Krupensky
Principal Planner
DuPage County DOT
130 N. County Farm Road
Wheaton, IL 60187-3997
(630) 682-7318
www.mcs.net/~msc/IPP/

17 Illinois Prairie Path— Geneva Branch

Endpoints: Geneva, West Chicago
Mileage: 9
Surface: crushed stone

Location: DuPage; Kane
Contact: Ruth Krupensky
Principal Planner
130 North County Farm Road
Wheaton, IL 60187-3997
(630) 682-7318
www.mcs.net/~msc/IPP/

18 Interurban Trail

Endpoints: Wabash Avenue and MacArthur Boulevard, Woodside Road (Springfield)
Mileage: 3

Surface: asphalt

Location: Sangamon
Contact: City of Springfield
300 South 7th Street
Springfield, IL 62701
(217) 789-2000

19 Jane Addams Trail

Endpoints: Freeport (Fairview Road), Illinois/Wisconsin state line
Mileage: 17
Surface: crushed stone

Location: Stephenson
Contact: Steve Ehlbeck
Superintendant of Parks; Chairman
Freeport Park District; Jane Addams Trail Commission
1200 Park Lane Drive
Freeport, IL 61032
(815) 235-6114
frprtparks@aol.com

20 Libertyville Trail

Endpoints: Libertyville
Mileage: 3
Surface: crushed stone

Location: Lake
Contact: Steve Magnusen
Director of Public Works
Town of Libertyville
200 East Cook Avenue
Libertyville, IL 60048-2090
(708) 362-2430

21 Lincoln Prairie Trail

Endpoints: Pana, Taylorville
Mileage: 14.8
Surface: asphalt

Location: Christian
Contact: Jim Deere
Office of Community
Development
120 East 3rd Street
Pana, IL 62557
(217) 562–3109
panail@mcleodusa.net

22 Long Prairie Trail

Endpoints: Winnebago county
line, McHenry county line
Mileage: 14.6
Surface: asphalt

Location: Boone
Contact: John Kremer
Executive Director
Boone County Conservation
District
7600 Appleton Road
Belvidere, IL 61008-3076
(815) 547–7935

23 Lost Bridge Trail

Endpoints: Rochester
Mileage: 5
Surface: asphalt

Location: Sangamon
Contact: Linda Shaw
Village Manager
Village of Rochester
P.O. Box 618
Rochester, IL 62563
(217) 498–7192
lindas@rpls.lib.il.us

24 Lowell Parkway Bicycle Path

Endpoints: Dixon, Lowell Park
Mileage: 3.5
Surface: asphalt, wood chips

Location: Lee
Contact: Dave Zinnen
Director of Administration and
Recreation
Dixon Park District
804 Palmyra Avenue
Dixon, IL 61021-1960
(815) 284–3306

25 Madison County Transit Nature Trail

Endpoints: Edwardsville (IL 159
and Longfellow Street), Pontoon
Beach (Lake Drive)
Mileage: 10
Surface: asphalt

Location: Madison
Contact: Joe Wright
Director of Marketing
RideFinders and Madison County
Transit
One Transit Way
Granite City, IL 62040
(618) 874–7433
jwright@mct.org
www.mcttrails.org/NatureTrail.html

26 McHenry County Prairie Trail

Endpoints: Kane county line, Wisconsin state line
Mileage: 25
Surface: asphalt, ballast

Location: McHenry
Contact: Steve Gulgrer
Planning Manager
McHenry County Conservation
District
6512 Harts Road
Ringwood, IL 60072-9641
(815) 678–4361

27 McHenry County Prairie Trail—North

Endpoints: Ringwood, Wisconsin state line
Mileage: 7.5
Surface: gravel, ballast

Location: McHenry
Contact: Mary Eysenbach
Assistant Director

McHenry County Conservation
District
6512 Harts Road
Ringwood, IL 60072-9641
(815) 678–4431

28 Nickel Plate Trail

Endpoints: Edwardsville (IL 159 and Longfellow Street), Glen Carbon Heritage Trail (Main Street)
Mileage: 4.6
Surface: crushed stone

Location: Madison
Contact: Joe Wright
Director of Marketing
RideFinders and Madison County
Transit
One Transit Way
Granite City, IL 62040
(618) 874–7433
jwright@mct.org
www.mcttrails.org/NickelPlateTrail.html

29 North Shore Bike Path

Endpoints: Lake Bluff, Mundelein
Mileage: 8
Surface: asphalt, crushed stone

Location: Lake
Contact: Bruce Christensen
Transportation Coordinator
Lake County Division of
Transportation
600 West Winchester Road

Libertyville, IL 60048-1381
(847) 362–3950
bchristensen@co.lake.il.us

30 Old Plank Road Trail

Endpoints: Joliet (Park Avenue),
Park Forest (Western Avenue)
Mileage: 21
Surface: asphalt

Location: Cook; Will
Contact: Forest Preserve District
of Will County
P.O. Box 1069
Joliet, IL 60434
(815) 727–8700
oprt.org/

31 O'Malley's Alley

Endpoints: Champaign
Mileage: 0.5
Surface: concrete

Location: Champaign
Contact: James Spencer
Director of Operations
Champaign Park District
706 Kenwood Drive
Champaign, IL 61821-4112
(217) 398–2550

32 Palatine Trail

Endpoints: Deer Grove Forest
Preserve, Winston and Anderson
Drives (Palatine)

Mileage: 15
Surface: asphalt

Location: Cook
Contact: Cheryl Scensny
Landscape Architect
Palatine Park District
250 E. Wood Street
Palatine, IL 60067-5332
(847) 705–5140
www.palatineparkdistrict.com

33 Pecatonica Prairie Path

Endpoints: East of Freeport (Rt.
75 and River Road), Village of
Winnebago
Mileage: 18
Surface: ballast

Location: Stephenson;
Winnebago
Contact: Rick Strader
Manager of Planning and
Development
Rockford Park District
1401 North Second Street
Rockford, IL 61107-3086
(815) 987–8865
rikstrader@home.com

34 Pimiteoui—Rock Island Trail

Endpoints: Peoria, Alta
Mileage: 7.5
Surface: asphalt, crushed stone

Location: Peoria
Contact: Peoria Park District
2218 N. Prospect Road
Peoria, IL 61603-2126
(309) 682–1200

35 Pioneer Parkway (Rock Island Trail Extension)

Endpoints: Peoria, Alta
Mileage: 2.5
Surface: crushed stone

Location: Peoria
Contact: Peoria Park District
2218 N. Prospect Road
Peoria, IL 61603-2126
(309) 682–1200

36 River Trail of Illinois

Endpoints: East Peoria, Morton
Mileage: 7
Surface: asphalt

Location: Tazewell
Contact: James Coutts
Director
Fon Du Lac Park District
201 Veterans Drive
East Peoria, IL 61611-2798
(309) 699–3923
www.fondulacpark.com

37 Robert McClory Bike Path

Endpoints: Winthrop Harbor, Lake Bluff
Mileage: 11

Surface: crushed stone

Location: Lake
Contact: Bruce Christensen
Transportation Coordinator
Lake County Division of
Transportation
600 West Winchester Road
Libertyville, IL 60048-1381
(847) 362–3950
bchristensen@co.lake.il.us

38 Rock Island Trail State Park

Endpoints: Alta Toulon
Mileage: 28.3
Surface: crushed stone

Location: Peoria; Stark
Contact: Melinda Kitchens
Site Superintendent
Illinois Department of Natural
Resources
P.O. Box 64
Wyoming, IL 61491
(309) 695–2225

39 Rock River Recreation Path

Endpoints: Rockford, Love's Park
Mileage: 8.5
Surface: asphalt

Location: Winnebago
Contact: Rick Strader
Planning and Development
Manager

Rockford Park District
1401 North Second Street
Rockford, IL 61107-3086
(815) 987–8865
rikstrader@home.com
www.rockfordparks.org/
recpaths.htm

40 Ronald J. Foster Heritage Trail

Endpoints: Glen Carbon
Mileage: 3.2
Surface: asphalt, gravel

Location: Madison
Contact: Bill Kleffman
Village Treasurer
Village of Glen Carbon
151 North Main Street
Glen Carbon, IL 62034-0757
(618) 288–1200
www.glen-carbon.il.us

41 Sam Vadalabene Great River Road Bike Trail

Endpoints: Alton, Pere
Marquette State Park
Mileage: 21
Surface: asphalt

Location: Jersey; Madison
Contact: James Easterly
District Engineer
Illinois Department of
Transportation
1100 Eastport Plaza Drive
P.O. Box 988
Collinsville, IL 62234-6198
(618) 346–3100

42 Schoolhouse Trail

Endpoints: Granite City
(Horseshoe Lake State Park), Troy
(IL 162 and Edwardsville/Troy
Roads)
Mileage: 11.5
Surface: asphalt

Location: Madison
Contact: Joe Wright
Director of Marketing
RideFinders and Madison County
Transit
One Transit Way
Granite City, IL 62040
(618) 874–7433
jwright@mct.org
www.mcttrails.org/Schoolhouse
Trail.html

43 Skokie Valley Bike Path

Endpoints: Lake Forest,
Highland Park
Mileage: 5.4
Surface: asphalt, crushed stone

Location: Lake
Contact: Bruce Christensen
Transportation Coordinator
Lake County Division of
Transportation
600 West Winchester Road
Libertyville, IL 60048-1381
(847) 362–3950
bchristensen@co.lake.il.us

44 Tunnel Hill State Trail

Endpoints: Harrisburg, Kamak
Mileage: 45
Surface: asphalt, crushed stone, gravel

Location: Saline; Johnson, Williamson
Contact: Kimberly Watson
Excecutive Director
Southeastern Regional Planning
and Development Commission
P.O. Box 606
Harrisburg, IL 62946-0606
(618) 252–7463

45 Vadalabene Nature Trail (Madison County Nature Trail)

Endpoints: Edwardsville, Pontoon Beach
Mileage: 7.9
Surface: asphalt, ballast

Location: Madison
Contact: George Arnold
Madison County Trail Volunteers
1306 St. Louis Street
Edwardsville, IL 62025-1310
(618) 656–3994

46 Village Bike Path

Endpoints: Dundee Road, Northbrook
Mileage: 1.1
Surface: asphalt

Location: Cook
Contact: Carl Peter
Village Engineer
Village of Northbrook
1225 Cedar Lane
Northbrook, IL 60062
(847) 272–5055

47 Virgil Gilman Nature Trail

Endpoints: Blisswoods Forest Preserve, Montgomery
Mileage: 14
Surface: asphalt, crushed stone

Location: Kane; Kendall
Contact: William Donnell
Landscape Architect
Fox Valley Park District
712 South River Street
Aurora, IL 60506-5911
(708) 897–0516

48 Watershed Trail

Endpoints: Edwardsville (West Union Street, Roxanna (Wanda Road)
Mileage: 5
Surface: asphalt

Location: Madison
Contact: Joe Wright
Director of Marketing
RideFinders and Madison County Transit
One Transit Way
Granite City, IL 62040
(618) 874–7433
jwright@mct.org
www.mct.org

INDIANA

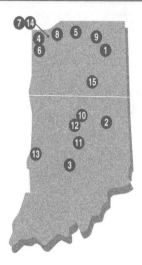

1 Auburn to Waterloo Bike Trail

Endpoints: Auburn, Waterloo
Mileage: 4
Surface: concrete

Location: DeKalb
Contact: Andrew Jagoda
Superintendent
Auburn Parks Department
P.O. Box 506
1500 South Cedar
Auburn, IN 46706-0506
(219) 925-8245

2 Cardinal Greenway

Endpoints: Muncie
Mileage: 10
Surface: asphalt, dirt

Location: Delaware
Contact: Bruce Moore
Director of Operations
Cardinal Greenway, Inc.
614 East Wysor Street
Muncie, IN 47305-1945
(765) 287-0399

3 Clear Creek Rail Trail

Endpoints: Bloomington, Victor
Mileage: 2.5
Surface: ballast

Location: Monroe
Contact: Dave Williams
Operations and Development
Director

Bloomington Parks and
Recreation
P.O. Box 848
Bloomington, IN 47402-0848
(812) 349–3700

4 Cross-Town Trail

Endpoints: Griffith, Highland
Mileage: 3.1
Surface: asphalt

Location: Lake
Contact: Highland Parks and
Recreation Department
2450 Lincoln Street
Highland, IN 46322
(219) 838–0114

5 East Bank Trail

Endpoints: South Bend (Dam
and Raceway downtown),
Roseland (Douglas Road and SR
933)
Mileage: 3
Surface: asphalt, cinder, gravel

Location: St. Joseph
Contact: Betsy Harriman
South Bend Parks Department
301 South St. Louis Boulevard
South Bend, IN 46617-3092
(219) 235–9401
www.indianatrails.org/East-Bank-Trail.htm

6 Erie Lackawanna Trail Linear Park

Endpoints: Erie Trail
(4)/Georgetown Lake Trail (1),
Hammond
Mileage: 21
Surface: asphalt

Location: Lake
Contact: Curtis Vosti
Administrator
Hammond Parks Department
5825 Sohl Avenue
Hammond, IN 46320-2358
(219) 853–6378

7 Iron Horse Heritage Trail

Endpoints: Portage
Mileage: 5
Surface: gravel

Location: Porter
Contact: Carl Fisher
Superintendent
City of Portage Parks and
Recreation
2100 Willowcreek Road
Portage, IN 46368-1596
(219) 762–1675
woodland@netnitco.net

8 Lake George Trail

Endpoints: Hammond (Sheffield
Avenue), Whiting (St. Joseph's
College)
Mileage: 1.5

Surface: asphalt

Location: Lake
Contact: 504 North Broadway
Suite 418
Gary, IN 46402

9 Mill Race portion of the Maple City Greenway

Endpoints: SR 4, CR 28 (Goshen)
Mileage: 2.7
Surface: asphalt, crushed stone

Location: Elkhart
Contact: Richard Fay
Goshen Park and Recreation
Department
607 West Plymouth Avenue
Goshen, IN 46526
(219) 534–2901

10 Monon Greenway in Carmel

Endpoints: 146th Street, 96th
Street
Mileage: 5.2
Surface: asphalt

Location: Hamilton
Contact: Jean Belcher
Office Administrator
Carmel Clay Parks and
Recreation
1055 Third Avenue SW
Carmel, IN 46032

(317) 848–7275
jbelcher@ci.carmel.in.us
www.ci.carmel.in.us

11 Monon Trail

Endpoints: Indianapolis
Mileage: 7.5
Surface: asphalt

Location: Marion
Contact: Ray Irvin
Administrator
Indianapolis Greenways
900 E. 64th Street
Indianapolis, IN 46220
(317) 327–7431
rirvin@indygov.org
www.indygreenways.org

12 Nancy Burton Memorial Trail

Endpoints: Zionsville
Mileage: 1.1
Surface: ballast

Location: Boone
Contact: Albert Smith
Parks Superintendent
Zionsville Town Hall
110 S. Fourth Street
Zionsville, IN 46077-1611
(317) 733–2273
zparks@iserve.net

13 National Road Heritage Trail

Endpoints: 13th Street, Twigg Rest Area (Terre Haute)
Mileage: 5.8
Surface: asphalt

Location: Vigo
Contact: Pat Goodwin
City Engineer
City of Terre Haute, Department of Engineering
City Hall, Room 200
17 Harding Avenue
Terre Haute, IN 47807
(812) 232–2727
wpgoodwin@cityofterrehaute.com

14 Prairie-Duneland Trail (Oak Savannah Trail)

Endpoints: Portage, Chesterton
Mileage: 9
Surface: asphalt

Location: Porter; Lake
Contact: Carl Fisher
Superintendent
City of Portage Parks and Recreation
2100 Willowcreek Road
Portage, IN 46368-1596
(219) 762–1675
woodland@netnitco.net

15 Sweetser Switch Trail

Endpoints: CR 400W (1 mile east of Main Street), CR 700W (2 miles west of Main Street)
Mileage: 3
Surface: asphalt

Location: Grant
Contact: Town of Sweetser
Sweetser Town Hall
113 N. Main Street
Sweetser, IN 46987
(765) 384–5333

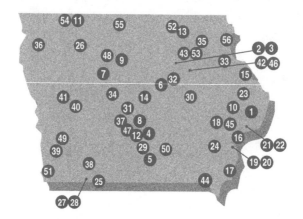

1 Brookfield Wildlife Refuge Trail

Endpoints: Brookfield Wildlife Refuge
Mileage: 2
Surface: grass, dirt

Location: Clinton
Contact: Al Griffiths
Director
Clinton County Conservation Board
P.O. Box 161
Grand Mound, IA 52751-0161
(319) 847-7202
cccb@netins.net

2 Cedar Prairie Trail

Endpoints: Cedar Falls
Mileage: 1
Surface: asphalt, concrete

Location: Black Hawk
Contact: Mark Ripplinger
Park Division Manager
Cedar Falls Parks Division
606 Union Road
Cedar Falls, IA 50613
(319) 273-8625
Mark_ripplinger@ci.cedar.falls.ia.us
www.ci.cedar.falls.ia.us

3 Cedar Valley Nature Trail

Endpoints: Hiawatha, Evansdale
Mileage: 53
Surface: asphalt, crushed stone

Location: Benton; Black Hawk; Buchanan; Linn
Contact: Steve Finegan

Executive Director
Black Hawk County Conservation
Board
2410 West Lone Tree Road
Cedar Falls, IA 50613-1093
(319) 277–1536
conservation@co.
black-hawk.ia.us
www.co.linn.ia.us/conservation/
activities/trails.html

4 Chichaqua Valley Trail

Endpoints: Bondurant, Baxter
Mileage: 21
Surface: asphalt

Location: Jasper; Polk
Contact: Ben Van Grundy
Director
Polk County Conservation Board
Jester Park
Granger, IA 50109
(515) 323–5300
pccb_info@cp.polk.ia.us
www.co.polk.ia.us

5 Cinder Path

Endpoints: Chariton, Humeston
Mileage: 13.5
Surface: crushed stone, ballast,
concrete

Location: Lucas; Wayne
Contact: Dwayne Clanin
Supervisor
Lucas County Conservation

P.O. Box 78
Chariton, IA 50049-0078
(515) 774–2314
Lucasccb@lucasco.net

6 Comet Trail

Endpoints: Conrad, Wolf Creek
Park
Mileage: 6
Surface: crushed stone, grass

Location: Grundy
Contact: Kevin Williams
Director
Grundy County Conservation
Board
P.O. Box 36
Morrison, IA 50657-0036
(319) 345–2688
gccb@starroute.com

7 Fort Dodge Nature Trail

Endpoints: Fort Dodge
Mileage: 3
Surface: crushed stone, gravel

Location: Webster
Contact: Tony Salvatore
Parks and Recreation Supervisor
813 First Avenue South
Fort Dodge, IA 50501-4725
(515) 573–5791

8 Four Mile Creek Greenway Trail

Endpoints: Altoona, Des Moines
Mileage: 8

Surface: asphalt

Location: Polk
Contact: Ben Van Grundy
Director
Polk County Conservation Board
Jester Park
Granger, IA 50109
(515) 323–5300
pccb_info@co.polk.ia.us
www.co.polk.ia.us

9 Franklin Grove Heritage Trail

Endpoints: Belmond
Mileage: 1.8
Surface: asphalt

Location: Wright
Contact: Wayne Pals
City of Belmond
112 Second Avenue NE
Belmond, IA 50421-1111
(515) 444–3386

10 Grant Wood Sesquicentennial Rail-Trail

Endpoints: Martelle, Olin
Mileage: 14
Surface: crushed stone

Location: Jones
Contact: Tom Neenan
Iowa Trails Council
1201 Central Avenue
Center Point, IA 52213-0131
(319) 849–1844

11 Great Lakes Spine Trail

Endpoints: Milford, Spirit Lake
Mileage: 12
Surface: asphalt

Location: Dickinson
Contact: John Walters
Director
Dickinson County
Conservation Board
1924 240th Street
Milford, IA 51351-1376
(712) 338–4786

12 Great Western Trail

Endpoints: Des Moines
(Waterworks Park), Martinsdale
Mileage: 18
Surface: asphalt

Location: Warren; Polk
Contact: Ben Van Grundy
Director
Polk County Conservation Board
Jester Park
Granger, IA 50109
(515) 323–5300
pccb_info@co.polk.ia.us
www.co.polk.ia.us

13 Harry Cook Nature Trail

Endpoints: Osage, Spring Park
Mileage: 2
Surface: crushed stone, gravel

Location: Mitchell
Contact: Ted Funk
Director
Parks and Recreation
Department
114 South Seventh Street
P.O. Box 29 City Hall
Osage, IA 50461-0029
(515) 732–3709

14 Heart of Iowa Nature Trail

Endpoints: Melbourne, Slater
Mileage: 32
Surface: crushed stone, dirt

Location: Marshall; Story
Contact: Steve Lekwa
Deputy Director
McFarland Park
56269 180th Street
Ames, IA 50010-9651
(515) 232–2516

15 Heritage Trail

Endpoints: Dubuque, Dyersville
Mileage: 27
Surface: crushed stone

Location: Dubuque
Contact: Robert Walton
Executive Director
Dubuque County Conservation

Board
13768 Swiss Valley Road
Peosta, IA 52068
(319) 556–6745

16 Hoover Nature Trail

Endpoints: Nichols, Conesville
Mileage: 7
Surface: crushed stone

Location: Muscatine
Contact: Charles Harper
President
Hoover Nature Trail
P.O. Box 531
Muscatine, IA 52761-0009
(319) 263–4043

17 Hoover Nature Trail– Burlington

Endpoints: Burlington
Mileage: 4
Surface: crushed stone

Location: Des Moines
Contact: Charles Harper
President
Hoover Nature Trail
P.O. Box 531
Muscatine, IA 52761-0009
(319) 263–4043

18 Hoover Nature Trail– Cedar Rapids

Endpoints: Cedar Rapids
Mileage: 2
Surface: crushed stone

Location: Linn
Contact: Charles Harper
President
Hoover Nature Trail
P.O. Box 531
Muscatine, IA 52761-0009
(319) 263–4043

19 Hoover Nature Trail– Columbus Junction

Endpoints: Columbus Junction
Mileage: 2
Surface: ballast

Location: Louisa
Contact: Charles Harper
President
Hoover Nature Trail
P.O. Box 531
Muscatine, IA 52761-0009
(319) 263–4043

20 Hoover Nature Trail– Morning Sun

Endpoints: Morning Sun
Mileage: 4
Surface: ballast

Location: Louisa
Contact: Charles Harper
President
Hoover Nature Trail
P.O. Box 531
Muscatine, IA 52761-0009
(319) 263–4043

21 Hoover Nature Trail– West Branch

Endpoints: West Branch
Mileage: 5
Surface: ballast

Location: Cedar; Johnson
Contact: Charles Harper
President
Hoover Nature Trail
P.O. Box 531
Muscatine, IA 52761-0009
(319) 263–4043

22 Hoover Nature Trail– West Liberty

Endpoints: West Liberty
Mileage: 5
Surface: crushed stone, ballast

Location: Cedar
Contact: Charles Harper
President
Hoover Nature Trail
P.O. Box 531
Muscatine, IA 52761-0009
(319) 263–4043

23 Jackson County Trail

Endpoints: Spragueville
Mileage: 3.3
Surface: crushed stone

Location: Jackson

Contact: Clark Schloz
County Road Engineer
201 West Platt
Maquoketa, IA 52060-2295
(319) 652–4782

24 Kewash Nature Trail

Endpoints: Keota, Washington
Mileage: 13
Surface: crushed stone

Location: Washington
Contact: Kathy Cuddeback
Washington County Conservation
Board
Courthouse
P.O. Box 889
Washington, IA 52353-0889
(319) 653–7765

25 Lamoni Recreational Trail

Endpoints: Lamoni (Cherry
Street), I–35
Mileage: 3
Surface: grass, gravel, ballast,
dirt

Location: Decatur
Contact: Louita Clothier
Friends of the Lamoni Rail-Trail
512 South Cherry
Lamoni, IA 50140

26 Laurens Trail

Endpoints: Laurens
Mileage: 1.5
Surface: crushed stone, ballast,

grass

Location: Pocahontas
Contact: Tom Neenan
Executive Director
Iowa Trails Council
1201 Central Avenue
Center Point, IA 52213-9638
(319) 849–1844

27 Little River Nature Trail

Endpoints: Leon
Mileage: 2
Surface: concrete

Location: Decatur
Contact: Brent Carll
City Clerk
City Hall
104 First Street
Leon, IA 50144
(515) 446–1446

28 Maple Leaf Pathway

Endpoints: Diagonal
Mileage: 3
Surface: crushed stone, gravel,
grass, cinder

Location: Ringgold
Contact: Rick Hawkins
Director
Ringgold County Conservation
Board
Box 83A, RR 1

Mount Ayr, IA 50854
(515) 464–2787

29 McVay Trail

Endpoints: East 5th Street,
Pickard Park (Indianola)
Mileage: 1.6
Surface: asphalt, concrete

Location: Warren
Contact: Glenn Cowan
Director
Indianola Parks and Recreation
Department
110 North First Street
Indianola, IA 50125-2527
(515) 961–9420

30 Old Creamery Trail

Endpoints: Vinton, Dysart
Mileage: 15.3
Surface: crushed stone

Location: Benton; Tama
Contact: Tom Neenan
Iowa Trails Council
1201 Central Avenue
P.O. Box 131
Center Point, IA 52213-0131
(319) 849–1844
TomNeenan1@aol.com

31 Perry to Rippey Trail (Three County Trail)

Endpoints: Perry, Rippey
Mileage: 9
Surface: ballast, grass, dirt

Location: Greene; Boone; Dallas
Contact: Tom Foster
Director
Boone County Conservation
Board
610 H Avenue
Ogden, IA 50212-7453
(515) 353–4237

32 Pioneer Trail

Endpoints: Holland, Grundy
Center, Morrison, Reinbeck
Mileage: 11.5
Surface: crushed stone

Location: Grundy
Contact: Kevin Williams
Director
Grundy County Conservation
Board
P.O. Box 36
Morrison, IA 50657-0036
(319) 345–2688
gccb@stroute.com
www.grundycenter.com/
grundycountyconservation

33 Pony Hollow Trail

Endpoints: Elkader
Mileage: 4
Surface: grass, dirt

Location: Clayton
Contact: Tim Engelhardt

Clayton County Conservation
Board
29862 Osborne Road
Elkader, IA 52043-8247
(319) 245–1516
cccb@mwci.net

34 Praeri Rail Trail

Endpoints: Roland, Zearing
Mileage: 10.5
Surface: crushed stone, grass,
dirt

Location: Story
Contact: Steve Lekwa
Deputy Director
McFarland Park
56269 180th Street
Ames, IA 50010-9651
(515) 232–2516

35 Prairie Farmer Recreation Trail (Winneshiek County Trail)

Endpoints: Calmar, Cresco
Mileage: 18
Surface: crushed stone

Location: Winneshiek
Contact: David Oestmann
Director
Winneshiek County Conservation
Board
2546 Lake Meyer Road
Fort Atkinson, IA 52144-7435
(319) 534–7145

36 Puddle Jumper Trail

Endpoints: Orange City, Alton
Mileage: 2
Surface: crushed stone

Location: Sioux
Contact: Todd Larsen
Director
Orange City Parks and
Recreation Department
City Hall
Orange City, IA 51041
(712) 737–4885

37 Raccoon River Valley Trail

Endpoints: Jefferson, Waukee
Mileage: 34
Surface: asphalt, grass

Location: Greene; Guthrie; Dallas
Contact: Tom Neenan
Executive Director
Iowa Trails Council
1201 Central Avenue
P.O. Box 151
Center Point, IA 52213-0131
(319) 849–1844
TomNeenan1@aol.com
www.dallascountyconservation.
org/raccoon.html

38 Ringgold Trailway

Endpoints: Mt. Ayr
Mileage: 2

Surface: ballast

Location: Ringgold
Contact: Rick Hawkins
Director
Ringgold County Conservation
Board
Box 83A, RR 1
Mount Ayr, IA 50854
(515) 464–2787

39 Rock Island – Old Stone Arch Nature Trail

Endpoints: I-80, Exit 40, Shelby
Mileage: 4
Surface: asphalt

Location: Pottawattamie, Shelby
Contact: Mel Hursey
City of Shelby
419 East Street
Shelby, IA 51570
(712) 544–2638
smu@fmctc.com

40 Russell White Nature Trail

Endpoints: Lanesboro, Highway 286
Mileage: 3.8
Surface: ballast, grass

Location: Carroll

Contact: David Olson
Director
Carroll County Conservation
Board
22811 Swan Lake Drive
Carroll, IA 51401-9801
(712) 792–4614

41 Sauk Rail Trail

Endpoints: Carroll, Lake View
Mileage: 33.2
Surface: asphalt, crushed stone

Other use: hunting
Location: Carroll; Sac
Contact: Chris Bass
Director
Sac County Conservation Board
2970 280th Street
Sac City, IA 50583-7474
(712) 662–4530

42 Sergeant Road Trail

Endpoints: Waterloo, Hudson
Mileage: 10
Surface: crushed stone

Location: Black Hawk
Contact: Kevin Blanshon
Transportation Director
INRCOG
501 Sycamore Street, Suite 333
Waterloo, IA 50703-4651
(319) 235–0311

43 Shell Rock River Trail (Butler County Trail)

Endpoints: Clarksville, Shell Rock
Mileage: 5.5
Surface: crushed stone

Location: Butler
Contact: Steve Brunsma
Director
Butler County Conservation Board
28727 Timber Road
Clarksville, IA 50619
(319) 278–4237

44 Shimek State Forest Trail

Endpoints: Shimek State Forest
Mileage: 4.5
Surface: ballast, grass, dirt

Location: Van Buren; Lee
Contact: Wayne Fuhlbrugge
Area Forester
Iowa Department of Natural
Resources
Shimek State Forest
RR 1, Box 95
Farmington, IA 52626
(319) 878–3811
www.state.ia.us/dnr/organiza/
forest/shimek

45 Solon–Lake Macbride Recreation Trail

Endpoints: Solon, Lake
Macbride State Park
Mileage: 5.3
Surface: crushed stone

Location: Johnson
Contact: Gwen Prentice
Park Ranger
Lake Macbride State Park
3525 Highway 382 NE
Solon, IA 52333-8911
(319) 644–2200
macbride@gte.net

46 South Riverside Trail

Endpoints: Cedar Falls Junction,
Waterloo
Mileage: 50 (2.6 miles are
rail-trail)
Surface: asphalt

Location: Black Hawk
Contact: Kevin Blanshon
Director of Transportation
501 Sycamore Street, Suite 333
Waterloo, IA 50703-5714
(319) 235–0311

47 Summerset Trail

Endpoints: Carlisle, Indianola
(near Highway 5)
Mileage: 12
Surface: asphalt

Location: Warren
Contact: www.iowatourism.org
/trails.html

48 Three Rivers Trail

Endpoints: Eagle Grove, Rolfe
Mileage: 36
Surface: crushed stone

Location: Humboldt;
Pocahontas; Wright
Contact: Jeanne Mae Ballgous
Director
Humboldt County Conservation
Board
Court House
Dakota City, IA 50529
(515) 332–4087

49 Upper Nish Habitat Trail

Endpoints: Irwin
Mileage: 6
Surface: crushed stone, ballast,
grass, dirt, concrete

Location: Shelby
Contact: Darby Sanders
Director
Shelby County Conservation Board
514 Maple Road
Harlan, IA 51537-6600
(712) 744–3403

50 Volksweg Trail

Endpoints: Fifield Park, Lake Red
Rock
Mileage: 14
Surface: asphalt

Location: Marion
Contact: George Wesselheft
City Planner
City of Pella
100 Truman Road
Pella, IA 50219-0345
(641) 628–1601
www.mvr.usace.army.mil/redrock/
recreation/trails/default.htm

51 Wabash Trace Nature Trail

Endpoints: Council Bluffs,
Blanchard
Mileage: 63
Surface: crushed stone

Location: Fremont; Mills; Page;
Pottawattamie
Contact: Lisa Hein
Iowa Natural Heritage
Foundation
505 Fifth Avenue, Suite 444
Des Moines, IA 50309-2382
(515) 288–1846
ihein@inhf.org
www.inhf.org

52 Wapsi–Great Western Trail

Endpoints: Riceville, Lake
Hendricks
Mileage: 14
Surface: crushed stone

Location: Howard; Mitchell

Contact: Elaine Govern
Chairman
Wapsi–Great Western Line
Committee
P.O. Box 116
Riceville, IA 50466-0116
(515) 985–4030

53 Waverly Rail-Trail

Endpoints: Waverly (west side of
Cedar River), Highway 63, north
of Denver
Mileage: 7.5
Surface: asphalt

Location: Bremer
Contact: Tab Ray
Director
Waverly Parks and Recreation
Department
200 1st Street NE
Waverly, IA 50677
(319) 352–6263
tab@ci.waverly.ia.us
www.waverlyia.com/rail_
welcome.asp

54 Winkel Memorial Trail

Endpoints: Sibley to Allendorf,
spur to Willow Creek County
Recreation Area
Mileage: 10
Surface: gravel

Location: Osceola
Contact: Ron Spengler

Director
Osceola County Convervation
Board
5945 Highway 9
Ocheyedan, IA 51354-7517
(712) 758–3709

55 Winnebago River Trail

Endpoints: Forest City
Mileage: 2.5
Surface: crushed stone, ballast,
wood chips

Location: Winnebago
Contact: Robert Schwartz
Executive Director
Winnebago County Conservation
Board
33496 110th Avenue
Forest City, IA 50436-9205
(515) 565–3390

56 Yellow River Forest Trail

Endpoints: Yellow River State
Forest
Mileage: 30
Surface: gravel, grass, dirt

Location: Allamakee
Contact: Bob Honeywell
Area Forester
Yellow River State Forest
729 State Forest Road
Harpers Ferry, IA 52146-7539
(319) 586–2254
RHwell@means.net
www.state.ia.us-forestry

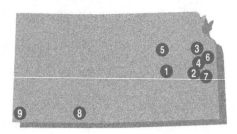

1 Flint Hills Nature Trail (Council Grove Segment)

Endpoints: Council Grove, 4 miles east of Council Grove
Mileage: 4
Surface: packed gravel

Location: Morris
Contact: Dan Pickert
Vice President
Kanza Rail-Trails Conservancy, Inc.
(785) 418–1088
www.kanzatrails.org

2 Flint Hills Nature Trail (Ottawa Segment)

Endpoints: Orlis Cox Ballfield Complex, Marais des Cygnes River (Ottawa)
Mileage: 1
Surface: packed gravel

Location: Franklin
Contact: Dan Pickert
Vice President

Kanza Rail-Trails Conservancy, Inc.
(785) 418–1088
dlpickert@juno.com
www.kanzatrails.org

3 Haskell Rail-Trail

Endpoints: 29th Street, 23rd Street (Lawrence)
Mileage: 1.1
Surface: crushed stone

Location: Douglas
Contact: Fred DeVictor
Director
Lawrence Parks and Recreation Department
Box 708
Lawrence, KS 66044-0708
(785) 832–3450

4 Landon Nature Trail

Endpoints: Sanneman Drive (Topeka city limits), Adams Road (south of Topeka)
Mileage: 1

Surface: packed gravel

Location: Shawnee
Contact: Dan Pickert
Vice President
Kanza Rail-Trails Conservancy, Inc.
(785) 418-1088
dlpickert@juno.com
www.kanzatrails.org

5 Manhattan Linear Park Trail

Endpoints: Casement Street,
Anneberg Park
Mileage: 9.4
Surface: crushed stone

Location: Riley
Contact: Manhattan Parks and
Recreation
Manhattan, KS 66502
(785) 587–2757

6 Mill Creek Streamway Park

Endpoints: Nelson Island on the
Kansas River, Olathe
Mileage: 17
Surface: asphalt

Location: Johnson
Contact: Michael Meadors
Director
Johnson County Park and
Recreation District
7900 Renner Road
Shawnee, KS 66217

(913) 831–3355
info@jcprd.com

7 Prairie Spirit Rail-Trail

Endpoints: Ottawa, Welda
Mileage: 33
Surface: asphalt, crushed stone

Location: Franklin; Anderson;
Allen
Contact: Trent McCown
Park Manager
Kansas Department of Wildlife &
Parks
419 South Oak
Garnett, KS 66032-1316
(785) 448–6767
www.ukans.edu/~hisite/
franklin/railtrail/

8 Short Grass Prairie Trail

Endpoints: Protection, Clark
county line
Mileage: 2
Surface: dirt, ballast

Location: Comanche
Contact: Richard Stein
Short Grass Prairie Trail, Inc.
P.O. Box 902
Ashland, KS 67831

9 Whistle Stop Park

Endpoints: Elkhart
Mileage: 1.8
Surface: asphalt

Location: Morton
Contact: Ed Johnson
Chairman
Whistle Stop Park Committee
Drawer 70
Elkhart, KS 67950-0070
(316) 697–2402

KENTUCKY

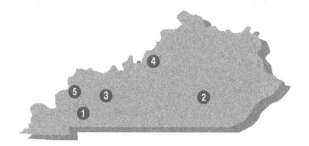

1 Cadiz Railroad Trail

Endpoints: Cadiz
Mileage: 1.5
Surface: asphalt

Location: Trigg
Contact: Stan White
Chairman
Cadiz Railroad Trail Committee
Drawer B
Cadiz, KY 42211
(502) 522–8483
cadiz@commandnet.net
www.kyrailtrail.org

2 Cathy Crockett Memorial Trail

Endpoints: Burnside, Alpine
Recreation Area
Mileage: 1.5
Surface: gravel, ballast

Location: Pulaski
Contact: Rick Bates
Tourism Development Specialist
University of Kentucky
2292 South Highway 27
Suite 310
Somerset, KY 42501-3602
(606) 677–6000
rbates@ca.uky.edu
www.kyrailtrail.org/lctf

3 Paradise Trail

Endpoints: Central City,
Greenville
Mileage: 6
Surface: asphalt

Location: Muhlenberg
Contact: Rodney Kirtley
P.O. Box 137
Greenville, KY 42345
(270) 338–2529
cojudge@muhlen.com
www.kyrailtrail.org

4 River Walk Trail

Endpoints: Belvedere, Chichasaw Park
Mileage: 6.9
Surface: asphalt

Location: Jefferson
Contact: Sushil Gupta
Manager of Urban Design and
Forestry
City of Louisville
City Hall, Room 217
601 West Jefferson
Louisville, KY 40202-2741
(502) 574–3921
www.kyrailtrail.org

5 Sturgis Rail Trail

Endpoints: Sturgis
Mileage: 1
Surface: asphalt

Location: Union
Contact: Cindy Loxley
Sturgis Elementary School
1101 North Grant Street
Sturgis, KY 42459
(207) 333–4088

1 Tammany Trace

Endpoints: Abita Springs, Slidell
(western city limits)
Mileage: 25
Surface: asphalt

Location: St. Tammany
Contact: Felicia Leonard
Transportation Planner
St. Tammany Parish Police Jury
428 East Boston Street
P.O. Box 628
Covington, LA 70433-2846
(504) 875–2601
For general information call
(504) 898–2529
www.stp.pa.sttammany.la.us/
departments/trace/trace.html

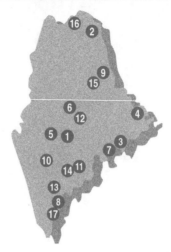

1 Anson to Bingham

Endpoints: Anson, Bingham
Mileage: 19
Surface: ballast

Location: Somerset
Contact: Roger Poulin
Kennebec Valley Trails
248 Madison Avenue
Skowhegan, ME 04976-1306

2 Aroostook Valley Trail (Bargona and Aroostook Trail)

Endpoints: Washburn, Van Buren
Mileage: 71
Surface: gravel, ballast

Other use: ATVs
Location: Aroostook
Contact: Scott Ramsey
Supervisor, Off-Road Vehicles
Bureau of Parks and Recreation
Department of Conservation
Station #22
Augusta, ME 04333-0022
(207) 287-3821

3 Brewer to Ellsworth

Endpoints: Brewer, Ellsworth
Mileage: 31
Surface: ballast

Location: Penobscot; Hancock
Contact: John Balicki
Bicycle and Pedestrian
Coordinator
Office of Passenger
Transportation
Maine Department of
Transportation

16 State House Station
Augusta, ME 04333-0016
(207) 624–3252
john.balicki@maine.gov
members.fortunecity.com/
railtrails/

4 Calais Waterfront Walkway

Endpoints: Calais
Mileage: 1.5
Surface: crushed stone, gravel

Location: Washington
Contact: Jim Porter
Community Development
Director
City of Calais
P.O. Box 413
Calais, ME 04619-0413
(207) 454–2521

5 Carrabassett River Trail (Woodabogan Trail)

Endpoints: Carrabassett,
Bigelow
Mileage: 19
Surface: grass, dirt

Location: Franklin
Contact: Susan Foster
Manager
Sugarloaf/USA Outdoor Center
RR 1, Box 5000
Kingfield, ME 04947-9799
(207) 237–6830
outdoor@somtel.com

6 Derby to Greenville

Endpoints: Derby, Greenville
Mileage: 60
Surface: gravel

Location: Piscataquis
Contact: Scott Ramsey
Supervisor, Off-Road Vehicles
Bureau of Parks and Recreation
Department of Conservation
Station #22
Augusta, ME 04333-0022
(207) 287–3821

7 Downeast Trail (Sunrise Trail)

Endpoints: Ellsworth, Calais (at
Canadian border)
Mileage: 113
Surface: ballast

Location: Hancock; Washington
Contact: Sally Jacobs
Chair
Sunrise Trail Coalition
91 Bennoch Road
Orono, ME 04473-1409
sjacobs@maine.edu
members.fortunecity.com/
railtrails/

8 Eastern Promenade Trail (Portland)

Endpoints: Portland
Mileage: 2.1
Surface: asphalt

Location: Cumberland
Contact: Alix Hopkins
Chair
Mountain Division Alliance
259 Libby Road
Pownal, ME 04069
awdeng@gwi.net
www.trails.org/map_files/
eastern_prom_page_
description.html

9 Houlton to Phair

Endpoints: Houlton, Phair
Mileage: 44
Surface: gravel, ballast

Other use: ATV, hunting
Location: Aroostook
Contact: Scott Ramsey
Supervisor, Off-Road Vehicles
Bureau of Parks and Recreation
Department of Conservation
Station #22
Augusta, ME 04333-0022
(207) 287–3821

10 Jay to Farmington Trail

Endpoints: Jay, Farmington
Mileage: 15
Surface: gravel, ballast

Other use: ATVs
Location: Franklin
Contact: Scott Ramsey
Supervisor, Off-Road Vehicles

Bureau of Parks and Recreation
Department of Conservation
Station #22
Augusta, ME 04333-0022
(207) 287–3821

11 Kennebec River Rail Trail

Endpoints: Hallowell, Augusta
Sanitary District
Mileage: 1.6
Surface: crushed stone

Location: Kennebec
Contact: Andrea LaPointe
Environmental Specialist
Friends of the Kennebec River
Rail Trail
10 Academy Street
Hallowell, ME 04347-1362
andrea.lapointe@state.me.us
www.bikemaine.org/krrt2.htm
www.krrt.org

12 Lagrange Right-of-Way Trail

Endpoints: South Lagrange,
Medford
Mileage: 15
Surface: gravel, ballast

Other use: ATV, hunting
Location: Piscataquis; Penobscot
Contact: Scott Ramsey
Supervisor, Off-Road Vehicles
Bureau of Parks and Recreation
Department of Conservation
Station #22
Augusta, ME 04333-0022
(207) 287–3821

13 Mountain Division Trail

Endpoints: Windham (Gambo Recreation Area), Standish (Johnson Field Recreation Area)
Mileage: 4
Surface: crushed stone, dirt

Location: Cumberland
Contact: Alix Hopkins, Chair
Mountain Division Alliance
259 Libby Road
Pownal, ME 04069
awdeng@gwi.net
www.mountaindivisiontrail.org

14 Old Narrow Gauge Volunteer Nature Trail

Endpoints: Randolph
Mileage: 2.4
Surface: ballast, dirt

Location: Kennebec
Contact: Wayne Libby
Town of Randolph
Code Enforcement and Public Works
P.O. Box 216
Randolph, ME 04345-0216
(207) 582–0335

15 Patten to Sherman

Endpoints: Patten, Sherman
Mileage: 7
Surface: gravel

Location: Aroostook; Penobsot
Contact: Scott Ramsey
Supervisor, Off-Road Vehicles
Bureau of Parks and Recreation
Department of Conservation
Station #22
Augusta, ME 04333-0022
(207) 287–3821

16 Saint John Valley Heritage Trail

Endpoints: Fort Kent, St. Francis
Mileage: 18
Surface: crushed stone

Other use: dogsledding
Location: Aroostook
Contact: Charles Rudelitch
Economic Development Director
Town of Fort Kent
111 West Main Street
Fort Kent, ME 04743-1040
(207) 834–3507
charles.redulitch@fortkent.org

17 South Portland Greenbelt

Endpoints: South Portland
Mileage: 3.5
Surface: asphalt

Location: Cumberland
Contact: Charles (Tex) Haeuser
Planning Director
City Hall
25 Cottage Road
South Portland, ME 04106-3604
(207) 767–7602
tex@ime.net

MARYLAND

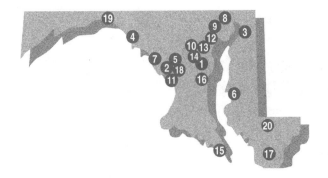

1 Baltimore and Annapolis Trail

Endpoints: Glen Burnie, Annapolis
Mileage: 13.3
Surface: asphalt

Location: Anne Arundel
Contact: David Dionne
Park Superintendent
Anne Arundel County Trails
1003 Cecil Avenue
Millersville, MD 21108
(410) 222–8820
trailman96@msn.com
www.his.com/~jmenzies/
urbanatb/rtrails/ba/ba.htm

2 Bethesda Trolley Trail

Endpoints: Bethesda, Rockville
Mileage: 1.3
Surface: asphalt

Location: Montgomery
Contact: Gail Tait-Nori
Montgomery County
Department of Transportation
101 Monroe Street
10th Floor
Rockville, MD 20850-2540
(301) 217–2145

3 Chesapeake & Delaware Canal Trail

Endpoints: Chesapeake City, Delaware City
Mileage: 15
Surface: crushed stone, dirt

Location: Cecil; New Castle
Contact: David Hawley
Civil Engineer
U.S. Army Corps of Engineers
P.O. Box 77
Chesapeake City, MD 21915-0077
(410) 885–5621

4 Chesapeake & Ohio Canal National Historic Park

Endpoints: Cumberland, Georgetown
Mileage: 184.5
Surface: crushed stone, gravel, dirt

Location: Allegany; Frederick; Montgomery; Washington
Contact: Douglas Faris
Superintendent
C&O National Historical Park
P.O. Box 4
Sharpsburg, MD 21782-0004
(301) 739–4200

5 College Park Trolley Line

Endpoints: College Park
Mileage: 1
Surface: asphalt

Location: Prince George's County
Contact: College Park Area

Bicycle Coalition
www.cpabc.org/

6 Cross Island Trail

Endpoints: Kent Island (Terrapin Nature Area to Kent Narrows)
Mileage: 5
Surface: asphalt

Location: Queen Anne's
Contact: Wes R. Johnson
Director
Queen Anne's County
Department of Parks and Recreation
P.O. Box 37
Centreville, MD 21617
(410) 758–0835
wjohnson@qac.org

7 Goldmine Loop Trail

Endpoints: Potomac (Great Falls Tavern)
Mileage: 3
Surface: dirt

Location: Montgomery
Contact: Faye Walmsley
Subdistrict Ranger
C&O Canal National Historic Park
11710 MacArthur Boulevard
Potomac, MD 20854-1659
(301) 299–3613

8 Lower Susquehanna Heritage Greenway

Endpoints: Susquehanna State Park, Conowingo Dam
Mileage: 5
Surface: crushed stone

Location: Harford; Cecil
Contact: Rick Smith
Manager
Susquehanna State Park
3318 Rocks Chrome Hill Road
Jarrettsville, MD 21084-1741
(410) 836–6735
www.marylandhistoricaltrust.net/
halsusq.html

9 MA & PA Heritage Trail

Endpoints: N. Tollgate Road to Mast Street (Bel Air), Rock Spring to Friends Park (Forest Hill)
Mileage: 3.65 (in two sections)
Surface: crushed stone

Location: Harford
Contact: Katherine Adams
Project Manager
Department of Parks and
Recreation
702 N. Tollgate Road
Bel Air, MD 21014-2482
(410) 638–3570

10 Mill Trail

Endpoints: Savage Park
Mileage: 1.5

Surface: crushed stone, gravel, ballast

Location: Howard
Contact: Clara Govin
Senior Park Planner
Howard County Recreation and
Parks
7120 Oakland Mills Road
Columbia, MD 21046-1621
(410) 313–4687
cgovin@co.ho.md.us

11 North Bethesda Trail

Endpoints: Bethesda, Rockville
Mileage: 1.3
Surface: asphalt

Location: Montgomery
Contact: Montgomery County
Department of Public Works and
Transportation
101 Monroe Street
9th Floor
Rockville, MD 20850
(240) 777–7220
bikewashington.org/trails/
bethesda/bethesda.htm

12 Northern Central Railroad Trail

Endpoints: Ashland, Pennsylvania line
Mileage: 21
Surface: crushed stone

Location: Baltimore
Contact: Rob Marconi
Area Manager
Gunpowder Falls State Park
P.O. Box 480
Kingsville, MD 21087
(410) 592–2897
www.dnr.state.md.us/
greenways/ncrt_trail

13 Number Nine Trolley Line

Endpoints: Catonsville, Oella
Mileage: 2
Surface: asphalt

Location: Baltimore
Contact: John Mickanis
Western Region Supervisor
Baltimore County Department of
Recreation and Parks
Banneker Center, Main and
Wesley Avenues
Catonsville, MD 21228
(410) 887–0956

14 Patuxent Branch Trail

Endpoints: Savage (Savage Park),
Columbia (Lake Elkhom)
Mileage: 4
Surface: asphalt, crushed stone

Location: Howard
Contact: Clara Gouin
Senior Park Planner

Howard County Recreation and
Parks
209 Oakland Mills Road
Columbia, MD 21046-1621
(410) 313–4687
cgouin@co.ho.md.us

15 Point Lookout Railroad Trail

Endpoints: Point Lookout State
Park (Scotland)
Mileage: 2
Surface: dirt

Location: Saint Mary's
Contact: Park Staff
Ranger
Point Lookout State Park
P.O. Box 48
Scotland, MD 20687
(301) 872–5688

16 Poplar Park Trail

Endpoints: Annapolis
Mileage: 0.5
Surface: asphalt

Location: Anne Arundel
Contact: Stephen Carr
Pathways Coordinator
City of Annapolis
2009 Homewood Road
Annapolis, MD 21402
(410) 757–5916
stevecarr@toad.net

17 Snow Hill Rail-Trail

Endpoints: Snow Hill, Stockton
Mileage: 3
Surface: crushed stone

Location: Worcester
Contact: Lisa Challenger
Tourism Coordinator
Worcester County Department of
Economic Development
105 Pearl Street
Snow Hill, MD 21863-1051
(410) 632–3110

18 Washington, Baltimore, & Annapolis Trail (WB&A Trail)

Endpoints: Near Lanham (corner
of Route 450 and 704), Past
Bowie to the Patuxent River
Mileage: 6.2
Surface: asphalt

Location: Prince George's; Anne
Arundel
Contact: Eileen Nivera
Trail Planner
MD-National Capital Park and
Planning Commission
Prince George's County
Department of Parks and
Recreation
6600 Kenilworth Avenue
Riverdale, MD 20737
(301) 699–2522
rivera.eileen@pgparks.com
www.pgparks.com
www.bikewashington.org/trails/
wba/wba.htm

19 Western Maryland Rail Trail

Endpoints: Big Pool through
Hancock, Polly Pond
Mileage: 20
Surface: asphalt

Location: Washington
Contact: Ralph Young
Park Manager
Fort Frederick State Park
Maryland Department of Natural
Resources
11100 Fort Frederick Road
Big Pool, MD 21711-1313
(301) 842–2155
www.dnr.state.md.us/publiclands/
wmrt.html

20 Winterplace Park Trail

Endpoints: Salisbury, Walston
Switch
Mileage: 2
Surface: grass, crushed stone,
wood chips, gravel, dirt, ballast

Location: Wicomico
Contact: Aaron Levinthal
Greenways Coordinator
Wicomico County Parks,
Recreation, and Tourism
500 Glen Avenue
Salisbury, MD 21804
(410) 548–4900, x112
alevinthal@wicomicocounty.org

MASSACHUSETTS

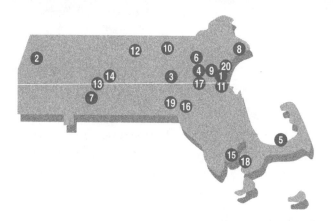

1 Alewife Linear Park

Endpoints: Somerville (Davis Square), Cambridge (Minuteman Path at Alewife T Station)
Mileage: 1.1
Surface: asphalt

Location: Middlesex
Contact: City of Somerville
93 Highland Avenue
Somerville, MA 02143
(617) 625-6600
www.ci.somerville.ma.us/
departments/recreation/
parksandplay.asp

2 Ashuwillticook Rail-Trail

Endpoints: Lanesborough, Adams (parallel to Route 8)
Mileage: 11
Surface: asphalt

Location: Berkshire
Contact: Allison Lassoe
Bikeways Planner
Department of Environmental
Management
P.O. Box 1433
Pittsfield, MA 01202
(413) 442-8928
www.massparks.org
www.berkshirebikepath.org

3 Assabet River Rail-Trail

Endpoints: 1.25 miles: Marlborough (Fairbanks Boulevard) to Hudson (I–290 Connector); 0.6 miles: Maynard (Great Road to White Pond Road)
Mileage: 1.85
Surface: asphalt

Location: Middlesex
Contact: Assabet River Rail-Trail
246 Essex Street
Marlborough, MA 01752
www.arrtinc.org

4 Bedford Narrow-Gauge Rail-Trail

Endpoints: Loomis Street (Bedford), Bedford-Billerica town line
Mileage: 3
Surface: crushed stone, asphalt

Location: Middlesex
Contact: Richard Warrington
Director
Town of Bedford
Department of Public Works
314 The Great Road
Bedford, MA 01730
(781) 275–7605
members.aol.com/depotpark/FBDP.htm

5 Cape Cod Rail Trail

Endpoints: Dennis, South Wellfleet
Mileage: 25
Surface: asphalt, grass, dirt, sand

Location: Barnstable
Contact: Daniel O'Brien

Bikeway and Rail Trail Planner
Department of Environmental Management
Box 66
100 Cambridge Street
Room 1404
South Carver, MA 02366
(617) 626–1388
danny.obrien@state.ma.us
www.state.ma.us/dem/parks/ccrt.htm
www.state.ma.us/dem/parks/nash.htm

6 Lowell Canal System Trails

Endpoints: Lowell
Mileage: 2.5
Surface: asphalt, concrete

Location: Middlesex
Contact: Christina Briggs
Planning Director
Lowell National Historical Park
67 Kirk Street
Lowell, MA 01852-5900
(508) 458–7653
www.nps.gov/lowe

7 Manhan Rail Trail

Endpoints: Easthampton (South Street) to Mt. Tom junction (Route 5, Connecticut River boat launch)
Mileage: 4.2
Surface: asphalt

Location: Hampshire

Contact: City Clerk
Town Hall, 43 Main Street
Easthampton, MA 01027
(413) 529-1460
cityclerk@easthampton.org
manhanrailtrail.tripod.com

8 Marblehead Rail-Trail (The Path)

Endpoints: Marblehead,
Swampscott; with spur to Salem
Mileage: 5
Surface: gravel, ballast, grass,
dirt

Location: Essex
Contact: Tom Hammond
Superintendent of Recreation
Marblehead Department of
Recreation, Park and Forestry
10 Humphrey Street
Marblehead, MA 01945-1906
(781) 631–3350

9 Minuteman Bikeway

Endpoints: Arlington, Bedford
Mileage: 10.5
Surface: asphalt

Location: Middlesex
Contact: Alan McClennen, Jr.
Director
Planning and Community
Development
Town of Arlington
730 Massachusetts Avenue
Arlington, MA 02174-4908
(781) 316–3091

amcclenn@town.arlington.ma.us
minutemanbikeway.org

10 Nashua River Rail Trail

Endpoints: Ayer (Main Street),
Hollis, N.H. (between Groton
Road/Nashua River)
Mileage: 11
Surface: asphalt

Location: Middlesex
Contact: Daniel O'Brien
Bikeway and Rail Trail Planner
Department of Environmental
Management
Box 66
100 Cambridge Street, Room
1404
South Carver, MA 02366
(617) 626-1388
danny.obrien@state.ma.us
www.state.ma.us/dem/parks/
nash.htm

11 Neponset Trail

Endpoints: Central Avenue
(Milton), Victory Road, Boston
(Dorchester)
Mileage: 2.5
Surface: asphalt

Location: Suffolk; Norfolk
Contact: Cathy Garnett
Metropolitan District Commission

Planning Office
20 Somerset Avenue
Boston, MA 02108
(617) 727-9693, ext. 264
catherine.garnett@state.ma.us
www.state.ma/us/mdc/
neponset.htm
www.massbike.org/bikeways/
nepon

12 North Central Pathway

Endpoints: Gardner
Mileage: 2.5
Surface: asphalt

Location: Worcester
Contact: Cynthia Boucher
North Central Pathway, Inc.
135 Gardner Road
Winchendon, MA 01475
commwtr@banet.net

13 Northampton Bikeway

Endpoints: Northampton
Mileage: 2.6
Surface: asphalt

Location: Hampshire
Contact: Wayne Feiden
Principal Planner
Northampton Office of Planning
and Development
210 Main Street, City Hall
Northampton, MA 01060-3110
(413) 586–6950
wfeiden@city.northampton.ma.us

www-unix.oit.umass.edu:-80/
~ditullio/Northamhome.html

14 Norwottuck Rail-Trail (Five College Bikeway)

Endpoints: Amherst,
Northampton
Mileage: 9
Surface: asphalt

Location: Hampshire
Contact: Daniel O'Brien
Bikeway and Rail Trail Planner
Department of Environmental
Management
100 Cambridge Street
Room 1404
South Carver, MA 02366
(617) 626–1338
danny.obrien@state.ma.us
www.state.ma.us/dem/parks/
nash.htm

15 Phoenix Rail-Trail

Endpoints: Fairhaven
Mileage: 4
Surface: asphalt

Location: Bristol
Contact: Friends of the Fairhaven
Bike Path
www.millicentlibrary.org/bike
trail/bike1.htm

16 Quarries Footpath

Endpoints: Quincy Quarries Historic Site
Mileage: 1
Surface: dirt

Location: Norfolk
Contact: Maggie Brown
Chief Ranger
Blue Hills Reservation, South Region
695 Hillside Street
Milton, MA 02186-5224
(617) 727–4573

17 Reformatory Branch Trail

Endpoints: Bedford (Railroad Avenue), Concord (Lowell Road)
Mileage: 4
Surface: dirt, cinder, sand

Location: Middlesex
Contact: Richard Warrington
Director
Town of Bedford
Department of Public Works
314 The Great Road
Bedford, MA 01730
(781) 275-7605
www.bedforddepot.org

18 Shining Sea Bikeway

Endpoints: Falmouth, Woods Hole
Mileage: 4
Surface: asphalt

Location: Barnstable
Contact: Kevin Lynch
Chairman
Falmouth Bikeways Committee
52 Town Hall Square
Falmouth, MA 02540
(508) 968–5293
avnyd@aol.com
http://members.aol.com/fal-bike/bike/bike/index.html

19 Southern New England Trunkline Trail

Endpoints: Franklin, Douglas
Mileage: 21
Surface: crushed stone, ballast

Location: Norfolk; Worcester
Contact: Tom LaVoie
Assistant Regional Director
Department of Environmental Management, Region III
P.O. Box 155
Jamaica Plain, MA 02130
(978) 368–0126

20 Southwest Corridor Park

Endpoints: Back Bay/South End
T Station, Forest Hills T–Jamaica
Plain (Boston)
Mileage: 5
Surface: asphalt

Location: Suffolk
Contact: Allan Morris
Parkland Manager
Southwest Corridor Park
38 New Heath Street
Jamaica Plain, MA 02130-1670
(617) 727–0057

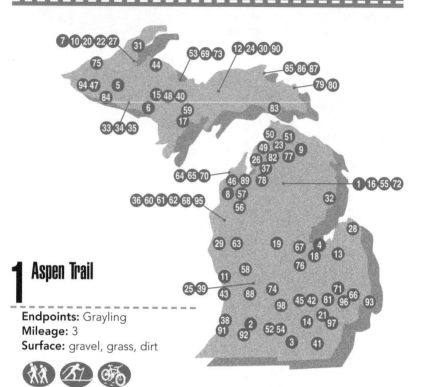

1 Aspen Trail

Endpoints: Grayling
Mileage: 3
Surface: gravel, grass, dirt

Location: Crawford
Contact: Robert Bacon
Management Unit Supervisor
Hartwick Pines State Park
Route 3, Box 3840
Grayling, MI 49738-9357
(517) 348–7068

2 Battle Creek Linear Park

Endpoints: Battle Creek
Mileage: 17
Surface: asphalt

Location: Calhoun
Contact: Linn Kracht
Recreation Superintendent
Battle Creek Department of
Parks and Recreation
35 Hambin Avenue
Battle Creek, MI 49017-4012
(616) 966–3431
www.bcparks.org/jsps/linear_
park.jsp

3 Baw Beese Trail

Endpoints: Osseo, Hillsdale
Mileage: 6
Surface: asphalt, ballast

Location: Hillsdale
Contact: Mark Reynolds
Director
Hillsdale Recreation Department
43 McCollum Street
Hillsdale, MI 49242-1630
(517) 437–3579

4 Bay Hampton Rail Trail

Endpoints: Bay City, Hampton
Township
Mileage: 6
Surface: asphalt

Location: Bay
Contact: Jim Bedell
Community Development
Planner
301 Washington Street
Bay City, MI 48708-5866
(517) 894–8154

5 Beaver Lodge Nature Trail

Endpoints: Ottawa National
Forest
Mileage: 1.3
Surface: grass, wood chips, dirt

Location: Houghton
Contact: Dawn Buss
Forestry Technician
Ottawa National Forest
1209 Rockland Road

Ontonagon, MI 49953-1731
(906) 884–2411

6 Beaver Pete's Trail

Endpoints: Dickinson/
Menominee county line, Iron
Mountain
Mileage: 20
Surface: ballast

Location: Dickinson
Contact: Allan Keto
Assistant, Resource Protection
Copper Country State Forest
Norway Forest Area
US-2
Norway, MI 49870
(906) 563–9247

7 Bergland to Sidnaw Rail Trail

Endpoints: Sidnaw, Bergland
Mileage: 45
Surface: gravel, ballast, dirt

Other use: ATV
Location: Houghton; Ontonagon
Contact: Martin Nelson
Unit Manager
Michigan Department of Natural
Resources
427 US Highway 41 North
Baraga, MI 49908-9627
(906) 353–6651

8 Betsie Valley Trail

Endpoints: Frankfort, Thompsonville (via Beulah)
Mileage: 22
Surface: asphalt, crushed stone

Location: Benzie
Contact: Dean Sandell
Michigan Department of Natural Resources
Cadillac Operations Service Center
8015 Mackinaw Trail
Cadillac, MI 49601
(231) 775–9727, ext. 6045
www.greenwaycollab.com/BVT.htm

9 Big Bear Lake Nature Pathway

Endpoints: Mackinaw State Forest
Mileage: 5
Surface: dirt

Location: Otsego
Contact: Bill O'Neill
Assistant Area Forester
Unit Manager
Michigan Department of Natural Resources
Gaylord Forest Management Division
P.O. Box 667
Gaylord, MI 49734
(517) 731–5806
oneillw@state.mi.us
www.dnr.state.mi.us

10 Bill Nicholls Trail

Endpoints: Houghton, McKeever
Mileage: 55
Surface: gravel, ballast, dirt, sand

Other use: ATV
Location: Ontonagon; Houghton
Contact: Martin Nelson
Unit Manager
Michigan Department of Natural Resources
427 US Highway 41 North
Baraga, MI 49908-9627
(906) 353–6651

11 Boardwalk of Grand Haven

Endpoints: Grand Haven
Mileage: 2.5
Surface: asphalt

Location: Ottawa
Contact: Laurel Nease
Visitors Bureau Coordinator
Grand Haven Visitors Bureau
1 South Harbor Drive
Grand Haven, MI 49417-1385
(616) 842–4499
inease@grandhavenchamber.org
www.grandhavenchamber.org

12 Bruno's Run Trail

Endpoints: Munising
Mileage: 7.3
Surface: dirt

Location: Alger
Contact: Dick Andersen
Recreation Supervisor
Hiawatha National Forest
Munising Ranger District
400 East Munising, RR #2 Box 400
Munising, MI 49862-1487
(906) 387–2512

13 Cass City Walking Trail

Endpoints: Cass City
Mileage: 1.4
Surface: gravel, ballast, grass, wood chips, dirt

Location: Tuscola
Contact: Jane Downing
Village Manager
6505 Main Street
P.O. Box 123
Cass City, MI 48726-1524
(517) 872–2911
ccvillag@avci.net

14 Chelsea Hospital Fitness Trail

Endpoints: Chelsea
Mileage: 1
Surface: wood chips

Location: Washtenaw
Contact: Philip Boham
Vice President

Chelsea Community Hospital
775 S. Main Street
Chelsea, MI 48118-1370
(313) 475–3998

15 Coalwood Trail

Endpoints: Shingleton, Chatham
Mileage: 24
Surface: ballast

Other use: ATV
Location: Alger; Schoolcraft
Contact: Dick Andersen
Recreation Supervisor
Hiawatha National Forest
Munising Ranger District
400 East Munising, RR #2
Box 400
Munising, MI 49862-1487
(906) 387–2512

16 Cross Country Ski and Mountain Bike Trail

Endpoints: Hartwick Pines State Park
Mileage: 9
Surface: gravel, grass, dirt

Location: Crawford
Contact: Jon Gregorich
Supervisor
Hartwick Pines State Park
4216 Ranger Road
Grayling, MI 49738
(517) 348–7068

17 Felch Grade Trail

Endpoints: Narenta, Felch
Mileage: 45
Surface: gravel, dirt

Other use: ATV
Location: Delta; Menominee; Dickinson
Contact: Russ MacDonald
Assistant Area Forest Manager
Escanaba Forest Area Office
Escanaba River State Forest
6833 US 2-41 & M-35
Gladstone, MI 49837
(906) 786–2354

18 Frank N. Anderson Trail

Endpoints: Bay City State Park
Mileage: 1.4
Surface: asphalt

Location: Bay
Contact: Karen Gillespie
Park Secretary
Bay City State Recreation Area
3582 State Park Drive
Bay City, MI 48706
(517) 684–6282

19 Fred Meijer Heartland Trail

Endpoints: Greenville, Alma
Mileage: 29
Surface: asphalt, gravel

Location: Gratiot; Montcalm
Contact: Carolyn Kane
Secretary
Friends of Fred Meijer Heartland Trail
P.O. Box 455
Edmore, MI 48829
ckane@cmsinter.net

20 Freda Trail

Endpoints: Freda, Bill Nicholls Trail
Mileage: 11.2
Surface: dirt

Other use: ATV
Location: Houghton
Contact: Dave Tuovila
District Fire and Recreation Specialist
Michigan Department of Natural Resources
427 US Highway 41 North
Baraga, MI 49908-9627
(906) 353–6651

21 Gallup Park Trail

Endpoints: Ann Arbor, Parker Mill
Mileage: 4.3
Surface: asphalt

Location: Washtenaw
Contact: Thomas Raynes
Manager of Park Planning
Ann Arbor Department of Parks
and Recreation
P.O. Box 8647
100 North Fifth Avenue
Ann Arbor, MI 48107-8647
(734) 994–2423
traynes@ci.ann-arbor.mi.us

22 Gay Trail

Endpoints: Gay, Mohawk
Mileage: 27
Surface: dirt

Location: Houghton; Keweenaw
Contact: Martin Nelson
Area Forest Manager
Michigan Department of Natural
Resources
427 US Highway 41 North
Baraga, MI 49908-9627
(906) 353–6651

23 Gaylord to Indian River

Endpoints: Gaylord, Indian River
Mileage: 33
Surface: gravel, dirt

walk, snowmobile, mt. bike
Location: Cheboygan, Otsego
Contact: Gaylord Area
Convention and Tourism Bureau
101 West Main Street

Gaylord, MI 49735
(989) 732–4000
info@gaylordmichigan.net
www.gaylord-mich.com/snow
mobile/

24 Grand Marais Trail

Endpoints: Shingleton, Grand
Marais
Mileage: 41.7
Surface: sand

Location: Alger; Schoolcraft
Contact: Jeff Stampfly
Area Forest Manager
Lake Superior State Forest
Shingleton Forest Area
M-28, P.O. Box 57
Shingleton, MI 49884
(906) 452–6227

25 Grand River Edges

Endpoints: Grand Rapids
Mileage: 0.5
Surface: asphalt

Location: Kent
Contact: Steve Pierpoint
Landscape Architect
Grand Rapids Planning
Department
300 Monroe Avenue, NW
Grand Rapids, MI 49503-2206
(616) 456–3031

26 Grass River Natural Area Nature Trail

Endpoints: Bellaire
Mileage: 8
Surface: crushed stone, ballast, dirt

Location: Antrim
Contact: Mark Randolph
Grass River Natural Area
P.O. Box 231
Bellaire, MI 49615-0231
(616) 533–8314
www.torchlake.com/grana

27 Hancock/Calumet Trail

Endpoints: Hancock, Calumet
Mileage: 13
Surface: asphalt, gravel, dirt

Other use: ATV
Location: Houghton
Contact: Martin Nelson
Unit Manager
Michigan Department of Natural Resources
427 US Highway 41 North
Baraga, MI 49908-9627
(906) 353–6651

28 Harbor Beach Bike-Pedestrian Path

Endpoints: Harbor Beach
Mileage: 1
Surface: asphalt

Location: Huron
Contact: Tom Youatt
City Administrator
City of Harbor Beach
766 State Street
Harbor Beach, MI 98441
(517) 479–3363

29 Hart-Montague Bicycle Trail State Park

Endpoints: Hart, Montague
Mileage: 22.5
Surface: asphalt

Location: Oceana; Muskegon
Contact: Peter LundBorg
Park Administrator
Silver Lake State Park
Management Unit
9679 West State Park Road
Mears, MI 49436-9667
(616) 873–3083
www.michigandnr.com/parks andtrails/parksandTrailsInfo. asp?id=452

30 Haywire Trail

Endpoints: Manistique, Shingleton
Mileage: 33
Surface: ballast, cinder

Other use: ATV
Location: Alger; Schoolcraft
Contact: Dick Andersen
Recreation Supervisor
Hiawatha National Forest
Munising Ranger District
400 East Munising, RR #2
Box 400
Munising, MI 49862-1487
(906) 387–2512

31 Houghton Waterfront Trail

Endpoints: Houghton
Mileage: 4.5
Surface: asphalt

Location: Houghton
Contact: Scott MacInnes
Assistant City Manager
City of Houghton
P.O. Box 406
Houghton, MI 49931-0406
(906) 482–1700

32 Huron Forest Snowmobile Trails

Endpoints: Huron National
Forest, Barton City
Mileage: 95
Surface: dirt

Other use: ATV
Location: Alcona; Oscoda
Contact: Nick Schmelter
Assistant Ranger
Huron National Forest
Huron Shores Ranger District
5761 Skeel Avenue

Oscoda, MI 48750
(517) 739–0728

33 Iron Range Trails— Beechwood to Sidnaw Trail

Endpoints: Beechwood, Gibbs
City
Mileage: 48
Surface: ballast

Location: Iron
Contact: Dave Tuovila
District Fire and Recreation
Specialist
Michigan Department of Natural
Resources
427 US Highway 41 North
Baraga, MI 49908-9627
(906) 353–6651

34 Iron Range Trails— Crystal Falls to Iron River Trail

Endpoints: Crystal Falls, Iron
River
Mileage: 25
Surface: ballast

Location: Iron
Contact: Dave Tuovila
District Fire and Recreation
Specialist
Michigan Department of Natural
Resources
427 US Highway 41 North
Baraga, MI 49908-9627
(906) 353–6651

35 Iron Range Trails— Crystal Falls to Stager Trail

Endpoints: Crystal Falls, Stager
Mileage: 11
Surface: ballast

Location: Iron
Contact: Dave Tuovila
District Fire and Recreation
Specialist
Michigan Department of Natural
Resources
427 US Highway 41 North
Baraga, MI 49908-9627
(906) 353–6651

36 Iron's Area Tourist Association Snowmobile Trail

Endpoints: Manistee National
Forest
Mileage: 22
Surface: ballast

Location: Lake; Manistee
Contact: John Hojnowski
Assistant Ranger
USDA Forest Service
Manistee Ranger District
412 Red Apple Road
Manistee, MI 49660
(616) 723–2211

37 Jordan River Pathway

Endpoints: Jordan River Valley
Mileage: 17.5
Surface: dirt

Location: Antrim
Contact: Bill O'Neill
Area Forest Manager
Michigan Department of Natural
Resources, Gaylord Field Office
P.O. Box 667
Gaylord, MI 49735-0667
(517) 732–3541

38 Kal-Haven Trail Sesquicentennial State Park Trail

Endpoints: Kalamazoo, South
Haven
Mileage: 33.5
Surface: crushed stone

Location: Kalamazoo; Van Buren
Contact: Kurt Maxwell
Trail Supervisor
Van Buren State Park
23960 Ruggles Road
South Haven, MI 49090-9492
(269) 637–4984

39 Kent Trails

Endpoints: Grand Rapids, Byron
Center
Mileage: 15
Surface: asphalt

Location: Kent
Contact: Roger Sabine
Director of Parks
Kent County Parks Department
1500 Scribner NW
Grand Rapids, MI 49504-3299
(616) 336–3697

40 Keweenaw Trail

Endpoints: Houghton, Calumet
Mileage: 58
Surface: grass, dirt

Location: Houghton; Keweenaw
Contact: Martin Nelson
Unit Manager
Michigan Department of Natural
Resources
427 US Highway 41 North
Baraga, MI 49908-9627
(906) 353–6651

41 Kiwanis Trail

Endpoints: Adrian (Trestle Park),
near Tecumseh (Occidental
Highway)
Mileage: 7
Surface: asphalt, ballast

Location: Lenawee
Contact: Mark Gasche
Community Services Director

Adrian City Hall
100 East Church Street
Adrian, MI 49221-2773
(517) 263–2161

42 Lakelands Trail State Park

Endpoints: Pinckney,
Stockbridge
Mileage: 13
Surface: crushed stone

Location: Ingham; Livingston;
Washtenaw
Contact: Jon LaBossiere
Pinckney Recreation Area
8555 Silver Hill
Pinckney, MI 48169-8901
(313) 426–4913

43 Lakeside Trail

Endpoints: Spring Lake
Mileage: 1.8
Surface: asphalt

Location: Ottawa
Contact: Andy Lukasik
Village Manager
Village of Spring Lake
102 W. Savidge Street
Spring Lake, MI 49456-1603
(616) 842–1393

44 L'Anse to Big Bay Trail

Endpoints: L'Anse, Big Bay
Mileage: 54
Surface: dirt

Location: Baraga; Marquette
Contact: Martin Nelson
Area Forest Manager
Michigan Department of Natural
Resources
427 US Highway 41 North
Baraga, MI 49908-9627
(906) 353–6651

45 Lansing River Trail

Endpoints: Lansing
Mileage: 6
Surface: asphalt

Location: Ingham
Contact: Dick Schaefer
Landscape Architect
Parks and Recreation
318 North Capital Avenue
Lansing, MI 48933-1605
(517) 483–4277

46 Leelanau Trail

Endpoints: Traverse City, Suttons
Bay
Mileage: 15.3
Surface: asphalt, gravel, dirt

Location: Grand Traverse;
Leelanau
Contact: Missy Luyk
Administrative Supervisor
TART Trails, Inc.
P.O. Box 252
Traverse City, MI 49865
missy@traversetrails.org
www.traversetrails.org/leelanau-
trail.shtml

47 Little Falls Trail

Endpoints: Ottawa National
Forest
Mileage: 6.5
Surface: ballast, grass

Location: Gogebic; Ontonagon
Contact: Wayne Petterson
Forestry Technician
Ottawa National Forest
P.O. Box 276
Watersmeet, MI 49969-0276
(906) 358–4551

48 Little Lake–Chatham Snowmobile Trail

Endpoints: Chatham, Little Lake
Mileage: 26
Surface: ballast, dirt, cinder

Location: Marquette; Alger

Contact: Bill Brondyke
Area Forest Manager
Gwinn Forest Area
410 West M-35
Gwinn, MI 49841
(906) 346–9201

49 Little Traverse Wheelway

Endpoints: Petoskey
Mileage: 2.3
Surface: asphalt

Location: Emmet
Contact: Melanie Chiodini
Top of Michigan Trails Council
445 East Mitchell Street
Petoskey, MI 49770

50 Mackinaw/Alanson Trail

Endpoints: Mackinaw Alanson
Mileage: 24
Surface: gravel, ballast, dirt, grass

Location: Emmet
Contact: Bill O'Neill
Unit Manager
Michigan Department of Natural Resources
Forest Management Unit
P.O. Box 667
Gaylord, MI 49734
(517) 731–5806
oneillw@state.mi.us
www.dnr.state.mi.us

51 Mackinaw to Hawks Trail

Endpoints: Hawks, Mackinaw City
Mileage: 59
Surface: ballast

Location: Cheboygan; Presque Isle
Contact: Melanie Chiodini
Top of Michigan Trails Council
445 East Mitchell Street
Petoskey, MI 49770

52 Main Trail

Endpoints: Whitehouse Nature Center, Albion College
Mileage: 0.5
Surface: gravel, grass, wood chips, dirt

Location: Calhoun
Contact: Tamara Crupi
Director
Albion College
Whitehouse Nature Center
KC 4868
Albion, MI 49224
(517) 629–0582
tcrupi@albion.edu

53 Mattson Lower Harbor Park Trail

Endpoints: Harvey, Marquette
Mileage: 8
Surface: asphalt

Location: Marquette
Contact: Leslie Hugh
Director
City of Marquette Parks and
Recreation Department
401 East Fair Avenue
Marquette, MI 49855
(906) 228–0460

54 McClure Riverfront Park

Endpoints: Albion
Mileage: 0.2
Surface: grass, wood chips

Location: Calhoun
Contact: Joe Domingo
Superintendent
Albion Department of Parks and
Recreation
112 West Cass Street
Albion, MI 49224
(517) 629–5535

55 Mertz Grade Trail

Endpoints: Grayling
Mileage: 2
Surface: gravel, grass, dirt

Location: Crawford
Contact: John Gregorich
Department of Natural Resources
Unit Supervisor
Hartwick Pines State Park
4216 Ranger Road
Grayling, MI 49738
(517) 348–7068

56 Michigan Shore to Shore Riding-Hiking Trail— Cadillac Spur

Endpoints: Cadillac
Mileage: 35
Surface: sand

Location: Wexford; Missaukee;
Grand Traverse
Contact: Steve Cross
Forest Management Specialist
Forest Management Division
8015 Mackinaw Trail
Cadillac, MI 49601-9746
(616) 775–9727

57 Michigan Shore to Shore Riding-Hiking Trail— Scheck's Place

Endpoints: Empire, Sheck's Place
Mileage: 40
Surface: sand

Location: Grand Traverse; Benzie
Contact: Steve Cross
Forest Management Specialist
Forest Management Division
8015 Mackinaw Trail
Cadillac, MI 49601-9746
(616) 775–9727

58 Musketawa Trail

Endpoints: Marne, Muskegon
Mileage: 26
Surface: asphalt

Location: Muskegon; Ottawa
Contact: Harold Drake
President
Village of Ravenna
12090 Crockery Creek Drive
Ravenna, MI 49451-9460
(616) 853–2360

59 Nahma Grade Trail

Endpoints: Rapid River, Alger
county line
Mileage: 32
Surface: dirt

Location: Delta
Contact: Anne Okonek
Assistant District Ranger
Hiawatha National Forest
Rapid River Ranger District
8181 US Highway 2
Rapid River, MI 49878-9501
(906) 474–6442

60 Nordhouse Dunes Trail System

Endpoints: Manistee National
Forest
Mileage: 14
Surface: grass, dirt

Location: Mason
Contact: Teresa Maday
Outdoor Recreation Planner
Manistee National Forest
Manistee/Cadillac Ranger District
412 Red Apple Road
Manistee, MI 49660-9616
(616) 723–2211

61 North Country National Scenic Trail—Baldwin

Endpoints: Baldwin
Mileage: 1.5
Surface: dirt

Other use: Snowshoeing
Location: Lake
Contact: Executive Director
North Country Trail Association
3777 Sparks Drive SE, Suite 105
Grand Rapids, MI 49546-6186

62 North Country National Scenic Trail—Manistee Ranger District

Endpoints: Red Bridge, Marilla
Trailhead
Mileage: 43
Surface: dirt

Location: Manistee; Mason; Lake
Contact: Ramona Venegas
Wilderness Ranger
Manistee Ranger District
USDA Forest Service
412 Red Apple Road
Manistee, MI 49660-9616
(616) 723–2211

63 North Country National Scenic Trail—White Cloud

Endpoints: White Cloud
Mileage: 0.3
Surface: dirt

Other use: Snowshoeing
Location: Newaygo
Contact: Executive Director
North Country Trail Association
3777 Sparks Drive SE
Suite 105
Grand Rapids, MI 49546-6186

64 Old Grade Nature Trail

Endpoints: Glen Lake
Mileage: 1
Surface: grass

Location: Leelanau
Contact: William Herd
Park Ranger
Sleeping Bear Dunes National
Lakeshore
9922 Front Street
Empire, MI 49630-0277
(616) 326–5134

65 Old Grade Trail

Endpoints: North Manitou Island
Mileage: 8
Surface: grass, dirt

Location: Leelanau
Contact: William Herd

Park Ranger
Sleeping Bear Dunes National
Lakeshore
9922 Front Street
Empire, MI 49630-0277
(616) 326–5134

66 Paint Creek Trailway

Endpoints: Rochester, Rochester
Hills, Oakland, Orion
Mileage: 8
Surface: crushed stone, ballast,
dirt

Location: Oakland
Contact: William Stark
Trailways Coordinator
Paint Creek Trailways
Commission
4349 Collins Road
Rochester, MI 48306-1619
(248) 651–9260
www.paintcreektrail.org

67 Pere Marquette Rail-Trail of Mid-Michigan

Endpoints: Midland, Clare
Mileage: 22
Surface: asphalt

Location: Midland
Contact: William Gibson
Director
Midland County Parks and
Recreation Department

220 W. Ellsworth Street
Midland, MI 48640-5194
(517) 832–6876
www.lmb.org/pmrt/

68 Pere Marquette State Trail

Endpoints: Baldwin, Clare
Mileage: 54.7
Surface: asphalt, ballast, sand

Location: Clare; Lake; Osceola
Contact: Paul Pounders
Director
Midland County Parks and
Recreation Department
220 W. Ellsworth Street
Midland, MI 48640-5194
(989) 832–6876
ppounders@col.midland.mi.us
www.co.midland.mi.us

69 Peshekee to Clowry ORV Trail

Endpoints: Near Champion
Mileage: 6.1
Surface: gravel, ballast, dirt

Location: Marquette
Contact: Al Keto
Recreation Specialist
1990 US-41 South
Marquette, MI 49855
(906) 228–6561

70 Platte Plains Trail

Endpoints: Sleepy Bear Dunes
National Lake Shore
Mileage: 14.7
Surface: grass, dirt, sand

Location: Benzie
Contact: William Herd
Park Ranger
Sleeping Bear Dunes National
Lakeshore
9922 Front Street
Empire, MI 49630-0277
(616) 326–5134

71 Polly Ann Trail

Endpoints: Orion Township
(Joslyn/Indianwood Roads),
Oakland/Lapeer county line at
Bordman Road
Mileage: 12.2
Surface: gravel, ballast, grass

Location: Lapeer, Oakland
Contact: Amy Murray
Manager
Polly Ann Trail Management
Council
23 E. Elmwood
P.O. Box 112
Leonard, MI 48367
(248) 969–8660
www.orion.lib.mi.us/patmc/

72 Railroad Trail

Endpoints: Gaylord, Indian River, Frederick
Mileage: 68 (22 are rail-trail)
Surface: grass, dirt

Location: Crawford; Otsego
Contact: Phil Silverio-Mazzela
Trail Coordinator
Alpine Snowmobile Trails, Inc.
2583 Old 27 South
Gaylord, MI 49735
(517) 732–7171

73 Republic/Champion Grade Trail

Endpoints: Champion, Republic
Mileage: 8.1
Surface: ballast

Other use: ATV
Location: Marquette
Contact: Dennis Nezich
Area Forest Manager
Ishpeming Forest Area
Escanaba River State Forest
1985 US-41
Ishpeming, MI 49849
(906) 485–1031

74 Rivertrail Park

Endpoints: Portland
Mileage: 3.7
Surface: asphalt

Location: Ionia
Contact: Mary Scheurer
Parks and Recreation
Department
City of Portland
259 Kent Street
Portland, MI 48875-1458
(517) 647–7985

75 Rockland to Mass Trail

Endpoints: Rockland
Mileage: 7
Surface: ballast

Location: Ontonagon
Contact: Martin Nelson
Area Forest Manager
Michigan Department of Natural
Resources
427 US Highway 41 North
Baraga, MI 49908-9627
(906) 353–6651

76 Saginaw Valley Rail Trail

Endpoints: St. Charles
(Lumberjack Park), 6 miles north
Mileage: 6
Surface: asphalt

Location: Saginaw
Contact: John Schmude
Director
Saginaw County Parks
Department
111 S. Michigan Avenue
Saginaw, MI 48602
Parks@saginawcounty.com
www.saginawcounty.com/Parks

77 Shingle Mill Pathway

Endpoints: Pigeon River Country Forest Management Unit
Mileage: 11
Surface: dirt

Location: Otsego
Contact: Joe Jarecki
Area Forest Manager
Pigeon River Country Forest Area
9966 Twin Lakes Road
Vanderbilt, MI 49795-9767
(517) 983–4101

78 Skegemog Lake Pathway

Endpoints: Skegemog Lake Wildlife Area
Mileage: 0.8
Surface: ballast

Location: Kalkaska
Contact: Jerry Grieve
Assistant Area Forest Manager
Tranerce City Unit
2089 North Birch
Kalkaska, MI 49646-9448
(616) 258–2711
grieveg@state.mi.us

79 Soo/Strongs Trail— Raco to Strongs

Endpoints: Raco, Strongs
Mileage: 12
Surface: ballast

Location: Chippewa
Contact: William Rhoe
District Ranger
Hiawatha National Forest
Sault Ste. Marie Ranger District
4000 I-75, Business Spur
Sault Ste. Marie, MI 49783
(906) 635–5511

80 Soo/Strongs Trail— Sault Ste. Marie to Raco

Endpoints: Sault Ste. Marie, Raco
Mileage: 20
Surface: ballast, dirt, sand

Other use: ATV
Location: Chippewa
Contact: Patrick Halfrisch
Assistant Unit Land Manager
Sault Ste. Marie Forest Area
Lake Superior State Forest
P.O. Box 798
Sault Ste. Marie, MI 49783-0798
(906) 635–5281

81 South Lyon Rail-Trail

Endpoints: South Lyon
Mileage: 3.3
Surface: asphalt

Location: Oakland
Contact: Rodney Cook
City Manager
City of South Lyon
335 South Warren

South Lyon, MI 48178-1377
(248) 437–1735
www.southlyonmi.org

82 Spring Brook Pathway

Endpoints: Mackinaw State Forest
Mileage: 6.3
Surface: ballast, dirt

Location: Charlevoix
Contact: Bill O'Neill
Area Forest Manager
Michigan Department of Natural Resources, Gaylord Field Office
P.O. Box 667
Gaylord, MI 49735-0667
(517) 732–3541

83 St. Ignace to Trout Lake

Endpoints: St. Ignace, Trout Lake
Mileage: 26
Surface: crushed stone

Location: Mackinac
Contact: Joe Hart
Assistant District Manager
Hiawatha National Forest
1498 W. US-2
St. Ignace, MI 49781
(906) 643–7900

84 State Line Trail

Endpoints: Wakefield, Stager
Mileage: 107
Surface: ballast

Other use: ATV
Location: Iron; Gogebic
Contact: Martin Nelson
Unit Manager
Michigan Department of Natural Resources
427 US Highway 41 North
Baraga, MI 49908-9627
(906) 353–6651

85 Tahquamenon Falls State Park–Clark Lake Loop

Endpoints: Tahquamenon Falls State Park
Mileage: 5
Surface: grass, dirt

Location: Chippewa; Luce
Contact: Jon Spieles
Park Interpreter
Tahquamenon Falls State Park
41382 West M-123
Paradise, MI 49768
(906) 492–3415
J.spieles@up.net

86 Tahquamenon Falls State Park–North Country Loop

Endpoints: Tahquamenon Falls State Park
Mileage: 23
Surface: grass, dirt

Location: Chippewa; Luce
Contact: Jon Spieles
Park Interpreter
Tahquamenon Falls State Park
41382 West M-123
Paradise, MI 49768
(906) 492–3415
J.spieles@up.net

87 Tahquamenon Falls State Park—Wilderness Loop

Endpoints: Tahquamenon Falls State Park
Mileage: 7.4
Surface: grass, dirt

Location: Chippewa; Luce
Contact: Jon Spieles
Park Interpreter
Tahquamenon Falls State Park
41382 West M-123
Paradise, MI 49768
(906) 492–3415
J.spieles@up.net

88 Thornapple Trail/Paul Henry Trail

Endpoints: 2.5 miles paved in Kentwood, 3.5 miles paved between Middleville and Irving
Mileage: 6
Surface: asphalt

Location: Kent, Barry
Contact: Mark Fritsma
Board Member

Thornapple Trail Association
P.O. Box 393
Middleville, MI 49333
trailfan.com
www.thornappletrail.com

89 Traverse Area Recreation Trail (TART)

Endpoints: Acme (Bunker Hill Road), Traverse City (M–22/M–72 intersection)
Mileage: 10
Surface: asphalt, concrete

Location: Grand Traverse
Contact: Bob Otwell
Executive Director
TART Trails, Inc.
P.O. Box 252
Traverse City, MI 49865
bob@traversetrails.org
www.traversetrails.org/
tart-trail.shtml

90 Tyoga Historical Pathway

Endpoints: Deerton
Mileage: 1.4
Surface: ballast

Location: Alger
Contact: Dennis Nezich
Area Forest Manager
Ishpeming Forest Area
Escanaba River State Forest
1985 US-41
Ishpeming, MI 49849
(906) 485–1031

91 Van Buren Trail State Park

Endpoints: Hartford, South Haven
Mileage: 14
Surface: gravel, ballast, dirt

Location: Van Buren
Contact: Kurt Maxwell
Trail Supervisor
Van Buren State Park
23960 Ruggles Road
South Haven, MI 49090-9492
(616) 637–2788

92 Vicksburg Recreation Area Trailway

Endpoints: Vicksburg
Mileage: 1.8
Surface: asphalt

Location: Kalamazoo
Contact: Matthew L. Crawford
Village Manager
Village of Vicksburg
126 N. Kalamazoo Avenue
Vicksburg, MI 49097
(646) 649–1919
mcrawford000@ameritech.net

93 Wadhams to Avoca Trail

Endpoints: Kimball Township
Mileage: 1.2
Surface: asphalt

Location: St. Clair
Contact: St. Clair County Parks and Recreation
200 Grand River Avenue, Suite 205
Port Huron, MI 48060
(801) 989–6960
countyparks@stclaircounty.org
www.stclaircounty.org/offices/parks/wadhams.asp

94 Watersmeet/Land O'Lakes Trail

Endpoints: Watersmeet, Land O'Lakes
Mileage: 8.8
Surface: ballast

Other use: ATV
Location: Gogebic
Contact: Wayne Petterson
Forestry Technician
Ottawa National Forest
P.O. Box 276
Watersmeet, MI 49969-0276
(906) 358–4551

95 Wellston Area Tourist Association Snowmobile Trail

Endpoints: Manistee National Forest
Mileage: 51.5
Surface: ballast

Location: Manistee; Lake
Contact: Teresa Maday

Outdoor Recreation Planner
Manistee National Forest
Manistee/Cadillac Ranger District
412 Red Apple Road
Manistee, MI 49660-9616
(616) 723–2211

96 West Bloomfield Trail Network

Endpoints: West Bloomfield
Township, Sylvan Manor Park
Mileage: 6.3
Surface: crushed stone

Location: Oakland
Contact: Dan Navarre
Director
West Bloomfield Parks and
Recreation Commission
4640 Walnut Lake Road
West Bloomfield, MI
48323-1940
(248) 738–2500
Trailnet88@aol.com

97 West Campus Bicycle Path

Endpoints: Eastern Michigan
University
Mileage: 1
Surface: asphalt

Location: Washtenaw
Contact: Daniel Klenczar
Project Manager
Eastern Michigan University
Physical Plant
Ypsilanti, MI 48197
(734) 487–1337

98 White Pine Trail State Park

Endpoints: Cadillac, Howard City
Mileage: 92
Surface: asphalt, crushed stone,
gravel, ballast

Location: Kent; Mecosta;
Montcalm; Osceola; Wexford
Contact: Paul Yauk
Staff Specialist
Michigan Department of Natural
Resources
Parks and Recreation Division
P.O. Box 30257
Lansing, MI 48909-7757
(517) 335–4824
http://multimag.com/city/mi/
reedcity/white.html

MINNESOTA

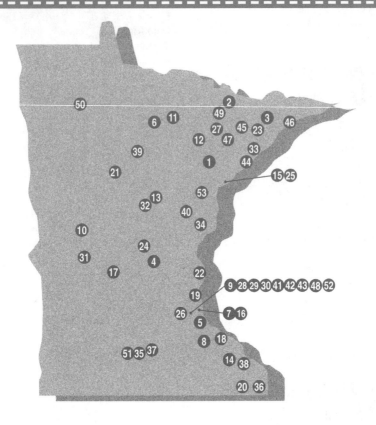

1 Alborn-Pengilly Greenway Trail

Endpoints: Alborn, Pengilly
Mileage: 42
Surface: gravel, ballast

Other Use: ATV
Location: Itasca; St. Louis
Contact: Jack Klassen
Trail Coordinator
Alborn Snow Devils

6697 Highway 47
Alborn, MN 55702-8234

2 Arrowhead State Trail

Endpoints: Taconite State Trail
(near tower), 3 miles south of
International Falls
Mileage: 135
Surface: ballast, grass, dirt

Location: St. Louis; Koochiching
Contact: Ann Bjorgo
Area Supervisor
Minnesota Department of
Natural Resources, Trails and
Waterways Unit
P.O. Box 388
406 Main Street
Tower, MN 55790-0388
(218) 753–6256
ann.bjorgo@dnr.state.mn.us
www.dnr.state.mn.us/state_trails/
arrowhead/index.html

3 Bear Island—Lake Trail

Endpoints: Bear Island State
Forest
Mileage: 13
Surface: ballast

Location: St. Louis
Contact: Mike Magnuson
Area Forester
Tower Area Forestry Office
609 North Second Street
P.O. Box 432
Tower, MN 55790
(218) 753–4500

4 Beaver Island Trail (Tileston Mill Spur)

Endpoints: St. Cloud
Mileage: 2.5
Surface: asphalt

Location: Stearns
Contact: Prentiss Foster
Park Management Assistant
St. Cloud Parks Division
400 Second Street South

St. Cloud, MN 56301-3699
(612) 255–7216
pfoster@ci.st.cloud.mn.us

5 Big Rivers Regional Trail

Endpoints: Mendota Heights
(near Minneapolis), Lillydale
Mileage: 4.2
Surface: asphalt

Location: Dakota
Contact: Parks Director
Dakota County Parks Department
Spring Lake Park
8500 127th Street East
Hastings, MN 55033
(651) 438–4660
parks@gsc.co.dakota.mn.us

6 Blue Ox Trail (Voyageur Trail)

Endpoints: Bemidji, International
Falls
Mileage: 107
Surface: ballast

Location: Beltrami; Itasca;
Koochiching
Contact: Forrest Boe
Regional Manager
Trails and Waterways
Minnesota Department of
Natural Resources
6603 Bemidji Avenue N.
Bemidji, MN 56601

7 Burlington Northern Regional Trailway

Endpoints: St. Paul, Maplewood
Mileage: 5
Surface: asphalt

Location: Ramsey
Contact: Don Ganje
Landscape Architect
City of St. Paul/Divison of Parks
and Recreation
300 City Hall Annex
25 West Fourth Street
St. Paul, MN 55102
(651) 266–6425
don.ganje@ci.stpaul.mn.us

8 Cannon Valley Trail

Endpoints: Cannon Falls, Red Wing
Mileage: 19.7
Surface: asphalt

Location: Goodhue
Contact: Scott Roepke
Cannon Valley Trail
306 West Mill Street
Cannon Falls, MN 55009
www.cannonfalls.org

9 Cedar Lake Trail

Endpoints: Hopkins at Southwest Regional LRT Trail, downtown Minneapolis via St. Louis Park
Mileage: 7.9

Surface: asphalt

Location: Hennepin
Contact: Jon Wertjes
Minneapolis Transportation
Department
City Hall
350 South Fifth Street, Room 233
Minneapolis, MN 55415-1316
(612) 673–2411

10 Central Lakes Trail

Endpoints: Osakis, Furgus Falls
Mileage: 63
Surface: gravel, asphalt, crushed stone

Location: Douglas; Grant; Otter Tail
Contact: Donald Lieffort
Park Superintendent
Douglas County Public Works
Department
P.O. Box 3
Alexandria, MN 56308
(320) 763–6001
al.lieffort@mail.co.douglas.mn.us
www.co.douglas.mn.us/central_
lakes_trail

11 Circle L Trail

Endpoints: Big Fork, George Washington State Forest
Mileage: 24.8
Surface: grass, dirt

Other use: ATV
Location: Itasca
Contact: Ben Anderson
Program Forester
Minnesota Department of
Natural Resources, Division of
Forestry
P.O. Box 95
Effie, MN 56639-0095
(218) 743–3694

12 Circle T Trail

Endpoints: Nashwauk, George
Washington State Forest
Mileage: 39.5
Surface: grass, dirt

Location: Itasca
Contact: Trail Manager
Minnesota Department of
Natural Resources, Division of
Forestry
1208 East Howard Street
Hibbing, MN 55746
(218) 262–6760

13 Cuyuna Trail

Endpoints: Aitkin to Crosby,
spurs to Deerwood, Riverton,
and Trommald
Mileage: 18.8
Surface: grass, dirt

Location: Aitkin, Crow Wing
Contact: Crosby Chamber of
Commerce
P.O. Box 23
Crosby, MN 56441-0023
(218) 546–8131

14 Douglas State Trail

Endpoints: Rochester, Pine
Island
Mileage: 12.5
Surface: asphalt, ballast

Location: Goodhue; Olmsted
Contact: Joel Wagar
Area Manager
Minnesota Department of
Natural Resources, Trails and
Waterways Unit
2300 Silver Creek Road NE
Rochester, MN 55906-4505
(507) 285–7176
www.dnr.state.mn.us

15 DWP Trail

Endpoints: Carlton, West Duluth
Mileage: 5
Surface: gravel

Location: St. Louis
Contact: Kelly Fleissner
City Forester
City of Duluth
Department of Public Works
110 N. Forty-second Avenue
West
City Hall Room 208
Duluth, MN 55802
(218) 723–3586

16 Gateway Segment of the Willard Munger Trail

Endpoints: St. Paul, Pine Point

Regional Park
Mileage: 18.3
Surface: asphalt, crushed stone

Location: Washington; Ramsey
Contact: Scott Kelling
Area Supervisor
Minnesota Department of
Natural Resources
1200 Warner Road
St. Paul, MN 55106-6793
(612) 297–2911
www.dnr.state.mn.us/state_trails/
gateway/index.html

17 Glacial Lakes State Trail

Endpoints: Willmar, Stearns
county line near Hawick
Mileage: 18
Surface: asphalt, crushed stone,
grass

Other use: Dogsledding
Location: Kandiyohi
Contact: Jeff Brown
Trail Manager
Minnesota Department of
Natural Resources
P.O. Box 508
New London, MN 56273-0508
(612) 354–4940
www.dnr.state.mn.us/compass
trails/glacial/glacial.html

18 Goodhue Pioneer Trail (R. J. Dorer Memorial Trail)

Endpoints: R. J. Dorer Hardwood
State Forest, Hay Creek
Mileage: 8.9
Surface: grass, dirt

Other use: Hunting
Location: Goodhue
Contact: Kyle Klatt
Planning Technician
City of Red Wing
P.O. Box 34
Red Wing, MN 55066-0034
(612) 385–3622
kyle.wklatt@ci.red-wing.mn.us

19 Hardwood Creek Trail

Endpoints: Forest Lake, Hugo
Mileage: 9.5
Surface: asphalt, grass

Location: Washington
Contact: John Elholm
Operations Coordinator/Parks
Planner
Washington County Parks
11660 Myeron Road N.
Stillwater, MN 55082
(651) 430–4303
john.elholm@co.washington.mn.us
www.co.washington.mn.us

20 Harmony—Preston Valley Trail (Root River Trail)

Endpoints: Fountain, Harmony
Mileage: 18

Surface: asphalt

Location: Fillmore
Contact: Craig Blommer
Area Supervisor
Minnesota Department of
Natural Resources, Trails and
Waterways Unit
2300 Silver Creek Road N.E.
Rochester, MN 55906-4505
(507) 280–5061
www.dnr.state.mn.us/state_trails/
blufflands/harmony_preston.html

21 Heartland State Trail

Endpoints: Park Rapids, Cass
Lake
Mileage: 51
Surface: asphalt, gravel

Location: Cass; Hubbard
Contact: Pat Tangeman
Trails and Waterways Technician
Heartland State Trail
P.O. Box 112
Nevis, MN 56467-0112
(218) 652–4054

22 Interstate State Park to Taylor Falls Trail

Endpoints: Interstate State Park,
Taylor Falls
Mileage: 1
Surface: grass

Location: Chisago
Contact: Steve Anderson
Park Manager
Interstate State Park
P.O. Box 254
Taylor Falls, MN 55084-0254
(612) 465–5711

23 Iron Ore Trail

Endpoints: Tower, Embarass
Mileage: 15
Surface: ballast

Location: St. Louis
Contact: Thomas Peterson
Area Supervisor
Minnesota Department of
Natural Resources, Trails and
Waterways Unit
500 Lafayette Road
St. Paul, MN 55155-4052
(218) 753–6256

24 Lake Wobegon Trail

Endpoints: Avon, Sauk Centre
Mileage: 28
Surface: asphalt

Location: Stearns
Contact: Pete Theismann
Park Technician
Stearns County Parks
1802 County Road 137
Waite Park, MN 56387
(320) 255–6172
pete.theismann@co.stearns.mn.us
www.lakewobegontrails.com

25 Lakewalk Trail—Duluth

Endpoints: Canal Park Museum, Twenty-sixth Avenue and London Road
Mileage: 3.8
Surface: asphalt

Location: St. Louis
Contact: Sue Moyer
Director
Duluth Parks and Recreation Department
City Hall, Room 330
411 W. First Street
Duluth, MN 55802-1102
(218) 723–3337
www.ci.duluth.mn.us

26 Luce Line State Trail

Endpoints: Plymouth, Cosmos
Mileage: 65
Surface: crushed stone, grass

Location: Hennepin; Carver; McLeod; Meeker
Contact: Richard Schmidt
Trails and Waterways Technician
Minnesota Department of Natural Resources, Trails and Waterways Unit
3980 Watertown Road
Maple Plain, MN 55359-9615
(612) 475–0371

27 Mesabi Trail

Endpoints: Grand Rapids; Ely
Mileage: 66
Surface: asphalt

Location: St. Louis; Itasca
Contact: Robert Manzaline
Director
St. Louis and Lake Countries Regional RR Authority
US Bank Place (Suite 6B)
230 First Street S.
Virginia, MN 55792
(218) 749–0697
info@mesabitrail.com
www.mesabitrail.com/frames/main.html

28 Minnehaha Trail

Endpoints: Fort Snelling State Park, Minneapolis
Mileage: 5
Surface: asphalt

Location: Hennepin
Contact: David Berg
Park Specialist
Fort Snelling State Park
1 Post Road
St. Paul, MN 55111
(612) 725–2389

29 Minnesota Valley State Trail

Endpoints: Minneapolis, Le Sueur
Mileage: 75
Surface: asphalt, crushed stone

Location: Dakota; Hennepin; Scott
Contact: Bill Weir
Trails Coordinator
Minnesota Department of Natural Resources
1200 Warner Road
St. Paul, MN 55106
(612) 722–7994

30 Minnetonka Loop Trail System

Endpoints: Minnetonka
Mileage: 32
Surface: crushed stone

Location: Hennepin; Carver
Contact: Dean Elstad
Loop Trail Coordinator
City of Minnetonka
14600 Minnetonka Boulevard
Minnetonka, MN 55345-1597
(612) 938–7245
delstad@ci.minnentonka.mn.us

31 Minnewaska Snowmobile Trail (D.A.T.A. Trail System)

Endpoints: Starbuck, Villard
Mileage: 25

Surface: gravel, dirt

Location: Pope
Contact: Bill Anderson
Trail Manager
Douglas Area Trails Association
P.O. Box 112
Alexandria, MN 56308-0112
(612) 834–2033

32 Paul Bunyan State Trail

Endpoints: Brainerd-Baxter, Bemidji, Hackensack
Mileage: 100
Surface: asphalt, ballast

Location: Beltrami; Cass; Crow Wing; Hubbard
Contact: Terry McGaughey
Volunteer Coordinator
Paul Bunyan Trail
P.O. Box 356
124 North Sixth Street
Brainerd, MN 56401-0356
terry@paulbunyantrail.com
www.brainerd.com/pbtrail/pbtrail.html

33 Pequaywam Lake Snowmobile Trail (Cloquet Valley Trail)

Endpoints: Cloquet Valley State Forest, Aurora
Mileage: 50
Surface: ballast, dirt

Location: St. Louis
Contact: Tom Peterson
Area Supervisor
Two Harbors Division of Trails and Waterways
1568 Highway 2
Two Harbors, MN 55616
(218) 834–6622
www.dnr.state.mn.us

34 Quarry Loop Trail

Endpoints: Banning State Park
Mileage: 2
Surface: gravel, ballast

Location: Pine
Contact: Randy Gordon
Park Manager
Banning State Park
P.O. Box 643
Sandstone, MN 55072
(320) 245–2668

35 Red Jacket Trail

Endpoints: Mankato, Rapidan
Mileage: 5.6
Surface: asphalt, crushed stone

Location: Blue Earth
Contact: Dean Ehlers
Park Superintendent
Parks Department
P.O. Box 3083
Mankato, MN 56002-3083
(507) 625–3282

36 Root River State Trail

Endpoints: Fountain, Houston
Mileage: 42
Surface: asphalt, grass

Location: Fillmore; Houston
Contact: Craig Blommer
Area Supervisor
Minnesota Department of Natural Resources, Trails and Waterways Unit
2300 Silver Creek Road, N.E.
Rochester, MN 55906-4505
(507) 280–5061
www.dnr.state.mn.us/state_trails/blufflands/root_river.html

37 Sakatah Singing Hills State Trail

Endpoints: Faribault, Mankato
Mileage: 39
Surface: asphalt, grass

Location: Blue Earth; Le Sueur; Rice
Contact: Randy Schoeneck
Trail Technician
Minnesota Department of Natural Resources
Sakatah State Park
P.O. Box 11
Elysian, MN 56028-0011
(507) 267–4772
www.dnr.mn.state.us

38 Silver Creek Bike Trail

Endpoints: Rochester
Mileage: 1.3
Surface: asphalt

Location: Olmsted
Contact: John Wellner
Infrastructure Manager
City of Rochester
201 4th Street S.E., Room 108
Rochester, MN 55904-3740
(507) 281–6197
jwellner@ci.rochester.mn.us

39 Soo Line ATV Trail—North Route

Endpoints: Cass Lake, Moose Lake State Park
Mileage: 112
Surface: gravel, ballast

Other use: ATVs
Location: Aitkin; Carlton; Cass
Contact: Bill Stocker
District Ranger
Chippewa National Forest
Route 3, Box 244
Cass Lake, MN 56633-8929
(218) 335–2283

40 Soo Line ATV Trail— South Route

Endpoints: Saunders Junction (near Superior, Wisconsin), Genola
Mileage: 114
Surface: ballast, gravel (11 miles paved for non-motorized use between Isle and Onamia)

Other use: ATVs
Location: Douglas (WI); Carlton; Pine; Aitkin; Mille Lacs; Morrison
Contact: www.dnr.state.mn.us/ohv/trails/sooline_south.html

41 Southwest Regional LRT Trail—North Corridor

Endpoints: Hopkins, Minnetonka
Mileage: 15
Surface: asphalt, crushed stone

Location: Carver; Hennepin
Contact: Delbert Miller
Trails Coordinator
Hennepin County Parks
12615 County Road 9
Plymouth, MN 55441-1299
(612) 559–6754
Dmiller@hennepinparks.org
www.hennepinparks.org/

42 Southwest Regional LRT Trail—South Corridor

Endpoints: Chanhassen, Hopkins
Mileage: 11.5
Surface: crushed stone

Location: Carver; Hennepin
Contact: Delbert Miller
Trails Coordinator
Hennepin County Parks
12615 County Road 9
Plymouth, MN 55441-1248
(612) 559–6754
Dmiller@hennepinparks.org/
www.hennepinparks.org/

43 St. Anthony Falls Heritage Trail (Stone Arch Bridge)

Endpoints: Minneapolis
Mileage: 1.5

Surface: concrete

Location: Hennepin
Contact: David Wiggins
Program Manager
Minnesota Historical Society
125 Main Street S.E.
Minneapolis, MN 55414-2143
(612) 627–5433

44 Superior Hiking Trail

Endpoints: Canadian border,
Two Harbors
Mileage: 220 (3 are rail-trail)
Surface: ballast, dirt

Other use: Snowshoeing
Location: St. Louis; Lake; Cook
Contact: Nancy Odden
Executive Director
Superior Hiking Trail Association
P.O. Box 4
Two Harbors, MN 55616-0004
suphike@mn.net
www.shta.org

45 Taconite State Trail

Endpoints: Ely, Grand Rapids
Mileage: 165
Surface: gravel, ballast, grass,
asphalt, dirt

Location: St. Louis
Contact: Ann Bjorgo

Area Supervisor
Minnesota Department of
Natural Resources
406 Main Street
P.O. Box 388
Tower, MN 55790
(218) 753–6256
www.dnr.state.mn.us/state_trails/
taconite/index.html

46 Tomahawk Trail

Endpoints: Ely, Little Marais
Mileage: 65
Surface: ballast, grass

Location: Lake; St. Louis
Contact: Minnesota Department
of Natural Resources
1568 Highway 2
Two Harbors, MN 55616
(218) 834–6626

47 Trailblazers Path (part of Mesabi Trail)

Endpoints: Hibbing, Lake Swan
Mileage: 10
Surface: asphalt, gravel, ballast

Location: Itasca; St. Louis
Contact: Douglas Swenson
Hibbing Trailblazers
P.O. Box 432
Hibbing, MN 55746-0432
senbay@uslink.net

48 29th Street Midtown Greenway

Endpoints: 31st Street
South/Chowen Avenue, 5th
Avenue South (Minneapolis)
Mileage: 2.8
Surface: asphalt

Location: Hennepin
Contact: Midtown Greenway
Coalition
118 E. 26th Street, Suite 100B
Minneapolis, MN 55404
www.midtowngreenway.org/
greenway

49 Virginia Trails

Endpoints: Virginia
Mileage: 1
Surface: crushed stone, gravel

Location: St. Louis
Contact: John Bachman
Director
City of Virginia Park and
Recreation Department
Virginia, MN 55792
(218) 741–3583

50 Wapiti Trail

Endpoints: Thief/River Falls, Grygla
Mileage: 50.2 (17 are rail-trail)
Surface: ballast, grass, dirt

Location: Marshall; Pennington
Contact: Alan Swanson
Goodrich Trailblazers
Snowmobile Club
Route 2, Box 28A
Goodridge, MN 56725-9724
www.dnr.state.mn.us

51 West Mankato Trail

Endpoints: Mankato City
Mileage: 1.5
Surface: asphalt

Location: Blue Earth
Contact: Floyd Roberts
Parks Superintendent
City of Mankato Parks and
Forestry
P.O. Box 3368
Mankato, MN 56002-3368
(507) 387–8650
Trailnet88@aol.com

52 West River Parkway

Endpoints: Boom Island, Minnehaha Falls (Minneapolis)
Mileage: 8.9
Surface: asphalt, concrete

Location: Hennepin
Contact: Bob Mattson
Park and Recreation Planner
Minneapolis Park and Recreation
Board
200 Grain Exchange
400 South Fourth Street
Minneapolis, MN 55415-1400
(612) 661–4824

53 Willard Munger State Trail (Alex Laveau Memorial Trail)

Endpoints: Hinckley, Duluth
Mileage: 72
Surface: asphalt

Location: Carlton; Pine
Contact: Kevin Arends
Area Supervisor
Minnesota Department of
Natural Resources, Trails and
Waterways Unit
Route 2, 701 South Kenwood
Moose Lake, MN 55767
(218) 485–5410

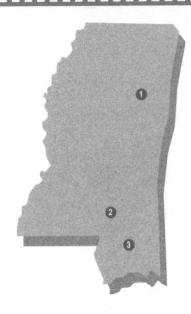

2 Longleaf Trace Trail

Endpoints: Prentiss, Hattiesburg (Varnado Switch)
Mileage: 39
Surface: asphalt

Location: Forrest; Jefferson Davis; Lamar
Contact: Herlon Pierce
Trail Manager
Pearl to Leaf River Rail-Trail
Recreation District
P.O. Box 15187
Hattiesburg, MS 39404-5187
(601) 264–8825
www.longleaftrace.org

1 Catherine "Kitty" Bryan Dill Memorial Parkway

Endpoints: West Point
Mileage: 1.2
Surface: concrete

Location: Clay
Contact: Dewel Brasher, Jr.
City Manager
City of West Point
P.O. Box 1117
West Point, MS 39773-1117
(601) 494–2573

3 Tuxachanie National Recreation Trail

Endpoints: DeSoto National Forest
Mileage: 22.8
Surface: dirt

Location: Harrison; Stone
Contact: Diane Tyrone
Forester
Desoto Ranger District
P.O. Box 248
654 West Frontage Road
Wiggins, MS 39577-0248
(601) 928–5291

MISSOURI

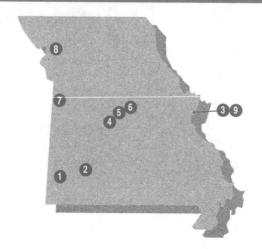

1 Frisco Greenway

Endpoints: Joplin, Webb City
Mileage: 4
Surface: crushed stone, ballast

Location: Jasper
Contact: Paul Teverow
President
Joplin Trails Coalition
P.O. Box 2102
Joplin, MO 64803-2102
teverow-p@mail.mssc.edu

2 Frisco Highline Trail

Endpoints: Walnut Grove, Willard
Mileage: 11.7
Surface: crushed stone, ballast

Location: Greene
Contact: Terry Whaley
Executive Director
Ozark Greenways
P.O. Box 50733
Springfield, MO 65805-0733
(417) 864–2015
terry@ozarkgreenways.org
www.ozarkgreenways.org

3 Grant's Trail

Endpoints: St. Louis (Orlando Gardens), Kirkwood (Highway 44)
Mileage: 8
Surface: asphalt, crushed stone, ballast

Location: St. Louis
Contact: Fred Earnie
Manager, Grant's Trail
Development
Trailnet, Inc.
3900 Reavis Barracks Road
St. Louis, MO 63125-2308
(314) 416–9930
granttrail@stlnot.com
www.trailnet.org

4 Katy Spur Trail

Endpoints: Jefferson City (Cedar
City Drive), North Jefferson City
(junction with main Katy Trail)
Mileage: 1
Location: Cole
Contact: Jefferson City
P.O. Box 166
Booneville, MO 65233-0166
(816) 882–8196

5 Katy Trail State Park

Endpoints: St. Charles (Route
370), North Clinton (Routes 7 and
13)
Mileage: 226
Surface: crushed stone

Location: Boone; Callaway;
Cooper; Henry; Howard;
Montgomery; Pettis; St. Charles;
Warren
Contact: Larry Larson
District Supervisor
Missouri River District
Missouri Department of Natural
Resources
P.O. Box 166
Booneville, MO 65233-0166
(660) 882–8196
nrlarsl@mail.dnr.state.mo.us

www.katy-trail.com
www.global-image.com/
katytrail/intro.html

6 M.K.T. Nature/Fitness Trail

Endpoints: Columbia, McBain
Mileage: 8.5
Surface: crushed stone

Location: Boone
Contact: Steve Saitta
Parks Development
Superintendent
Columbia Parks and Recreation
Department
P.O. Box N
Columbia, MO 65205-5013
(573) 874–7203

7 Trolley Track Trail

Endpoints: Brookside and Volker
Boulevards, 85th Street east of
Main Street (Kansas City)
Mileage: 4.5
Surface: crushed stone

Location: Jackson
Contact: Ron Guglielmino
Kansas City Area Transportation
Authority
1200 East 18th Street
Kansas City, MO 64108
(816) 346–0235
metro@kcata.org
www.kcata.org/country_club_trail.
html

8 Urban Trail System (St. Joseph Trail System)

Endpoints: Ferndale Street, 28th and Commercial Streets (St. Joseph)
Mileage: 5
Surface: asphalt

Location: Buchanan
Contact: Andrew Clements
Transportation Planning Manager
City of St. Joseph, MO
1100 Frederick Avenue
St. Joseph, MO 64501
(816) 271–4653
andyc@ci.st-joseph.mo.us
www.ci.st-joseph.mo.us/pwt.html

9 West Alton Trail

Endpoints: West Alton (St. Charles Street), Lincoln Shields Recreation Area
Mileage: 1.3
Surface: crushed stone

Location: St. Charles
Contact: Ted Curtis
Executive Director
Trailnet, Inc.
3900 Reavis Barracks Road
St. Louis, MO 63125-2308
(314) 416–9930, ext. 105
tedcurtis@trail.net
www.trailnet.org

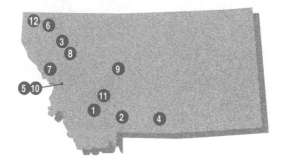

1 Butte to Toll Mountain Cross-Country Ski Trail

Endpoints: Deerlodge National Forest
Mileage: 7
Surface: ballast

Location: Jefferson
Contact: Wendell Beardsley
Trails Program Coordinator
USDAFS, Region 1
200 East Broadway
P.O. Box 7669
Missoula, MT 59802-4598
(406) 329–3150

2 Gallagator Linear Trail

Endpoints: (East Story and South Church Streets, 3rd Street and Kagy Boulevard (Bozeman)
Mileage: 1.5
Surface: gravel, ballast

Location: Gallatin
Contact: Gary Vodehnal
Resource Specialist
Gallatin Valley and Land Trust
P.O. Box 7021
Bozeman, MT 59771-7021
(406) 587–8404
gvlt@mon.net
www.gvlt.org

3 Great Northern Historical Trail

Endpoints: Kalispell city limits, 3.75 miles west of Kalispell city limits
Mileage: 3.75
Surface: gravel

Location: Flathead
Contact: Mark Crowley
Trails Coordinator
Flathead County Planning Office
800 S. Main Street
Kalispell, MT 59901
(406) 758–5965
mcrowley@co.flathead.mt.us

4 Heights Bike Trail (Kiwanis Bike Trail)

Endpoints: Billings Boulevard at Yellowstone River, Main Street (Billings)
Mileage: 5
Surface: asphalt, crushed stone

Location: Yellowstone
Contact: Mike Hink
Director
Department of Parks, Recreation and Public Lands
510 North Broadway
4th Floor Library
Billings, MT 59101-1156
(406) 657–8369

5 Kim Williams Nature Trail

Endpoints: 5th Street (Missoula), Clark Fork River (2.5 miles west of Missoula)
Mileage: 2.5
Surface: ballast

Location: Missoula
Contact: Jim Van Fossen
Director
Missoula Parks and Recreation Department
100 Hickory Street
Missoula, MT 59801-1859
(406) 721–7275
www.marsweb.com/~missoula/feetfrst.html

6 Kootenai Trail

Endpoints: Rexford, Eureka (Kootenai National Forest)
Mileage: 7.5
Surface: gravel

Location: Lincoln
Contact: Resource Forester
Kootenai National Forest
1299 Highway 93 North
Eureka, MT 59917
(406) 296–2536

7 NorPac Trail

Endpoints: Lolo National Forest, Idaho State Line at Lookout Pass
Mileage: 12.1
Surface: ballast

Location: Mineral
Contact: Carol Johnson
Lolo National Forest
Superior Ranger District
P.O. Box 460
Superior, MT 59872
(406) 822–4233

8 Northern Pacific Rail-Trail

Endpoints: Routes 82 and 93, Kalispell Bay (Somers)
Mileage: 1
Surface: asphalt

Location: Flathead
Contact: Mark Crowley
Trails Coordinator
Flathead County Planning Office
800 South Main Street
Kalispell, MT 59901
(406) 758–5965
mcrowley@co.flathead.mt.us

9 River's Edge Trail

Endpoints: First Avenue North Bridge, Crooked Falls (Great Falls)
Mileage: 13
Surface: asphalt

Location: Cascade
Contact: Doug Wicks
Vice President
Recreational Trails, Inc.
P.O. Box 553
Great Falls, MT 59403-0553
trailsrus@in-tch.com

10 Southside Trail

Endpoints: McCormick Park, Kim Williams Nature Trail (Missoula)
Mileage: 1.5
Surface: asphalt, gravel, ballast

Location: Missoula
Contact: Jim Van Fossen
Director
Missoula Parks and Recreation Department
100 Hickory Street
Missoula, MT 59801-1859
(406) 721–7275

11 Spring Meadow Lake and Centennial Park Trail

Endpoints: Spring Meadow Lake, Carroll College (Helena)
Mileage: 4.6
Surface: crushed stone

Location: Lewis and Clark
Contact: Randy Lilje
Park Manager
Helena Area Resource Office of Fish, Wildlife and Parks
930 Custer West
Helena, MT 59620
(405) 447–8463

12 Tobacco River Memorial Trail

Endpoints: Eureka Park, Rexford (Kootenai National Forest)
Mileage: 6
Surface: gravel

Location: Lincoln
Contact: Resource Forester
Kootenai National Forest
1299 Highway 93 North
Eureka, MT 59917
(406) 296–2536

NEBRASKA

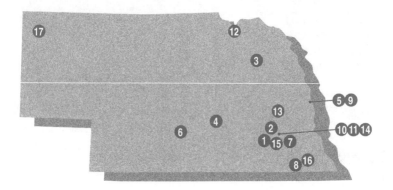

1 Belt Line Trail

Endpoints: St. Joe Trail at Ada Street (Grand Island), Cherry Street (Grand Island)
Mileage: 2.72
Surface: asphalt

Location: Hall
Contact: Steven Paustian
Director of Parks and Recreation
City of Grand Island
City Hall—100 East 1st Street
Box 1968
Grand Island, NE 68802-1968
(308) 385–5444, ext. 290
spaustian@ci.grand-island.ne.us

2 Cottonmill—Fort Kearny Trail

Endpoints: Kearney, Fort Kearny
Mileage: 3.1

Surface: asphalt, crushed stone, concrete

Location: Buffalo
Contact: Neil Lewis
Kearney Parks and Recreation Department
P.O. Box 1180
Kearney, NE 68848-1180
(308) 233–3230

3 Cowboy Trail

Endpoints: Norfolk, Neligh, O'Neill, Valentine
Mileage: 47 (in 3 sections)
Surface: crushed stone, concrete

Location: Antelope; Cherry; Holt
Contact: Larry Voecks
State Trail Coordinator

Nebraska Games and Parks
Commission
2201 North Thirteenth Street
Norfolk, NE 68701-2267
(402) 370–3374
netrails@ngpc.state.ne.us
lvoecks@ngpc.state.ne.us
www.ngpc.state.ne.us
admserver.ngpc.state.ne.us/
infoeduc/cbtrail.ht

4 Dannebrog Rail-Trail

Endpoints: Dannebrog
Mileage: 3
Surface: wood chips, concrete

Location: Howard
Contact: Shirley Johnson
Treasurer and Public Relations
Dannenbrog Trail Association
P.O. Box 216
522 East Roger Welsch Avenue
Dannenbrog, NE 68831-0216
(308) 226–2237

5 Field Club Trail

Endpoints: 38th Avenue and
Leavenworth Street, 35th Avenue
and Vinton Street (Omaha)
Mileage: 2
Surface: concrete

Location: Douglas
Contact: Jerry Leahy
Assistant Director
Douglas County Environmental
Services
3015 Menke Circle

Omaha, NE 68134-4638
(402) 444–7775
www.co.douglas.ne.us/dept/
envserv/field.htm

6 Fort Kearny Hike-Bike Trail

Endpoints: Basswood Strip State
Wildlife Area, Fort Kearny State
Recreation Area
Mileage: 1.8
Surface: ballast, cinder

Location: Kearney; Buffalo
Contact: Eugene Hunt
Superintendent
Fort Kearny State
Recreation Area
Route 4
1020 V. Road
Kearney, NE 68847-9804
(308) 865–5305
www.ngpc.state.ne.us

7 Hickman Linear Bike Trail

Endpoints: Hickman (Main City
Park)
Mileage: 0.8
Surface: asphalt

Location: Lancaster
Contact: Jim Plouzek
Mayor
City of Hickman
P.O. Box 127
Hickman, NE 68372-0127
(402) 792–2212
www.hickmannebraska.com/
recreation.htm

8 Iron Horse Trail Lake Park

Endpoints: Nemaha Natural Resources District
Mileage: 2.9
Surface: ballast

Other use: Hunting
Location: Pawnee
Contact: Pat Foote
SCORP
Nebraska Game and Parks Commission
220 North Thirty-third Street
Lincoln, NE 68503-3303
(402) 471–0641
www.nemahanrd.org/iron_horse.htm

9 Keystone Trail

Endpoints: Omaha (90th and Fort Streets), Bellevue (Haworth Park)
Mileage: 12
Surface: concrete

Location: Douglas; Sarpy
Contact: Dolores Silkworth
Park and Recreation Planner
Parks, Recreation and Public Property
Omaha/Douglas Civic Center
1819 Farnam Street , Suite 1111
Omaha, NE 68183-0111
(402) 444–4985
www.ngpc.state.ne.us/parks/trails/showtrail.ihtml?trailID=112

10 MoPac East Trail

Endpoints: Lincoln (84th Street), Wabash
Mileage: 25
Surface: crushed stone

Location: Lancaster; Cass
Contact: Dan Schulz
Resources Coordinator
Lower Platte South Natural Resource District
3125 Portig Street
P.O. Box 83581
Lincoln, NE 68501-3581
(402) 476-2729
dan@lpsnrd.org
www.lpsnrd.org

11 MoPac Trail

Endpoints: 33rd Street. 84th Street (Lincoln)
Mileage: 4
Surface: concrete

Location: Lancaster
Contact: Lynn Johnson
Planning and Construction Manager
City of Lincoln Parks and Recreation Department
2740 A Street
Lincoln, NE 68502
(402) 441–8255

12 Niobrara Trail

Endpoints: Niobrara State Park
Mileage: 2.1
Surface: crushed stone

Location: Knox
Contact: Tom Motacek
Superintendent
Niobrara State Park
P.O. Box 226
Niobrara, NE 68760-0226
(402) 857–3373
www.ngpc.state.ne.us/parks/trails/
showtrail

13 Oak Creek Trail

Endpoints: Brainard, Valparaiso
Mileage: 12
Surface: crushed stone

Location: Saunders; Butler
Contact: Dan Schulz
Resources Coordinator
Lower Platte South Natural
Resources District
3125 Portia Street
P.O. Box 83581
Lincoln, NE 68501-3581
(402) 476–2729
dan@lpsnrd.org
www.lpsnrd.org

14 Rock Island Trail

Endpoints: 17th Street and Old
Cheney, City Campus at 19th and
Vine (Lincoln)
Mileage: 5
Surface: concrete

Location: Lancaster
Contact: Lynn Johnson
Planning and Construction
Manager
Lincoln Department of Parks and
Recreation
2740 A Street
Lincoln, NE 68502-3113
(402) 441–7847
www.gptn.org/rock_island.htm

15 St. Joe Trail

Endpoints: Ada Street (Grand
Island), U.S. 34 (Grand Island)
Mileage: 1.4
Surface: asphalt

Location: Hall
Contact: Steven Paustian
Director of Parks and Recreation
City of Grand Island
City Hall—100 East 1st Street
Box 1968
Grand Island, NE 68802-1968
(308) 385–5444, ext. 290
spaustian@ci.grand-island.ne.us

16 Steamboat-Trace Trail

Endpoints: Brownville, Peru
Mileage: 9.5
Surface: crushed stone

Location: Otoe; Nemaha
Contact: Paul Rohrbaugh
Nemaha Natural Resources
District
125 Jackson Street
Tecumseh, NE 68450-2133
(402) 335–3325

17 White River Trail

Endpoints: Andrews, Harrison
Mileage: 10
Surface: ballast

Location: Dawes; Sioux
Contact: Jim Lemmon
Fort Robinson State Park
P.O. Box 392
Crawford, NE 69339
(308) 665–2900

1 Historic Railroad Hiking Trail

Endpoints: Lake Mead National
Recreation Area
Mileage: 6
Surface: gravel, dirt

Location: Clark
Contact: Karen Whitney
Public Affairs Officer
Lake Mead National Recreation
Area
601 Nevada Highway
Boulder City, NV 89005-2426
(702) 293–8907

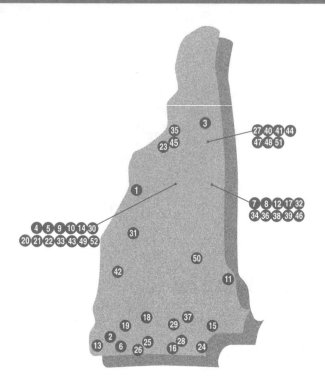

1 Ammonoosuc Rail Trail

Endpoints: Littleton (Industrial Road), Woodsville
Mileage: 19
Surface: gravel, ballast, dirt

Other Use: ATV
Location: Grafton
Contact: Paul Gary
Chief, Bureau of Trails

Division of Parks and Recreation
172 Pembroke Road
P.O. Box 1856
Concord, NH 03301-1858
(603) 271–3254
pgray@dred.state.nh.us
http://members.fortunecity.com/
railtrails/NH/WW/WL-home.html

2 Ashuelot Rail Trail

Endpoints: Hinsdale, Keene South
Mileage: 23
Surface: gravel, ballast, dirt, sand, cinder

Location: Cheshire
Contact: Bob Spoerl
Program Specialist
N.H. Division of Parks and
Recreation, Trails Bureau
172 Pembroke Road
P.O. Box 1856
Concord, NH 03302-1856
(603) 271–3254
members.fortunecity.com/
railtrails/NH/DK/DK-S0061.htm

3 Berlin Branch

Endpoints: Jefferson, Gorham
Mileage: 17
Surface: ballast

Location: Coos
Contact: Bob Spoerl
Program Specialist
N.H. Division of Parks and
Recreation, Trails Bureau
172 Pembroke Road
P.O. Box 1856
Concord, NH 03301-1858
(603) 271-3254

4 Black Pond Trail

Endpoints: White Mountain
National Forest
Mileage: 0.8
Surface: dirt
Location: Grafton
Contact: Dave Hrdlicka
Trails Coordinator

White Mountain National Forest
Pemigewassett Ranger District
RFD 3, Route 175, Box 15
Plymouth, NH 03264
(603) 536–1310

5 Cedar Brook Trail

Endpoints: White Mountain
National Forest
Mileage: 5.7
Surface: ballast

Location: Grafton
Contact: Dave Hrdlicka
Trails Coordinator
White Mountain National Forest
Pemigewassett Ranger District
RFD 3, Route 175, Box 15
Plymouth, NH 03264
(603) 536–1310

6 Cheshire Rail Trail

Endpoints: Massachusetts state
line, Keene
Mileage: 27
Surface: gravel, ballast, dirt,
cedar, sand

Location: Cheshire
Contact:
members.fortunecity.com/
railtrails/NH/WB/WB-S0679.htm

7 Dry River Trail

Endpoints: White Mountain
National Forest
Mileage: 11
Surface: ballast

Location: Carroll
Contact: Eric Swett
Forest Technician
White Mountain National Forest
Saco Ranger District
33 Kancamagus Highway
Conway, NH 03818-6019
(603) 447–5448

8 East Branch Trail

Endpoints: White Mountain
National Forest
Mileage: 8
Surface: ballast

Location: Carroll
Contact: Eric Swett
Forest Technician
White Mountain National Forest
Saco Ranger District
33 Kancamagus Highway
Conway, NH 03818-6019
(603) 447–5448

9 East Pond Trail

Endpoints: White Mountain
National Forest
Mileage: 5
Surface: gravel, grass, dirt

Location: Grafton
Contact: Dave Hrdlicka
Trails Coordinator
White Mountain National Forest
Pemigewassett Ranger District
RFD 3, Route 175, Box 15
Plymouth, NH 03264
(603) 536–1310

10 Ethan Pond Trail

Endpoints: White Mountain
National Forest
Mileage: 5.6
Surface: ballast, grass, dirt

Location: Grafton
Contact: Dave Hrdlicka
Trails Coordinator
White Mountain National Forest
Pemigewassett Ranger District
RFD 3, Route 175, Box 15
Plymouth, NH 03264
(603) 536–1310

11 Farmington Branch Rail-Trail

Endpoints: Rochester,
Farmington
Mileage: 6
Surface: gravel, ballast, dirt,
cedar, sand

Location: Strafford
Contact: members.fortunecity.
com/railtrails/NH/

12 Flat Mountain Pond Trail

Endpoints: White Mountain National Forest
Mileage: 9
Surface: ballast

Location: Carroll
Contact: Eric Swett
Forest Technician
White Mountain National Forest
Saco Ranger District
33 Kancamagus Highway
Conway, NH 03818-6019
(603) 447–5448

13 Fort Hill Branch

Endpoints: Hinsdale
Mileage: 9
Surface: gravel, ballast, dirt, cedar, sand

Location: Cheshire
Contact: Bob Spoerl
Program Specialist
N.H. Division of Parks and Recreation, Trails Bureau
172 Pembroke Road
P.O. Box 1856
Concord, NH 03302-1856
(603) 271–3254
b_spoerl@gwsmtp.dred.state.nh.us

14 Franconia Brook Trail

Endpoints: White Mountain National Forest
Mileage: 7.2
Surface: ballast

Location: Grafton
Contact: Dave Hrdlicka
Trails Coordinator
White Mountain National Forest
Pemigewassett Ranger District
RFD 3, Route 175, Box 15
Plymouth, NH 03264
(603) 536–1310

15 Fremont Branch Rail-Trail

Endpoints: Fremont, Epping
Mileage: 4.4
Surface: gravel, grass, dirt, sand, cedar

Other use: ATVs
Location: Rockingham
Contact: members.fortunecity.com/railtrails/NH/MP/MR-home.htm

16 Granite Town Rail-Trail

Endpoints: Milford (Department of Public Works garage on South Street), Brookline town line
Mileage: 3
Surface: cedar, grass, dirt

Location: Hillsborough
Contact: Conservation Commission
1 Union Square
Milford, NH 03055
(603) 672–1070
www.ci.milford.nh.us/
conservation/RRTrail.html

17 Guinea Pond Trail

Endpoints: White Mountain National Forest
Mileage: 4
Surface: ballast

Location: Carroll
Contact: Dave Hrdlicka
Trails Coordinator
White Mountain National Forest
Pemigewassett Ranger District
RFD 3, Route 175, Box 15
Plymouth, NH 03264
(603) 536–1310

18 Hillsborough Branch Rail-Trail

Endpoints: Hillsborough, Bennington
Mileage: 7.8
Surface: gravel, ballast, dirt, cedar, sand

Location: Hillsborough
Contact: members.fortunecity.com/railtrails/NH/WC/BH-home.htm

19 Industrial Heritage Trail

Endpoints: Railroad Square on Main Street, Eastern Avenue (Keene)
Mileage: 1
Surface: asphalt

Location: Cheshire
Contact: Ian Ferguson
President
Pathways for Keene
P.O. Box 226
Keene, NH 03421
iferguson@fibermark.com
www.tlaorg.org/pathways/

20 Lincoln Brook Trail

Endpoints: White Mountain National Forest
Mileage: 6.7
Surface: gravel, dirt

Location: Grafton
Contact: Dave Hrdlicka
Trails Coordinator
White Mountain National Forest
Pemigewassett Ranger District
RFD 3, Route 175, Box 15
Plymouth, NH 03264
(603) 536–1310

21 Lincoln Woods Trail

Endpoints: White Mountain National Forest
Mileage: 2.7
Surface: ballast

Location: Grafton
Contact: Dave Hrdlicka
Trails Coordinator
White Mountain National Forest
Pemigewassett Ranger District
RFD 3, Route 175, Box 15
Plymouth, NH 03264
(603) 536-1310

22 Little East Pond Trail

Endpoints: White Mountain
National Forest
Mileage: 1.7
Surface: ballast

Location: Grafton
Contact: Dave Hrdlicka
Trails Coordinator
White Mountain National Forest
Pemigewassett Ranger District
RFD 3, Route 175, Box 15
Plymouth, NH 03264
(603) 536-1310

23 Littleton to Woodsville

Endpoints: Littleton, Woodsville
Mileage: 19
Surface: ballast

Location: Grafton
Contact: Paul Gray
Bureau Chief

New Hampshire Bureau of Trails
P.O. Box 1856
Concord, NH 03302-1856
(603) 271-3254

24 Manchester and Lawrence Branch

Endpoints: Salem, Windham
Mileage: 8.2
Surface: gravel, ballast, dirt,
cedar, sand

Location: Rockingham
Contact: members.fortunecity.
com/railtrails/NH/MP/MP-
S0020.htm

25 Mason Railroad Trail

Endpoints: Wilton, Townsend,
MA
Mileage: 6.7
Surface: ballast

Location: Hillsborough
Contact: Liz Fletcher
Commissioner
Mason Conservation Commission
Mann House
Darling Hill Road
Mason, NH 03048
(603) 878-2070

26 Monadnock Branch Rail-Trail

Endpoints: Massachusetts state line, Jaffrey
Mileage: 7.2
Surface: gravel, grass, dirt, cedar

Location: Cheshire
Contact: Bob Spoerl
Program Specialist
N.H. Division of Parks and
Recreation, Trails Bureau
172 Pembroke Road
P.O. Box 1856
Concord, NH 03301-1858
(603) 271-3254

27 Moriah Brook Trail

Endpoints: White Mountain National Forest
Mileage: 5.3
Surface: gravel, dirt

Location: Coos
Contact: Terri Marceron
Assistant Ranger
White Mountain National Forest
Androscoggin Ranger District
300 Glen Road
Gorham, NH 03581-1322
(603) 466–2713

28 Nashua-Worcester Rail Trail

Endpoints: Nashua
Mileage: 1.3
Surface: asphalt, grass

Location: Hillsborough
Contact: Mark Archambault
Long Range Planner
Community Development
Divison of the City of Nashua
229 Main Street
Nashua, NH 03060
(603) 594–3360
archambaultm@nashuanh.org

29 New Boston Railroad Bed Trail

Endpoints: New Boston (4–H Grounds), Goffstown (Parker Station)
Mileage: 5
Surface: ballast

Location: Hillsborough
Contact: Cyndie Wilson
Conservation Commissioner
Town of New Boston
New Boston, NH 03070
www.new-boston.nh.us/orgs/
conservation/nbcon_trails.htm

30 North Twin Trail

Endpoints: White Mountain National Forest
Mileage: 4.3
Surface: dirt

Location: Grafton
Contact: Roger Collins

Forest Technician
White Mountain National Forest
Ammonusac Ranger District
P.O. Box 239
Bethlehem, NH 03574-0239
(603) 869–2626

Forest Technician
White Mountain National Forest
Saco Ranger District
33 Kancamagus Highway
Conway, NH 03818-6019
(603) 447–5448

31 Northern Rail-Trail

Endpoints: Lebanon (downtown), Grafton (Kilton Pond)
Mileage: 23
Surface: crushed stone, gravel, ballast, grass, dirt, cedar, sand

Location: Grafton
Contact: Bob Spoerl
Program Specialist
N.H. Division of Parks and
Recreation, Trails Bureau
172 Pembroke Road
P.O. Box 1856
Concord, NH 03301-1858
(603) 271-3254
www.northernrailtrail.org

32 Oliverian Trail

Endpoints: White Mountain
National Forest
Mileage: 3.5
Surface: dirt

Location: Carroll
Contact: Eric Swett

33 Osseo Trail

Endpoints: White Mountain
National Forest
Mileage: 5.8
Surface: gravel, dirt

Location: Grafton
Contact: Dave Hrdlicka
Trails Coordinator
White Mountain National Forest
Pemigewassett Ranger District
RFD 3, Route 175, Box 15
Plymouth, NH 03264
(603) 536–1310

34 Pine Bend Brook Trail

Endpoints: White Mountain
National Forest
Mileage: 4.3
Surface: gravel

Location: Carroll
Contact: Eric Swett
Forest Technician
White Mountain National Forest
Saco Ranger District
33 Kancamagus Highway
Conway, NH 03818-6019
(603) 447–5448

35 Pondicherry Trail

Endpoints: Whitefield, Jefferson
Mileage: 2
Surface: gravel, grass, dirt, crushed stone

Location: Coos
Contact: David Govatski
Jefferson Conservation
Commission
Route 115, Box 157-A
Jefferson, NH 03583
(603) 869–2626
dgovatski@fs.fed.us

36 Rob Brook Trail

Endpoints: White Mountain
National Forest
Mileage: 2
Surface: ballast

Location: Carroll
Contact: Eric Swett
Forest Technician
White Mountain National Forest
Saco Ranger District
33 Kancamagus Highway
Conway, NH 03818-6019
(603) 447–5448

37 Rockingham Recreational Trail

Endpoints: Manchester,
Newfields
Mileage: 25
Surface: gravel, ballast

Other use: Dogsledding
Location: Hillsborough;
Rockingham
Contact: Paul Gray
Chief, Bureau of Trails
Division of Parks and Recreation
172 Pembroke Road
P.O. Box 1856
Concord, NH 03302-1856
(603) 271–3254
pgray@dred.state.nh.us

38 Rocky Branch Trail

Endpoints: White Mountain
National Forest
Mileage: 9
Surface: ballast

Location: Carroll
Contact: Eric Swett
Forest Technician
White Mountain National Forest
Saco Ranger District
33 Kancamagus Highway
Conway, NH 03818-6019
(603) 447–5448

39 Sawyer River Trail

Endpoints: White Mountain National Forest
Mileage: 4
Surface: ballast

Location: Carroll
Contact: Eric Swett
Forest Technician
White Mountain National Forest
Saco Ranger District
33 Kancamagus Highway
Conway, NH 03818-6019
(603) 447–5448

40 Shelburne Trail

Endpoints: White Mountain National Forest
Mileage: 7.2
Surface: dirt

Location: Coos
Contact: Terri Marceron
Assistant Ranger
White Mountain National Forest
Androscoggin Ranger District
300 Glen Road
Gorham, NH 03581-1322
(603) 466–2713

41 Spider Bridge Loop Trail

Endpoints: White Mountain National Forest
Mileage: 4.5
Surface: gravel

Location: Coos
Contact: George Pozzuto
District Ranger
White Mountain National Forest
Androscoggin Ranger District
300 Glen Road
Gorham, NH 03581-1322
(603)466–2713

42 Sugar River Recreation Trail

Endpoints: Newport, Claremont
Mileage: 8
Surface: gravel, ballast

Location: Sullivan
Contact: Bob Spoerl
Program Specialist
N.H. Division of Parks and Recreation, Trails Bureau
172 Pembroke Road
P.O. Box 1856
Concord, NH 03302-1856
(603) 271–3254

43 Thoreau Falls Trail

Endpoints: White Mountain National Forest
Mileage: 5.1
Surface: ballast, dirt

Location: Grafton
Contact: Dave Hrdlicka
Trails Coordinator
White Mountain National Forest
Pemigewassett Ranger District
RFD 3, Route 175, Box 15
Plymouth, NH 03264
(603) 536–1310

44 Trestle Trail

Endpoints: White Mountain National Forest
Mileage: 1
Surface: dirt

Location: Coos
Contact: Roger Collins
Forest Technician
White Mountain National Forest
Ammonusac Ranger Distict
P.O. Box 239
Bethlehem, NH 03574-0239
(603) 869–2626

45 Upper Coos Railroad Trail

Endpoints: Whitefield, Jefferson
Mileage: 1.8
Surface: gravel, ballast, dirt, cedar

Location: Coos
Contact: Bob Spoerl
Program Specialist
N.H. Division of Parks and Recreation, Trails Bureau
172 Pembroke Road
P.O. Box 1856
Concord, NH 03301-1858
(603) 271-3254

46 Upper Nanamocomuck Trail

Endpoints: White Mountain National Forest
Mileage: 9.3
Surface: ballast

Location: Carroll
Contact: Eric Swett
Forest Technician
White Mountain National Forest
Saco Ranger District
33 Kancamagus Highway
Conway, NH 03818-6019
(603) 447–5448

47 West Milan Trail

Endpoints: White Mountain National Forest
Mileage: 4.5
Surface: gravel

Location: Coos

Contact: George Pozzuto
District Ranger
White Mountain National Forest
Androscoggin Ranger District
300 Glen Road
Gorham, NH 03581-1322
(603) 466–2713

48 Wild River Trail

Endpoints: White Mountain
National Forest
Mileage: 4.5
Surface: gravel, dirt

Location: Coos
Contact: Terri Marceron
Assistant Ranger
White Mountain National Forest
Androscoggin Ranger District
300 Glen Road
Gorham, NH 03581-1322
(603) 466–2713

49 Wilderness Trail

Endpoints: White Mountain
National Forest
Mileage: 8.9
Surface: ballast, dirt

Location: Grafton
Contact: Dave Hrdlicka
Trails Coordinator
White Mountain National Forest
Pemigewassett Ranger District
RFD 3, Route 175, Box 15
Plymouth, NH 03264
(603) 536–1310

50 Wolfeboro/Sanbornville Recreational Trail— Russell Chase Path

Endpoints: Wolfeboro Falls,
Sanbornville
Mileage: 12
Surface: crushed stone, gravel,
dirt

Location: Carroll
Contact: Sue Glenn
Director of Parks and Recreation
Town of Wolfeboro
P.O. Box 629
Wolfeboro, NH 03894-0629
(603) 271–3254

51 York Pond Trail

Endpoints: White Mountain
National Forest
Mileage: 6.5
Surface: dirt

Location: Coos
Contact: George Pozzuto
District Ranger
White Mountain National Forest
Androscoggin Ranger District
300 Glen Road
Gorham, NH 03581-1322
(603) 466–2713

52 Zealand Trail

Endpoints: White Mountain
National Forest, Bethlehem
Mileage: 2.5
Surface: dirt

Location: Grafton
Contact: Roger Collins
Forest Technician
White Mountain National Forest
660 Trudeau Road
P.O. Box 239
Bethlehem, NH 03574-0239
(603) 869–2626
rcollins/R9_whiteMTN@fed.us

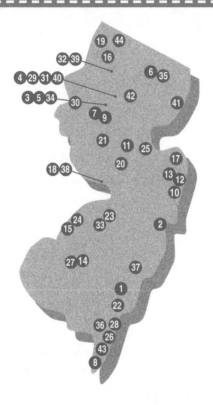

NEW JERSEY

1 Atlantic County Bikeway— East

Endpoints: Mays Landing (Atlantic County VoTech High School), Egg Harbor (Shore Mall)
Mileage: 7.5
Surface: asphalt

Location: Atlantic
Contact: Harry Tillett
Department Head
Atlantic County Parks and Recreation
Park Headquarters

109 Highway 50
Mays Landing, NJ 08330
(609) 625–1897
www.aclink.org/PARKS
www.aclink.org/Planning/MainPages/Bikew

2 Beachwood Borough Trail

Endpoints: Beachwood Borough
Mileage: 1
Surface: asphalt

Location: Ocean

Contact: Beachwood Borough
1600 Pinewald Avenue
Beachwood, NJ 08722-2897
(732) 286–6000
www.beachwoodusa.com

3 Berkshire Valley Management Area Trail

Endpoints: Gordon Road,
Minnisink (Roxbury)
Mileage: 2.1
Surface: ballast

Location: Morris
Contact: John Piccolo
Black River Wildlife
Management Area
275 North Road
Chester, NJ 07930-2332
(908) 879–6252
www.state.nj.us/dep/fgw/
wmaland.htm

4 Black River County Park Trail

Endpoints: Chester
Mileage: 9.4
Surface: dirt

Location: Morris
Contact: Al Kent
Commissioner
Morris County Park Commission
P.O. Box 1295
Morristown, NJ 07962-1295
(201) 326–7600

5 Black River Wildlife Management Area Trail

Endpoints: Chester (Pleasant Hill
Road), Ironia (Main Street)
Mileage: 4
Surface: ballast,

Location: Morris
Contact: John Piccolo
Black River Wildlife Management
Area
275 North Road
Chester, NJ 07930-2332
(908) 879–6252
www.state.nj.us/dep/fgw/
wmaland.htm

6 Boulevard Trolley Line Path

Endpoints: Mountain Lakes
(Crane Road), Mountain Lakes
(Fanny Road)
Mileage: 2.5
Surface: asphalt

Location: Morris
Contact: Mountain Lakes
Recreation Department
400 Boulevard
Mountain Lakes, NJ 07046
(973) 334–3183
recreation@mtnlakes.org
www.mtnlakes.org

7 Capoolong Creek Wildlife Management Area

Endpoints: Pittstown (Quakertown Road), Landsdown (Landsdown Road)
Mileage: 3.7
Surface: grass, dirt, cinder

Location: Hunterdon
Contact: Steve Smysler
Land Management Supervisor
Clinton Wildlife Management Area
7 Van Syckel's Road
Hampton, NJ 08827
(908) 735–8793

8 Cold Spring Bike Path

Endpoints: Sandman Boulevard, Sally Marshall Crossing (Lower Township)
Mileage: 2.7
Surface: asphalt

Location: Cape May
Contact: Lenora Boninfante
Communications Director
Cape May County
4 Moore Road
Cape May Court House, NJ 08120
(609) 463–6678
pubinfo@co.cape-may.nj.us
http://www.capemaycounty
gov.net/Cit-e-Access/News/
archnews.cfm?NID=906&TID=5
&jump2=0

9 Columbia Trail

Endpoints: High Bridge, Flanders
Mileage: 16.2
Surface: asphalt, crushed stone, ballast, concrete

Location: Hunterdon, Morris
Contact: John Trontis
Director
Hunterdon County Parks System
1020 Highway 13
Lebanon, NJ 08833
(908) 782–1158
parks@co.hunterdon.nj.us
www.co.morris.nj.us/transporta
tion/bike_ped/columbia.htm

10 Crossley Preserve Rail-Trail

Endpoints: Berkeley Township (Crossley Preserve)
Mileage: 1
Surface: sand

Location: Ocean
Contact: nynjctbotany.org/
njoptofc/crossley.html

11 Delaware and Raritan Canal State Park Trail

Endpoints: Frenchtown to Trenton, Trenton to New Brunswick
Mileage: 68
Surface: crushed stone, gravel

Location: Hunterdon; Mercer; Somerset
Contact: Susan Herron
Superintendent
Delaware and Raritan Canal State Park Trail
625 Canal Road
Somerset, NJ 08873-7309
(732) 873–3050

12 Edgar Felix Memorial Bikeway

Endpoints: Manasquan (N. Main Street), Wall (Hospital Road)
Mileage: 3.6
Surface: asphalt

Location: Monmouth
Contact: Thomas White
Director
Wall Township Parks and Recreation
2700 Allaire Road
Wall, NJ 07719-9570
(908) 449–8444

13 Freehold and Jamesburg Railroad Trail

Endpoints: Allenwood (Hospital Road), Farmingdale (Route 547)
Mileage: 4.5
Surface: gravel, dirt

Location: Monmouth

Contact: Nicholas DeMicco
Superintendent
Allaire State Park
P.O. Box 220
Farmingdale, NJ 07727-0220
(908) 938–2371

14 Glassboro Wildlife Management Area Trail

Endpoints: Glassboro Wildlife Management Area
Mileage: 3
Surface: dirt

Location: Gloucester
Contact: www.glassboroonline.com/glassboro_nj_comm_parks.htm

15 Gloucester Township Bikeway

Endpoints: Blackwood, Grenloch
Mileage: 2
Surface: asphalt

Location: Camden
Contact: Rosemary DiJosie
Township Clerk
Gloucester Township
1261 Chews Landing Road
Blackwood, NJ 08012
(856) 374–3520
glotwp@glotwp.com
www.glotwp.com

16 Hamburg Mountain Wildlife Management Area

Endpoints: Ogdensburg, Franklin

Mileage: 3
Surface: ballast, dirt, cinder

Location: Sussex
Contact: Vincent Mercurio
Supervisor WMA
N.J. Division of Fish, Game and
Wildlife
150 Fradon-Springdale Road
Newton, NJ 07860-5217
(201) 383–0918

17 Henry Hudson Trail

Endpoints: Atlantic Highlands,
Aberdeen
Mileage: 9
Surface: asphalt

Location: Monmouth
Contact: Laura Kirkpatrick
Public Information Officer
Monmouth County Park System
850 Newman Springs Road
Lincroft, NJ 07738
(732) 842–4000
www.monmouthcountyparks.
com/parks/hudson.html

18 Johnson Trolley Line Trail

Endpoints: Lawrence Township
Mileage: 2.5
Surface: asphalt, gravel, grass,
dirt

Location: Mercer

Contact: Andrew Link
Planner
Lawrence Township
(609) 844–7071

19 Karamac Trail

Endpoints: Pahaquarry
Mileage: 1.5
Surface: dirt, cinder

Location: Warren
Contact: Wayne Valentine
New Jersey District Ranger
Delaware Watergap National
Recreation Area
2 Walpack-Flatbrookville Road
Layton, NJ 07851
(973) 948–6500
wayne-valentine@nps.gov

20 Kingston Branch Loop Trail

Endpoints: Kingston, Rocky Hill
Mileage: 3.7
Surface: crushed stone, gravel

Location: Somerset
Contact: D&R Canal State Park

625 Canal Road
Somerset, NJ 08873-7309
(732) 873–3050

21 Landsdown Trail

Endpoints: Franklin Township
(Lower Landsdown Road), Clinton
Borough
Mileage: 1.8

Surface: dirt

Location: Hunterdon
Contact: John Trontis
Director
Hunterdon County Department
of Parks and Recreation
1020 Highway 31
Lebanon, NJ 08833
(908) 782–1158
parks@co.hunterdon.nj.us
www.co.hunterdon.nj.us/dept/
parks/guides/Landsdown.htm

22 Linwood Bikepath (George K. Francis Bikepath)

Endpoints: Pleasantville (Black
Horse Pike), Somers Point (Bethel
Road)
Mileage: 5.6
Surface: asphalt

Location: Atlantic
Contact: Gary Gardner
City Clerk
Linwood City Hall
400 Poplar Avenue
Linwood, NJ 08221-1899
(609) 927–4108

23 Medford Leas Trail

Endpoints: Medford Township
Mileage: 1
Surface: asphalt

Location: Burlington
Contact: Beth Richmond
Director of Recreation

Cranberry Hall
17 N. Main Street
Medford, NJ 08055
(609) 654–2512
recreation@medfordtownship.com
www.medfordtownship.com/
recreation1.htm

24 Merchantville Bike Path

Endpoints: Merchantville
Mileage: 1.5
Surface: asphalt

Location: Camden
Contact: Sue Walker
Borough Clerk
Merchantville Borough
One West Maple Avenue
Merchantville, NJ 08109
(856) 662–2474, ext. 101
http://merchantvillenj.com

25 Middlesex Greenway

Endpoints: Metuchen (Middlesex
Avenue), Woodbridge (Crows Mill
Road)
Mileage: 3.5
Surface: dirt

Location: Middlesex
Contact: Walter Stochel, Jr.
Vice President
Edison Greenways
Group/Middlesex Greenway
Coalition
2118 Oaktree Road
Edison, NJ 08820-1404
www.edisongreenways.org

26 Middle Township Bike Path

Endpoints: Goshen Road near Church Street, Dennisville Road near 4-H Grounds (Middle Township)
Mileage: 0.8
Surface: asphalt

Location: Cape May
Contact: Lenora Boninfante
Communications Director
Cape May County
4 Moore Road
Cape May Court House, NJ 08210
(609) 463–6678
pubinfo@co.cape-may.nj.us
www.capemaycountygov.net/
Cit-e Access/News/index.cfm?
NID=1349&TID=5&jump2=0

27 Monroe Township Bikepath

Endpoints: Williamstown (Church Street and Railroad Avenue), Downer (Fries Road)
Mileage: 3.5
Surface: asphalt

Location: Gloucester
Contact: Frank Campisi
Community Affairs Director
Monroe Township Parks and Recreation
301 Bluebell Road
Williamstown, NJ 08094
(609) 728–9840
mtdca@buyrite.com

28 Ocean City Trail

Endpoints: Ocean City
Mileage: 0.9
Surface: asphalt

Location: Cape May
Contact: George Savastano
Director of Public Works
Ocean City Public Works Department
1040 Haven Avenue
Ocean City, NJ 08226
(609) 525–9261

29 Ogden Mine Railroad Path

Endpoints: Hurdtown (Mahlon Dickerson Reservation)
Mileage: 2.5
Surface: crushed stone, ballast, dirt, cinder

Location: Morris; Sussex
Contact: Al Kent
Commissioner
Morris County Park Commission
P.O. Box 1295
Morristown, NJ 07962-1295
(201) 326–7600
nynjctbotany.org/njhltofc/ogdenmrr.

30 Oxford Bikeway

Endpoints: Oxford (Pequest Road), Oxford (Lower Denmark Road)
Mileage: 1.5
Surface: asphalt

Location: Warren
Contact: Municipal Building
11 Green Street
Oxford, NJ 07863
(908) 453–3098

31 Patriots' Path

Endpoints: East Hanover, Washington
Mileage: 12
Surface: asphalt, gravel, dirt

Location: Morris
Contact: Al Kent
Trail Coodinator
Morris County Park Commission
P.O. Box 1295
Morristown, NJ 07962-1295
(973) 326–7600
www.co.morris.nj.us/transport
ation/bike-ped/patriot.html

32 Paulinskill Valley Trail

Endpoints: Sparta Junction, Columbia
Mileage: 27
Surface: ballast, dirt, cinder

Location: Warren; Sussex
Contact: Park Superintendent
Kittatinny Valley State Park
P.O. Box 621
Andover, NJ 07821-0621
(973) 786–6445
kittvlly@warwick.net

community.nj.com/cc/pvtc

33 Pemberton Rail-Trail

Endpoints: Pemberton (Hanover Street), Birmingham (Birmingham Road)
Mileage: 3
Surface: asphalt

Location: Burlington
Contact: Jerry Jerome
Pemberton Rotary Club
128 Hanover Street
Pemberton, NJ 08068
TQJ@jersey.net

34 Pequest Wildlife Management Area Trail

Endpoints: Buttzville (Routes 31 and 46), Townsbury (Pequest Road)
Mileage: 4.2
Surface: ballast

Location: Warren
Contact: John Piccolo
Black River Wildlife Management Area
275 North Road
Chester, NJ 07930-2332
(908) 879–6252

35 Ramsey Bike Path

Endpoints: East Oak Street (Municipal Pool), Route 17 (interstate shopping center)

Mileage: 1.7
Surface: asphalt

Location: Bergen
Contact: John Solarino
Ramsey Recreation
Municipal Building
North Central Avenue
Ramsey, NJ 07446
(201) 825–8299
www.ramseynj.com

36 Seashore Line Trail

Endpoints: Belleplain State
Forest, Woodbine
Mileage: 10
Surface: ballast, dirt

Location: Cape May;
Cumberland
Contact: Tom Keck
Superintendent
Belleplain State Forest
Route 550, Box 450
Woodbine, NJ 08270-0450
(609) 861–2404
belleplain.st.forest@
jerseycape.com

37 Smithville Park

Endpoints: Easthampton
(Smithville Park)
Mileage: 2
Surface: dirt

Location: Burlington

Contact: Jeff Kerchner
Superintendent of Parks
Burlington County
13 Park Avenue
P.O. Box 6000
Mt. Holly, NJ 08060
(609) 265–5858
www.njht.org/profiles/smithville-
park.html
www.co.burlington.nj.us/dept/
parks/index2.htm

38 Somers Point Bike Path

Endpoints: Somers Point
Mileage: 1
Surface: asphalt

Location: Mercer
Contact: Celeste Tracy
Supervising Planner
N.J. Department of
Environmental Protection
Division of Parks and Forestry
P.O. Box 404
22 South Clinton Street
Trenton, NJ 08625-0404
(609) 984–1173
ctracy@dep.state.nj.us

39 Sussex Branch Railroad Trail

Endpoints: Byram Township
(Waterloo Road), Branchville
(Main Street)
Mileage: 21.2
Surface: ballast, cinder

Location: Sussex
Contact: Park Superintendent
Kittatinny Valley State Park
P.O. Box 621
Andover, NJ 07821-0621
(973) 786–6445
kittvlly@warwick.net

40 Traction Line Recreation Trail

Endpoints: Morristown (Morris Avenue), Madison (Danforth Road)
Mileage: 3.2
Surface: asphalt

Location: Morris
Contact: Janet McMillen
Trails Coordinator
Morris County Park Commission
P.O. Box 1295
Morristown, NJ 17962-1295
(973) 326–7604
www.co.morris.nj.us/transporta
tion/bike_ped/traction.html

41 West Essex Trail

Endpoints: Little Falls (north of Francisco Avenue), Verona (end of Arnold Way)

Mileage: 2.8
Surface: gravel, cinder

Location: Essex
Contact: Vincent Bucci
Chief Engineer
Essex County Department of Parks
115 Clifton Avenue
Newark, NJ 07104-1017
(973) 268–3500

42 Wharton Rail Trail (part of Patriot's Path)

Endpoints: North Main Street, East Dewey Avenue (Wharton)
Mileage: 0.5
Surface: asphalt

Location: Morris
Contact: Borough of Wharton
10 Robert Street
Wharton, NJ 07885
(973) 361–8444
www.whartonnj.com

43 Woodbine Railroad Trail

Endpoints: Woodbine
Mileage: 3
Surface: asphalt

Location: Cape May
Contact: Lisa Garrison
Borough of Woodbine
501 Washington Avenue
Woodbine, NJ 08270
(609) 861–2153
www.boroughofwoodbine.net

44 Wood Duck Nature Trail

Endpoints: Wantage (Wallkill
River National Wildlife Refuge)
Mileage: 1.5
Surface: ballast, dirt

Other use: hunting access
Location: Sussex
Contact: Wallkill River National
Wildlife Refuge
1547 Route 565
Sussex, NJ 07461
(973) 702–7266
wallkillriver@fws.gov
http://wallkillriver.fws.gov/
visitor%20opportunities.htm

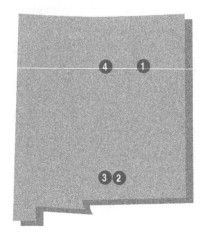

1 Gillinas Hiking Trail

Endpoints: Las Vegas
Mileage: 1.5
Surface: asphalt

Location: San Miguel
Contact: Stella Mason
Las Vegas Recreation
Department
P.O. Box 179
Las Vegas, NM 87701-0179
(505) 454–1158

2 Grandview Trail

Endpoints: High Rolls
Mileage: 1.5
Surface: ballast

Location: Otero
Contact: Tom Springer
Chairperson
New Mexico Rail-Trail
Association
P.O. Box 1361
Plotcroft, NM 88317
nmrails@zianet.com

3 Mexican Canyon Trestle Trail (Cloud-Climbing Trail)

Endpoints: Lincoln National Forest
Mileage: 3.5 (3 sections)
Surface: ballast

Location: Otero
Contact: Johnny Wilson
Staff Officer
Lincoln National Forest
1101 New York Avenue
Alamagordo, NM 88310-6992
(505) 434–7200

4 Santa Fe Rail-Trail

Endpoints: Santa Fe (Santa Fe Southern Railroad Depot), near Lamy (U.S. 84/285)
Mileage: 11.5
Surface: dirt

Location: Santa Fe
Contact: Lesli Kunkle-Ellis
Planner
Santa Fe County Planning Department
102 Grant Avenue
P.O. Box 276
Santa Fe, NM 87504-0276
(505) 986–6215
lellis@co.santa-fe.nm.us

NEW YORK

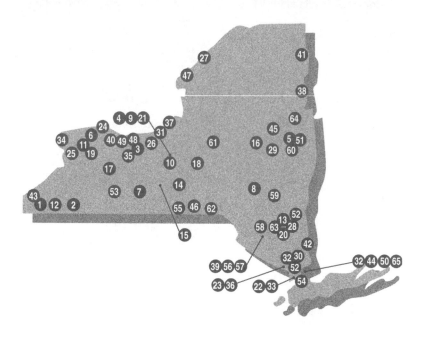

1 Alison Wells Ney Nature Trail

Endpoints: Brocton (Bliss Road), Ellicott Road
Mileage: 4.5
Surface: gravel, dirt

Location: Chautauqua
Contact: Les Johnson
Hollyloft Ski and Bike
600 Fairmount Avenue
Jamestown, NY 14701-2638
(716) 483–2330
www2.cecomet.net/railtrails/

2 Allegheny River Valley Trail

Endpoints: Allegany, Olean
Mileage: 5.6
Surface: asphalt

Location: Cattaraugus
Contact: George Schanzenbacher
Chief Operating Officer
American Chamber of Commerce
Greater Olean
120 N. Union Street
Olean, NY 14760-2735
(716) 372–4433
cooficer@Oleanny.com

3 Auburn Trail

Endpoints: Pittsford, Farmington
Mileage: 9
Surface: gravel, grass, dirt, crushed stone, original ballast

Location: Monroe, Ontario
Contact: Charlene Berry-Pickering
Director of Parks and Recreation
Town of Victor Parks and Recreation
85 E. Main Street
Victor, NY 14564-1302
(716) 742–7026
www.victorhikingtrails.org

4 Auburn-Fleming Trail

Endpoints: Auburn (Dunning Avenue), Fleming (Route 34)
Mileage: 1.6
Surface: ballast, dirt

Location: Cayuga
Contact: Michele Beelman
Park Director
Cayuga County Parks and Trail Commission
East Lake Road
Auburn, NY 13021
(315) 253–5611
www.co.cayuga.ny.lls

5 Bog Meadow Brook Trail

Endpoints: Saratoga Springs
Mileage: 1.9
Surface: ballast, grass, dirt

Location: Saratoga
Contact: Cynthia Beham
Project Director
Saratoga Springs Open Space Project
110 Spring Street
Saratoga Springs, NY 12866-3302
(518) 587–5554

6 Canalway Trail

Mileage: 95
Surface: dirt

Location: Cayuga; Monroe; Niagara; Onondaga; Orleans
Contact: John DiMura
Canalway Trail Program Manager
New York State Canal Recreation Way Commission
200 Southern Boulevard
Albany, NY 12209-2098
(518) 436–3034
www.canals.state.ny.us/exvac/trail/index.html

7 Catherine Valley Trail

Endpoints: Montour Falls, Watkins Glen
Mileage: 2
Surface: asphalt, crushed stone, ballast

Location: Schuyler
Contact: Rick Manning
Northeast Greenways
Collaborative
114 Dey Street
Ithaca, NY 14850
(607) 277–0178
manning@lightlink.com

8 Catskill Scenic Trail

Endpoints: Bloomville, Grand Gorge
Mileage: 19
Surface: crushed stone, dirt, cinder

Location: Delaware; Schoharie
Contact: Dave Riordan
Executive Director
Catskill Revitalization
Corporation
P.O. Box 310
Railroad Avenue
Stamford, NY 12167-0310
(607) 652-2821
fun@durr.org
www.durr.org

9 Cayuga County Trail

Endpoints: Ira, Victory, Sterling
Mileage: 20
Surface: dirt, cinder

Location: Cayuga
Contact: Thomas Higgins
Principal Planner
Cayuga County Planning
Department
160 Genesee Street
Auburn, NY 13021-3424
(315) 253–1276
thiggins@co.cayuga.ny.us
www.co.cayuga.ny.us/park/trails

10 Charlie Major Nature Trail

Endpoints: Old Seneca Turnpike, Crow Hill Road (Skaneateles)
Mileage: 1.2
Surface: dirt, cedar

Location: Onondaga
Contact: www.greyhound walkingclub.com

11 Clarence Pathways

Endpoints: Clarence, Akron
Mileage: 9.5
Surface: asphalt

Location: Erie
Contact: Michael Lex
Clarence Conservation Advisory
Council
4620 Christian Drive
Clarence, NY 14031-1803
(716) 633–4018
mslex@peoplepc.com
www.nypca.org/greenways/map
_files/5.sht

12 Conservation Trail

Endpoints: Allegheny State
Forest, Niagara Falls
Mileage: 175 (18 are rail-trail)
Surface: ballast

Location: Cattaraugus; Erie;
Genesse; Niagara; Wyoming
Contact: Terry Dailey
Allegheny State Park
2373 DSP Route 1
Salamana, NY 14779
(716) 354–9101

13 D&H Canal Heritage Corridor (O&W Rail-Trail)

Endpoints: Kingston
(Washington Avenue), Ellensville
Mileage: 35
Surface: crushed stone, cinder

Location: Hurley; Marbleton;
Rochester; Sullivan; Ulster
Contact: Rich Caraluzzo
Sullivan County Division of Public
Works
P.O. Box 5012
Monticello, NY 12701
(914) 794–3000

14 Dryden Lake Park Trail

Endpoints: Dryden, Harford
Mileage: 3.3
Surface: ballast, grass

Location: Cortland; Tompkins
Contact: James Schug
Supervisor
Town of Dryden
65 East Main Street
Dryden, NY 13053-9505
(607) 844–8619
drydent@lightlink.com

15 East Ithaca Recreation Way

Endpoints: Ithaca, Dryden
Mileage: 2.2
Surface: asphalt, gravel, cinder

Location: Tompkins
Contact: George Frantz
Assistant Town Planner
Town of Ithaca
126 East Seneca Street
Ithaca, NY 14850-4352
(607) 273–1747

16 Erie Canal Trail

Endpoints: Amsterdam,
Schoharie Crossing State Historic
Site
Mileage: 90
Surface: asphalt

Location: Montgomery
Contact: Micheal Kayes
Director
Planning and Development
Department
Park Street
P.O.Box 1500
Fonda, NY 12068
(518) 853–8155

17 Genesee Valley Greenway

Endpoints: North Cuba,
Rochester
Mileage: 50
Surface: gravel, grass

Location: Livingston, Monroe
Contact: Frances Gotesik
Executive Director
Friends of the Genesee Valley
Greenway, Inc.
P.O. Box 42
Mt. Morris, NY 14510-1202
(716) 658–2569
fogvg@aol.com
www.netacc.net/~fogvg/
index.htm

18 Gorge Trail

Endpoints: Cazenovia
Mileage: 2.2
Surface: crushed stone, ballast,
cinder

Location: Madison
Contact: Gene Gissin
Cazenovia Preservation
Foundation
P.O. Box 627
Cazenovia, NY 13035-0432
(315) 655–2224

19 Groveland Secondary Trail

Endpoints: Alexander, York
Mileage: 20
Surface: ballast

Other use: ATV
Location: Genessee
Contact: Jim Peck
Supervising Forester
New York State Department of
Environmental Conservation
7291 Coon Road
Bath, NY 14810-7742
(607) 776–2165
jrpeck@gw.dec.state.ny.us

21 Hojack Trail

Endpoints: Redcreek, Hannibal
Mileage: 8
Surface: crushed stone, gravel,
ballast

Location: Cayuga
Contact: Michele Beilman
Parks Director
Cayuga County Parks and Trails
Commission
Emerson Park, East Lake Road
Auburn, NY 13021
(312) 253–5611
www.co.cayuga.ny.us

20 Harlem Valley Rail Trail

Endpoints: Millerton to Wassaic,
Alander to Copake Falls
Mileage: 15 (2 sections)
Surface: asphalt

Location: Columbia; Dutchess
Contact: Charlie Drum
Commissioner
Dutchess County Department of
Parks, Recreation and
Conservation
85 Sheafe Road
Wappinger Falls, NY 12590-1103
(914) 297–1224
www.hvrt.org

22 John Kieran Nature Trail

Endpoints: Bronx (Van Cortlandt
Park)
Mileage: 1
Surface: wood chips, dirt

Location: Bronx
Contact: Marianne Anderson
Van Cortlandt and Pelham Bay
Parks Administration
1 Bronx River Parkway
Bronx, NY 10462-2869
(718) 430–1890
www.nycparks.org

23 Joseph Clarke Rail-Trail

Endpoints: Tappan, Blauvelt
Mileage: 3
Surface: crushed stone, dirt

Location: Rockland
Contact: Richard Rose
Superintendent of Parks
Town of Orangetown
81 Hunt Road
Orangeburg, NY 10962-2517
(845) 359–6503
otownrec@aol.com
www.orangetown.com

24 Keuka Lake Outlet Trail

Endpoints: Penn Yan (northern
tip of Keuka Lake), Dresden (near
Seneca Lake)
Mileage: 8.2
Surface: asphalt, ballast, cedar

Location: Yates
Contact: Friends of the Finger
Lakes Outlet
P.O. Box 231
Penn Yan, NY 14527
www.naturalhighs.net/waterfalls/
falls99/keukaoutlet-p0.htm

25 Lehigh Memory Trail

Endpoints: Amherst
Mileage: .71
Surface: asphalt

Location: Erie
Contact: William Wutz
Trustee
Municipality of Village of
Williamsville
5565 Main Street
Williamsville, NY 142217
(716) 632–4120
www.williamsvill.org
www.nypca.org/greenways/trails/
5-1.shtml

26 Lehigh Valley Trail

Endpoints: Victor, Mendon
Mileage: 1.7
Surface: ballast

Location: Monroe, Ontario
Contact: Carl Foss
President
The Mendon Foundation
P.O. Box 231
Mendon, NY 14506
(716) 385–6503
www.victorhikingtrails.com

27 Maple City Trail

Endpoints: Ogdensburg
Mileage: 1.8
Surface: asphalt

Location: St. Lawrence
Contact: John Rishe
Ogdensburg Planning
Department
330 Ford Street
Ogdensburg, NY 13669-1626
(315) 393–7150

28 Maybrook Rail-Trail

Endpoints: East Fishkill
Mileage: 12
Surface: ballast

Location: Dutchess
Contact: Brad Barclay
Senior Planner
Duchess County Department of
Public Works
County Office Building
22 Market Street
Poughkeepsie, NY 12601
(914) 486–2900

29 Mohawk-Hudson Bikeway

Endpoints: Albany, Rotterdam
Junction

Mileage: 41
Surface: asphalt, crushed stone

Location: Albany; Schenectady
Contact: Kathleen DeCataldo
Supervisor
Town of Niskayuna
One Niskayuna Circle
Schenectady, NY 12309
(518) 386–4503
nisky@crisny.org
www.canals.state.ny.us

30 North County Trailway

Endpoints: Mount Pleasant
(Eastview), Somers (Baldwin
Place)
Mileage: 22.1
Surface: asphalt

Location: Westchester
Contact: David DeLucia
Director of Park Facilities
Westchester County Parks and
Recreation
25 Moore Avenue
Mount Kisco, NY 10549-3102
(914) 242–6300
www.westchestergov.com/parks/
brochures/Trailways/Northcounty
main.htm

31 O&W Railroad Pedestrian Promenade and Bikeway

Endpoints: East Cayuga Street, East Mohawk Street (Oswego)
Mileage: 0.5
Surface: asphalt

Location: Oswego
Contact: Robert Farrell
Director
City of Oswego Parks and Recreation
13 West Oneida Street
Oswego, NY 13126
(315) 342–8169
bfarrell@oswegony.org
www.oswegony.org

32 Old Erie Path (part of Nyack Rail Trail)

Endpoints: Grand View-on-Hudson, Sparkill
Mileage: 3.2
Surface: crushed stone, gravel, ballast, grass, dirt

Location: Rockland
Contact: Thom Kleiner
Town Supervisor
Town of Orangetown
Town Hall
26 Orangeburg Road
Orangeburg, NY 10962-1706
(845) 359–5100

supervisor@orangetown.com
www.orangetown.com

33 Old Putnam Trail

Endpoints: Van Cortland Park
Mileage: 1.2
Surface: dirt

Location: Bronx
Contact: Marianne Anderson
Van Cortland and Pelham Bay Parks Administration
1 Bronx River Parkway
Bronx, NY 10462-2869
(718) 430–1890

34 Ongiara Trail System

Endpoints: Whirlpool State Park, Devil's Hole State Park
Mileage: 1.5
Surface: crushed stone, grass, dirt

Other use: Birdwatching
Location: Niagara
Contact: James Ford
Regional Manager
New York State Parks—Niagara Region
Niagara Reservation State Park
P.O. Box 1132
Niagara Falls, NY 14303-0132
(716) 285–3891

35 Ontario Pathway

Endpoints: Canandaigua to Stanley
Mileage: 11
Surface: dirt

Location: Ontario
Contact: Ontario Pathways, Inc.
P.O. Box 996
Canandaigua, NY 14424
www.ontariopathways.org

36 Orange Heritage Trail

Endpoints: Goshen, Monroe
Mileage: 10.5
Surface: asphalt, crushed stone

Location: Orange
Contact: Graham Skea
Commissioner
Orange County Department of
Parks, Recreation and
Conservation
211 Route 416
Montgomery, NY 12549-9803
(914) 457–4900
ocgparks@warwick.net
www.ocgovernment1home.html

37 Oswego Recreational Trail

Endpoints: Fulton, Cleveland
Mileage: 26
Surface: ballast

Other use: ATV
Location: Oswego
Contact: Edward Marx
Director of Planning
Oswego County Planning
Department
46 East Bridge Street
Oswego, NY 13126-2123
(315) 349-8292
marxe@co.oswego.ny.us

38 Outlet Trail

Endpoints: Penn Yan, Dresden
Mileage: 7.5
Surface: asphalt, ballast, cinder

Location: Yates
Contact: Philip Whitman
President
Friends of the Outlet Trail, Inc.
1939 Perry Point Road
P.O. Box 231
Dresden, NY 14441

39 Parksville Rail Trail

Endpoints: Main Street, 1.5 miles north of Fox Mt. Road (Parksville)
Mileage: 3.2
Surface: cedar

Location: Sullivan
Contact: Raymond Kelly
Parksville Rails to Trail Group
Parksville, NY 12768

40 Pittsford Trail System (Railroad Loop Trail)

Endpoints: Pittsford
Mileage: 11.4
Surface: asphalt, crushed stone, ballast

Location: Monroe
Contact: Mary Ann Burdett
Pittsford Parks and Recreation Department
35 Lincoln Avenue
Pittsford, NY 14534
(716) 248–6280

41 Plattsburgh Bicycle/Pedestrian Trail

Endpoints: Intersection of Jay and Hamilton Streets, Nevada Oval East—within former USAF base (Plattsburgh)
Mileage: 1.5
Surface: asphalt

Location: Clinton
Contact: Rosemary Schoomaker
Director of Community Development
City of Plattsburgh
41 City Place
Plattsburgh, NY 12901
(518) 563–7642

42 Putnam Trailway

Endpoints: Near Somers (Baldwin Place), Mahopac (Bucks Hollow Road)
Mileage: 1.8
Surface: asphalt

Location: Putnam, Westchester
Contact: Barry Leibowitz
President
Putnam Rail Trails Association Inc.
P.O. Box 801
Mahopac, NY 10541-0801
baleibowitz@prodigy.net

43 Ralph C. Sheldon Nature Trail

Endpoints: Sherman-Titus Road, Summerdale Road
Mileage: 6
Surface: dirt, sand

Location: Chautauqua
Contact: Les Johnson
Chautauqua Rails to Trails
600 Fairmount Avenue
Jamestown, NY 14701-2638
www2.cecomet.net/railtrails/

44 Raymond G. Esposito Trail

Endpoints: South Nyack, Village of South Nyack (Town of Orangetown)
Mileage: 1
Surface: crushed stone, gravel, dirt

Location: Rockland
Contact: Irene Murphy
Deputy Village Clerk
Village of South Nyack
282 South Broadway
South Nyack, NY 10960-4639
(914) 358–0287

45 Remsen–Lake Placid Travel Corridor

Endpoints: Lake Placid, Remsen
Mileage: 119
Surface: ballast

Location: Essex; Franklin; Hamilton; Herkimer; Oneida; St. Lawrence
Contact: Rick Fenton
Supervising Forester
New York State Department of Environmental Conservation
P.O. Box 458
Northville, NY 12134
(518) 863–4545
rtfenton@gw.dec.state.ny.us

46 Ridgeway Trail

Endpoints: Caroline
Mileage: 3.3
Surface: crushed stone

Location: Tompkins
Contact: Tompkins County Greenway Coalition
1456 Hanshaw Road
Ithaca, NY 14850-2754

47 Rivergate Trail

Endpoints: Clayton to La Fargeville, Theresa to Philadelphia
Mileage: 13
Surface: ballast

Other use: ATV
Location: Jefferson
Contact: Thousand Islands Land Trust
P.O. Box 238
Clayton, NY 13624-0238
(315) 686–5345

48 Rochester, Syracuse and Eastern Trail

Endpoints: Perinton, Fairport
Mileage: 6
Surface: crushed stone

Location: Monroe
Contact: David Morgan
Director of Parks
Town of Perinton
1350 Turk Hill Road
Fairport, NY 14450-8751
(716) 223–5050

49 Rochester's Genesee Riverway Trail

Endpoints: Erie Canal Trail, Lake Ontario (Rochester)
Mileage: 12
Surface: asphalt

Location: Monroe
Contact: Edward Doherty
Commissioner-Environmental
Services
City of Rochester
30 Church Street
City Hall, Room 300B
Rochester, NY 14614
(585) 428–6855
edoherty@cityofrochester.gov
www.cityofrochester.gov/rivertrail
brochure.htm

50 Samuel G. Fisher Mount Ivy Environmental Park

Endpoints: Pomona, Mount Ivy
Mileage: 2
Surface: ballast, grass, wood chips, dirt, cedar

Location: Rockland
Contact: R. Allen Beers
Coordinator
County of Rockland
50 Sanatorium Road
Building P
Ponoma, NY 10970
(845) 364–2670
beersa@co.rockland.ny.us
www.co.rockland.ny.us

51 Saratoga Springs Bicycle/Pedestrian Path

Endpoints: Saratoga Springs
Mileage: 39.6
Surface: asphalt

Location: Saratoga
Contact: Cynthia Beham
Project Director
Saratoga Springs Open Space
Project
110 Spring Street
Saratoga Springs, NY 12866-3302
www.openspaceproject.org

52 Shawmut Recreational Trail

Endpoints: Hornell, Town of Hornellsville
Mileage: 1.3
Surface: gravel

Location: Steuben
Contact: Shawn Hogan
Mayor
City of Hornell
82 Main Street
Hornell, NY 14843
(607) 324–7421
mayor@infoblvd.net

53 Skaneateles Nature Trail (Charlie Major Nature Trail)

Endpoints: Skaneateles
Mileage: 2
Surface: dirt, cinder

Location: Onondaga
Contact: Matthew Major
Recreation Supervisor
Town of Skaneateles
Recreation Department
24 Jordan Street
Skaneateles, NY 13152-1110
(315) 685-5607

54 South County Trailway

Endpoints: Eastview (Saw Mill
River Road), Yonkers (Barney
Street)
Mileage: 14
Surface: asphalt

Location: Westchester
Contact: Westchester County
Department of Parks, Recreation,
and Conservation
25 Moore Avenue
Mt. Kisco, NY 10549
(914) 864–PARK
www.westchestergov.com/parks/
images/maps2/sctrailwaymaps/
sctrail.htm

55 South Hill Recreation Way

Endpoints: Ithaca
Mileage: 3.3
Surface: grass

Location: Tompkins
Contact: George Frantz
Assistant Town Planner
Town of Ithaca
126 East Seneca Street
Ithaca, NY 14850-4352
(607) 273–1747

56 Sullivan County Rail-Trail—Hurleyville to Mountain Dale

Endpoints: Hurleyville to
Woodridge, Mountain Dale
Mileage: 9
Surface: gravel, dirt

Location: Sullivan
Contact: Dennis Hewston
Sullivan County Rails-to-Trails
Conservancy, Inc.
195 Lake Louise Marie Road
Rock Hill, NY 12775-6613

57 Sullivan County Rail-Trail—Monticello to Hartwood

Endpoints: Monticello, Hartwood
Mileage: 5
Surface: gravel, dirt

Location: Sullivan
Contact: Dennis Hewston
Sullivan County Rails-to-Trails Conservancy, Inc.
195 Lake Louise Marie Road
Rock Hill, NY 12775-6613

58 Sullivan County Rail-Trail—Summitville to Westbrookville

Endpoints: Summitville to Wurtsboro, Westbrookville
Mileage: 10
Surface: gravel, dirt

Location: Sullivan
Contact: Steve Levine
Town Supervisor
Railroad Plaza
South Fallsburg, NY 12779
(914) 434–8810

59 Tannersville Bike Path (Huckleberry Multi-Use Trail)

Endpoints: Bloomer Road, Clum Hill Road (Tannersville)
Mileage: 2.7
Surface: gravel, dirt

Location: Greene
Contact: Lee McGunnigle
Mayor
Village of Tannersville
P.O. Box 967
Tannersville, NY 12485
(518) 589–5850
www.nypca.org/greenways/trails/1-17.shtml

60 Uncle Sam Bikeway

Endpoints: Troy
Mileage: 3.5
Surface: asphalt

Location: Rensselaer
Contact: Bob Barns
Recreation Supervisor
City of Troy Bureau of Parks and Recreation
1 Movement Square
Troy, NY 12180
(518) 270–4553

61 Verona Beach State Park Trail

Endpoints: Verona Beach State Park
Mileage: 8
Surface: grass, dirt

 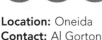

Location: Oneida
Contact: Al Gorton
Verona Beach State Park
P.O. Box 245
Verona Beach, NY 13162-0245
(315) 762–4463

62 Vestal Rail Trail

Endpoints: North Main Street, African Road (Vestal)
Mileage: 2.1
Surface: asphalt, gravel

Location: Broome
Contact: Gary Campo
Engineering Director
Town of Vestal
605 Vestal Parkway West
Vestal, NY 13850-1493
(607) 748–1514
www.nypca.org/greenways/trails/9-3.shtml

63 Wallkill Valley Rail-Trail

Endpoints: Gardiner, Rosendale
Mileage: 12.5
Surface: crushed stone, ballast

Location: Ulster
Contact: George Danskin
Wallkill Valley Rail Trail
Association, Inc.
P.O. Box 1048
New Paltz, NY 12561-0020
www.gorailtrail.com

64 Warren County Bikeway

Endpoints: Lake George, Glens Falls
Mileage: 12.5
Surface: asphalt

Location: Warren
Contact: Patrick Beland
Director
Warren County Parks and
Recreation Department
261 Main Street, Box 10
Warrensburg, NY 12885-1122
(518) 623–5576

65 White Plains Greenway

Endpoints: White Plains
Mileage: 0.7
Surface: wood chips

Location: Westchester
Contact: Michael Graessle
Commissioner of Planning
City of White Plains
Planning Department
255 Main Street
White Plains, NY 10601
(914) 422–1374
Trailnet88@aol.com

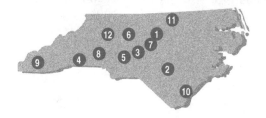

1 American Tobacco Trail

Endpoints: Durham (Morehead Avenue), Wake County
Mileage: 14.2 (in three sections)
Surface: asphalt

Location: Chatham; Durham; Wake
Contact: Christy Cornell
Wake County Parks and Recreation
P.O. Box 550, Suite 1000
Raleigh, NC 27602
(919) 856–6673
ccornell@co.wake.nc.us
www.ncrail-trails.org/trtc/

2 Dunn-Erwin Rail-Trail

Endpoints: Dunn, Erwin
Mileage: 5.3
Surface: crushed stone

Location: Harnett

Contact: Dana Cochran
Secretary
Dunn-Erwin Rail-Trail Authority
P.O. Box 310
Dunn, NC 28335
(910) 892–3282
dana@dunnchamber.com
www.dunnchamber.com

3 Eagles Spur Rail-Trail

Endpoints: Stage Coach Road, Jordan Lake (south of Durham)
Mileage: 2.2
Surface: gravel

Location: Durham
Contact: www.ncrail-trail.org

4 Forrest Hunt Greenway

Endpoints: Forest City (Alexander Mills Community), Forrest Hunt Elementary School
Mileage: 1
Surface: cinder

Location: Rutherford
Contact: www.ncrail-trail.org

5 Gold Hill Rail-Trail

Endpoints: Gold Hill, Cabarrus County Line
Mileage: 2
Surface: crushed stone

Location: Rowen
Contact: The Land Trust for Central North Carolina
P.O. Box 4284
Salisbury, NC 28145-4284
(704) 647–0302
www.landtrustcnc.org

6 Lake Brandt Greenway

Endpoints: Guilford Courthouse National Military Park, Bur-Mil Park
Mileage: 3.5
Surface: asphalt

Location: Guilford
Contact: Mike Simpson
Lakes, Trails and Greenways Director
Greensboro Parks and Recreation Department
5834 Owls Roost Road
Greensboro, NC 27410
(336) 545–5955
mike.simpson@ci.greensboro.nc.us

7 Libba Cotton Trail

Endpoints: Carrboro (central business district), Chapel Hill (University of North Carolina campus)
Mileage: 1
Surface: asphalt

Location: Orange
Contact: Kenneth Withrow
Transportation Planner
Town of Carrboro
3071 West Main Street
Carrboro, NC 27510
(919) 968–7713
carrplan@redial.net

8 Lincolnton Rail-Trail

Endpoints: Lincolnton
Mileage: 0.7
Surface: asphalt

Location: Lincoln
Contact: www.ncrail-trails.org

9 Nantahala Bikeway

Endpoints: Nantahala Center, Nanatahala Gorge (raft launch site)
Mileage: 1.3
Surface: asphalt

Location: Swain
Contact: www.ncrail-trails.org

10 River to Sea Bikeway

Endpoints: Wilmington, Wrightsville Beach
Mileage: 12
Surface: asphalt, concrete

Location: New Hanover
Contact: Bill Austin
Senior Transportation Planner
City of Wilmington
P.O. Box 1810
Wilmington, NC 28402-1810
(910) 341–5891
www.co.newhanover.nc.us/plan/menu.html

11 Sabina Gould Walkway (on Roanoke Valley Trail corridor)

Endpoints: Littleton
Mileage: 1.2
Surface: asphalt, crushed stone

Location: Halifax; Warren
Contact: www.ncrail-trails.org

12 Strollway

Endpoints: Winston-Salem (business district), historic Old Salem
Mileage: 1.2
Surface: crushed stone

Location: Forsyth
Contact: Nick Jameson
Recreation and Parks Director
Winston-Salem Recreation and Parks Department
City of Winston-Salem
P.O. Box 2511
Winston-Salem, NC 27102
(336) 727–2227
www.ci.winston-salem.nc.us

NORTH DAKOTA

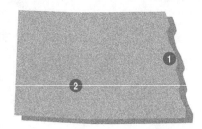

1 Grand Forks–East Grand Forks Bikeway

Endpoints: Grand Forks, East Grand Forks
Mileage: 4
Surface: asphalt

Location: Grand Forks
Contact: Charles Durrenburger
Senior Planner
Grand Forks–East Grand Forks
Metropolitan Planning
Organization
255 North Fourth Street
P.O. Box 5200
Grand Forks, ND 58206-5200
(701) 746–2656

2 Roughrider Trail

Endpoints: Fort Lincoln State Park, Fort Rice Historic Site
Mileage: 22
Surface: gravel, grass, dirt

Other use: ATV
Location: Morton
Contact: Randy Harmon
Trail Coordinator
Department of Parks and
Recreation
1835 East Bismarck Expressway
Bismarck, ND 58504-6708
(701) 328–5357
rharmon@state.nd.us

OHIO

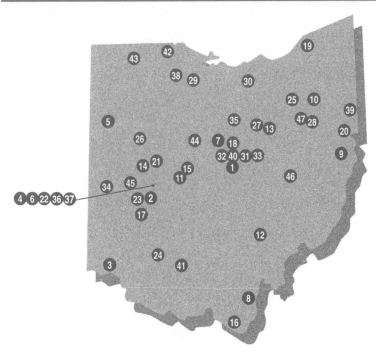

1 Blackhand Gorge Bikeway

Endpoints: Blackhand Gorge
State Nature Preserve
Mileage: 4.5
Surface: asphalt

Location: Licking
Contact: Greg Seymour
Preserve Manager
Blackhand Gorge State Nature
Preserve
5213 Rockhaven Road S.E.
Newark, OH 43055
(614) 763–4411

2 Buck Creek Trail

Endpoints: Near Buck Creek
State Park (Pumphouse Road at
Old Reid Park), Springfield
(Veteran's Park downtown)
Mileage: 3.1
Surface: asphalt

Location: Clark
Contact: James Campbell
Open Space Manager
National Trail Parks and
Recreation District
Springfield City Hall
76 East High Street
Springfield, OH 45502

OHIO   193

(937) 328–7275
jcampbell@ci.springfield.oh.us
www.intellweb.com/trails/buck.
htm
http://nationaltrailparksandrec.
org/trails.htm

3 California Junction Trail

Endpoints: California Woods
Nature Preserve
Mileage: 1
Surface: ballast, wood chips, dirt

Location: Hamilton
Contact: Clare Thorn
Director
Cincinnati Park Board
California Woods Nature
Preserve
5400 Kellogg Avenue
Cincinnati, OH 45228
(513) 231–8678

4 Cedarville Trail (Ohio to Erie Trail)

Endpoints: Xenia, South
Charleston
Mileage: 19
Surface: asphalt

Location: Greene
Contact: James Schneider
Assistant Director/Trail Manager
Greene County Parks
651 Dayton-Xenia Road
Xenia, OH 45385-2699

(740) 562–7445
Jschneider@co.greene.oh.us
www.intellweb.com/trails/ohio
erie.htm

5 Celina-Coldwater Bikeway

Endpoints: Celina, Coldwater
Mileage: 4.6
Surface: asphalt

Location: Mercer
Contact: Mike Sovinski
Celina Engineering Department
426 West Market Street
Celina, OH 45822-2127
(419) 586–1144

6 Creekside Trail (H-Connector)

Endpoints: Xenia (Xenia Station),
Dayton (Eastwood Metro Park)
Mileage: 17.8
Surface: asphalt

Location: Montgomery; Greene
Contact: James Schneider
Assistant Director/Trail Manager
Greene County Parks
651 Dayton-Xenia Road
Xenia, OH 45385-2699
(740) 562–7445
Jschneider@co.greene.oh.us

7 Delaware County 3C Trail (Ohio to Erie Trail)

Endpoints: Genoa Township (State Route 3 at Highland Lakes Avenue), State Route 3 at Lewis Center
Mileage: 3.5
Surface: asphalt

Location: Delaware
Contact: Randy Bennett
President
Delaware County Friends of the Trail
rqbikes@aol.com
www.ohiotoerietrail.org

8 Gallia County Hike and Bike Trail

Endpoints: Kerr Road to State Route 554, Mill Creek Road to McCormick Road
Mileage: 5.3
Surface: asphalt, crushed stone

Location: Gallia
Contact: Josette Baker
Director
O.O. McIntyre Park District
18 Locust Street
Gallipolis, OH 45631-1262
(614) 446-6275
oompd@zoomnet.nel
www.galliacounty.org/recreation/hike_bike.html

9 Harrison County Conotton Creek Trail

Endpoints: Bowerston, Jewett
Mileage: 11.4
Surface: asphalt

Location: Harrison
Contact: Dee Ann Hortsman
Chair
Conotton Creek Trail Committee
90151 Kilgore Road
Scio, OH 43988
sciomuseum@eohio.net
www.crossroads.org/hctrail

10 Headwaters Trail

Endpoints: Garrettsville, Hiram Station
Mileage: 3
Surface: crushed stone

Location: Portage
Contact: Christine Craycroft
Director
Portage County Park District
449 South Meridian Street
Ravenna, OH 44266
(330) 673-9404
ccraycr@earthlink.net

11 Heritage Trail

Endpoints: Hilliard (historic district), Plain City
Mileage: 6.1
Surface: asphalt

Location: Franklin
Contact: David Meeks
Economic Development Director
City of Hilliard
3800 Municipal Way
Hilliard, OH 43026
(614) 334–2357
dmeeks@cityofhilliard.com
www.cityofhilliard.com
www.heritagerailtrail.org

12 Hockhocking Adena Bikeway

Endpoints: Athens, Nelsonville
Mileage: 17
Surface: asphalt

Location: Athens
Contact: Athens County
Commissioner's Office
15 South Court Street
Athens, OH 45701
(740) 592–3219

13 Holmes County Trail

Endpoints: Holmesville, Millersburg
Mileage: 6
Surface: crushed limestone

Other use: Amish buggy
Location: Holmes
Contact: Shelly Venis
Holmes County Rails to Trails
Coalition
P.O. Box 95
Millersburg, OH 44654

14 Huffman Prairie Overlook Trail

Endpoints: Fairborn (Central Avenue), Greene/Montgomery county line
Mileage: 6
Surface: ballast, grass, dirt

Location: Greene
Contact: Elwood Ensor
Miami Valley Regional Bicycle
Committee
1304 Horizon Drive
Fairborn, OH 45324-5816
ejensor@prodigy.com

15 Interstate—670 Bikeway

Endpoints: Airport Drive, Cleveland Avenue (Columbus)
Mileage: 3.5
Surface: asphalt

Location: Franklin
Contact: Dale Hooper
City of Columbus
Division of Traffic Engineering
109 North Front Street
Columbus, OH 43215-2835
(614) 645–7790

16 Ironton Rail-Trail

Endpoints: Ironton
Mileage: 3
Surface: dirt

Location: Lawrence
Contact: Joe Unger
Ironton Chamber of Commerce
304 S. 3rd Street
Ironton, OH 45638
(740) 532–5954

17 Jamestown Connector

Endpoints: Jamestown
Mileage: 1.1
Surface: asphalt

Location: Greene
Contact: James Schneider

Assistant Director/Trail Manager
Greene County Parks
651 Dayton-Xenia Road
Xenia, OH 45385-2699
(740) 562–7445
jschneider@co.greene.oh.us

18 Kokosing Gap Trail

Endpoints: Mt. Vernon, Danville
Mileage: 14
Surface: asphalt

Location: Knox
Contact: Knox County
Convention and Visitors Bureau
8 West Vine Street
Mount Vernon, OH 43050
(800) 837–5282
info@visitknoxohio.org
www.kokosinggaptrail.org

19 Lake County Metroparks Greenway

Endpoints: Painesville (Jackson Street), Concord Township (Ravenna Road)
Mileage: 4.5
Surface: ballast, dirt

Location: Lake
Contact: Vince Urbanski
Lake Metroparks
11211 Spear Road
Concord Township, OH
44077-9542
(440) 639–7275

vurbanski@lakemetroparks.com
www.lakemetroparks.com

20 Little Beaver Creek Greenway Trail

Endpoints: Lisbon (State Route 164, South Lincoln Avenue), Leetonia
Mileage: 12
Surface: asphalt, gravel

Location: Columbiana
Contact: Dave Goerig
Columbiana County Park District
130 West Maple Street
Lisbon, OH 44432
(330) 424–9078
ccecondev@valuenet.com
www.bicycletrail.com/ghome.htm

21 Little Miami Scenic Trail (Clark County)

Endpoints: Springfield, Yellow Springs
Mileage: 9
Surface: asphalt

Location: Clark
Contact: Tim Smith
Director
Springfield Parks and Recreation
City Hall
76 East High Street
Springfield, OH 45502-1236
(513) 324–7348

22 Little Miami Scenic Trail (Greene County)

Endpoints: Yellow Springs, Spring Valley
Mileage: 15
Surface: asphalt

Location: Greene
Contact: James Schneider
Assistant Director/Trail Manager
Greene County Parks
651 Dayton-Xenia Road
Xenia, OH 45385-2699
(740) 562–7445
jschneider@co.greene.oh.us

23 Little Miami State Park Trail

Endpoints: Spring Valley, Millford
Mileage: 50
Surface: asphalt, ballast

Location: Clermont; Greene; Hamilton; Warren
Contact: Chuck Thiemann
Manager
Little Miami Scenic State Park
8570 East State Route 73
Waynesville, OH 45068-9719
(513) 897–3055
www.greenlink.org/miami/
lmtrail.html

24 Luther E. Warren Peace Path

Endpoints: Mulberry Street, Nelson Avenue (Wilmington)
Mileage: 1
Surface: asphalt

Location: Clinton
Contact: Eugene McKibben
President and Co-Founder
Clinton Rails-to-Trails Coalition
520 Dana Avenue
Wilmington, OH 45177
emckibben@cinci.rr.com
www.clintonrailtrails.org

25 Metro Parks Bike and Hike Trail

Endpoints: Walton Hills, Kent, and Stow
Mileage: 27
Surface: asphalt, crushed stone

Location: Summit
Contact: Keith Shy
Director
Metro Parks (serving Summit County)
975 Treaty Line Road
Akron, OH 44313-5898
(330) 867–5511
ametropa@neo.rr.com
www.neo.rr.com/Metro Parks

26 Miami & Erie Canal

Endpoints: Cross Trace, Laramie Creek
Mileage: 9
Surface: dirt

Location: Lucas; Miami
Contact: John Neilson
Manager
Piqua Historical Area State Memorial
9845 North Hardin Road
Piqua, OH 45356-9707
(513) 773–2522

27 Mohican Valley Trail

Endpoints: Brinkhaven, Danville
Mileage: 4.8
Surface: crushed stone, sand

Other use: horse drawn vehicles
Location: Knox
Contact: Mary Ridgway
Board Secretary
Mohican Valley Trail, Inc.
P.O. Box 261
Howard, OH 43028-0261
ridgwaym@kenyon.edu
clik.to/mohicanvalleytrail

28 Nickelplate Trail

Endpoints: Louisville
Mileage: 3
Surface: asphalt

Location: Stark
Contact: Darrin Metzger
Parks Supervisor
City of Louisville Parks
Department
215 South Mill Street
Louisville, OH 44641-1665
(216) 875–5644

29 North Coast Inland Trail

Endpoints: Clyde, Fremont
Mileage: 6.5
Surface: asphalt

Location: Huron; Lorain; Ottawa;
Sandusky; Wood
Contact: Steve Gruner
Director-Secretary
Sandusky County Park District
1970 Countyside Drive
Freemont, OH 43430-9574
(419) 334–4495
steve@scpd-parks.org
www.clydeohio.org/trail.htm
www.scpd-parks.org

30 Oberlin Bike Path

Endpoints: Kipton, Elyria
Mileage: 25
Surface: Asphalt

Location: Lorain
Contact: Ronald Twining
City of Oberlin
85 South Main Street
Oberlin , OH 44074-1626
(216) 775–1531

31 Ohio Canal Greenway

Endpoints: Hebron, State Route
79 West
Mileage: 2.8
Surface: crushed stone

Location: Licking
Contact: Russell Edgington
Director
Licking Park District
P.O. Box 590
Granville, OH 43023-0590
(740) 587–2535
lpd@msmisp.com
www.msmisp.com/lpd

32 Olentangy-Scioto Bike Path

Endpoints: Columbus
Mileage: 17
Surface: asphalt, concrete

Location: Franklin
Contact: Mollie O'Donnell
Landscape Architect
City of Columbus Recreation and
Parks Department
200 Greenlawn Avenue
Columbus, OH 43223
(614) 645–3300

33 Panhandle Trail

Endpoints: Newark, Licking
county line
Mileage: 10
Surface: dirt

Location: Licking
Contact: Russell Edgington
Licking Park District
P.O. Box 590
Granville, OH 43023
(614) 587–2538
lpd@msmisp.com
www.lickingparkdistrict.com

34 Piqua City Linear Park

Endpoints: Troy-Sidney Road,
Spiker Road (Piqua)
Mileage: 5.5
Surface: asphalt

Location: Miami
Contact: Marcia Scherer
Secretary
City of Piqua Parks and
Recreation
635 Gordon Street
Piqua, OH 45356
(937) 778–2085
mscherer@piquaoh.org

35 Richland B&O Trail

Endpoints: Butler, Mansfield
Mileage: 18.4
Surface: asphalt

Location: Richland
Contact: Steve McKee
Director
Richland County Park District
2295 Lexington Avenue
Mansfield, OH 44907-3027
(419) 884-3764
www.intellweb.com/trails/
nchland.htm

36 Simon Kenton Trail— Champaign County

Endpoints: Woodburn Road near
Cedar Bog Nature, State Route
55 south of Urbana
Mileage: 2.5
Surface: asphalt

Location: Champaign
Contact: Nancy Lokai-Baldwin

President
Simon Kenton Pathfinders
3420 Urbana-Moorefield Pike
P.O. Box 91
Urbana, OH 43078-0091
nlb@foryou.net
www.simonkentontrail.org

37 Simon Kenton Trail– Clark County

Endpoints: Buck Creek Trail (near Springfield), Villa Road and State Route 72
Mileage: 2.6
Surface: asphalt

Location: Clark
Contact: James Campbell
Open Space Manager
National Trail Parks and Recreation District
Springfield City Hall
76 East High Street
Springfield, OH 45502
(937) 328–7275
jcampbell@ci.springfield.oh.us
nationaltrailparksandrec.org/trails.htm
www.intellweb.com/trails/simon.htm

38 Slippery Elm Trail

Endpoints: Bowling Green, Baltimore
Mileage: 13
Surface: asphalt

Location: Wood

Contact: Andrew Kalmar
Director
Wood County Park District
18729 Mercer Road
Bowling Green, OH 43402-9688
(419) 353–1897
wcpd@wcnet.org
wcnet.org/ wcpd/

39 Stavich Bicycle Trail

Endpoints: Struthers, New Castle, Penn.
Mileage: 11
Surface: asphalt

Location: Mahoning; Lawrence
Contact: Gary Slaven
Falcon Foundry
Sixth and Water Street
Lowellville, OH 44436

40 Thomas J. Evans Bike Trail

Endpoints: Newark, Johnstown
Mileage: 14.5
Surface: asphalt

Location: Licking
Contact: Russell Edgington
Director
Licking Park District
P.O. Box 590
Granville, OH 43023-9509
(614) 587–2535
1pd@msmisp.com
www.msmisp.com/1pd

41 Tri-County Triangle Trail (Frankfort)

Endpoints: South Main Street, Maple Grove Road (Frankfort)
Mileage: 7
Surface: asphalt

Location: Fayette; Highland; Ross
Contact: tricotrail.tripod.com

42 University-Parks Bike-Hike Trail

Endpoints: Toledo
Mileage: 8.5
Surface: asphalt

Location: Lucas
Contact: Jean Ward
Director
Metroparks—Toledo Area
5100 West Central
Toledo, OH 43615-2100
(419) 535–3050

43 Wabash Cannonball Trail

Endpoints: Maumee to Montpelier, spur to Liberty Center
Mileage: 28
Surface: cinder

Location: Fulton; Henry; Lucas; Williams
Contact: Gene Markley
Vice President

Northwestern Ohio Rails-to-Trails Association
P.O. Box 234
Delta, OH 43515-0234
(800) 951–4788
140years@powersupply.net
www.toltbbs.com/~norta/

44 Westerville Bikeway

Endpoints: Westerville (State Street), Westerville (Maxtown Road)
Mileage: 2.2
Surface: asphalt

Location: Franklin
Contact: Jody Stower
Director
Westerville Parks and Recreation
64 East Walnut Street
Westerville, OH 43081
(614) 890–8544
www.ci.westerville.oh.us

45 Wolf Creek Bikeway

Endpoints: Trotwood, Verona
Mileage: 13
Surface: asphalt

Location: Montgomery
Contact: Dick Peddemors
Superintendent of Parks
Five Rivers Metro Parks
1375 East Siebenthaler Avenue
Dayton, OH 45414
(937) 222–2291
peddemors@juno.com
www.intellweb.com/trails/wolf.htm

46 Zanesville Riverfront Bikepath

Endpoints: Zanesville
Mileage: 2.9
Surface: asphalt

Location: Muskingum
Contact: Ernest Bynum
Recreation Director
City of Zanesville
401 Market Street
Zanesville, OH 43701-3520
(614) 455–0609
Recreation@co2.org

47 Zoar Valley Trail

Endpoints: Fort Laurens in
Bolivar, Schoenbrunn Village
Mileage: 20
Surface: asphalt, ballast, grass,
dirt

Location: Tuscarawas
Contact: Barb Watson
Trustee
Camp Tuscazoar Foundation, Inc.
2030 N. Wooster Avenue
Dover, OH 44622
babs_49_us@yahoo.com
www.tuscazoar.org/ZoarValley
Trail.htm

OKLAHOMA

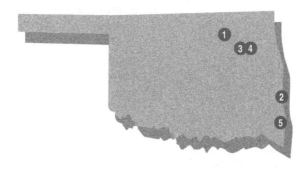

1 Cleveland Trail

Endpoints: Cleveland, Osage
Mileage: 3
Surface: asphalt

Location: Pawnee
Contact: Ed Callison
City Manager
City of Cleveland
P.O. Drawer 190
Cleveland, OK 74020-3829
(918) 358–3600

2 Indian Nations Recreation Trail

Endpoints: Stigler, Porum, Warner
Mileage: 39 (3 sections)
Surface: asphalt, ballast

Location: Haskell
Contact: Paul West
President
Indian Nations Recreation Trail, Inc.
P.O. Box 945
Warner, OK 74469-0945
(918) 463–2931

3 Katy Trail

Endpoints: Sand Springs, Tulsa
Mileage: 6.5
Surface: asphalt

Location: Tulsa
Contact: Jackie Bubenik
Executive Director
River Parks Authority
717 South Houston, Suite 510
Tulsa, OK 74127-9000
(918) 596–2006
jbubenik@ci.tulsa.ok.us

4 Midland Valley Trail & River Parks Pedestrian Bridge

Endpoints: Tulsa
Mileage: 2
Surface: asphalt

Location: Tulsa
Contact: Jackie Bubenik
Executive Director
River Parks Authority
707 South Houston, Suite 202
Tulsa, OK 74127-9000
(918) 596–2006
jbubenik@ci.tulsa.ok.us

5 Old Frisco Trail

Endpoints: Poteau, Wister
Mileage: 8.2
Surface: gravel

Location: Le Flore
Contact: Esther Canada
Director
Old Frisco Trail
Lake Wister Association
P.O. Box 890
Wister, OK 74966-0890
(918) 655–7216

OREGON

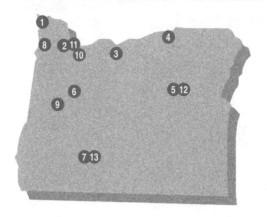

1 Astoria Riverwalk

Endpoints: Astoria—Smith Point,
Tongue Point
Mileage: 5.1
Surface: asphalt, gravel, ballast,
grass, concrete

Location: Clatsop
Contact: Paul Benoit
Community Development
Director
City of Astoria
City Hall
1095 Duane Street
Astoria, OR 97103-4524
(503) 325–5821
bencliff@seasurf.com

2 Banks-Vernonia State Trail

Endpoints: Banks, Vernonia
Mileage: 21
Surface: asphalt, gravel

Location: Columbia; Washington
Contact: Scott Green
Park Ranger
Banks/Vernonia State Trail
24600 N.W. Bacona Road
Buxton, OR 97109
(503) 324–06061

3 Deschutes River Trail

Endpoints: Deschutes State
Park, Mac's Canyon Campground
Mileage: 17
Surface: dirt

Location: Sherman
Contact: Peter Bond
State Trail Coordinator
Oregon Parks and Recreation
Department
1115 Commercial Street N.E.

Salem, OR 97310-1000
(503) 378–6378
peter.d.bond@state.or.us

4 Lake Wallula Scenic River Hiking Trail

Endpoints: Hat Rock State Park, McNary Beach Park
Mileage: 4.9
Surface: gravel

Location: Umatilla
Contact: Jeff Phillip
Park Ranger
Corps of Engineers
McNary Dam
P.O. Box 1230
Umatilla, OR 97882-1230
(503) 922–3211

5 Malheur Trail

Endpoints: Malheur National Forest
Mileage: 12.5
Surface: ballast

Location: Grant
Contact: Tim Kimble
Recreation Staff Officer
Malheur National Forest
139 N.E. Dayton Street
John Day, OR 97845-1202
(503) 575–1731

6 Mill City

Endpoints: Mill City
Mileage: 2
Surface: asphalt, gravel

Location: Linn
Contact: Roel Lundquist
City Administrator
City of Mill City
252 S.W. Cedar Street
P.O. Box 256
Mill City, OR 97360-2466
(503) 897–2302
millcity@wvi.com

7 OC&E Woods Line State Trail

Endpoints: Bly, Klamath Falls, Sprague River
Mileage: 100
Surface: asphalt, gravel, ballast, dirt, wood chips

Location: Klamath
Contact: Jim Beauchemin
Park Manager
Oregon State Parks and
Recreation Department
Collier State Park
4600 Highway 97 North
Chiloquin, OR 97624
(541) 783–2471
www.u-rhere.com/OCE

8 Oregon Electric ROW Trail and Linear Park

Endpoints: Beaverton
Mileage: 1
Surface: asphalt, wood chips

Location: Washington
Contact: Jim McElhinny
Director
Planning and Natural Resources
Tualatin Hills Parks and
Recreation District
15707 Southwest Walker Road
Beaverton, OR 97006-5941
(503) 645–6433

9 Row River Trail

Endpoints: Culp Creek, Cottage
Grove (Mosby Creek)
Mileage: 14
Surface: asphalt, stone

Location: Lane
Contact: Bryant Smith
Outdoor Recreation Planner
Eugene District Bureau of Land
Management
2890 Chad Drive
P.O. Box 10226
Eugene, OR 97408-7336
(541) 440–4930
or090mb@or.blm.gov
www.recreation.gov/detail.cfm?ID
=1752

10 Springwater Corridor

Endpoints: Portland (near
Tideman Johnson Park),
Gresham (Rugg Road and 267th
Avenue)
Mileage: 14
Surface: asphalt

Location: Clackamas,
Multnomah
Contact: Patty Freeman
Portland Parks and Recreation
1120 S.W. Fifth Avenue, #1302
Portland, OR 97204-1933
(503) 823–5592
pkpatty@ci.portland.or.us

11 Springwater on the Willamette

Endpoints: Portland (SE Ivon),
Portland (SE Umatilla)
Mileage: 3
Surface: asphalt

Location: Multnomah
Contact: Patty Freeman
Portland Parks and Recreation
1120 S.W. Fifth Avenue, #1302
Portland, OR 97204-1933
(503) 823–5592
pkpatty@ci.portland.or.us
www.parks.ci.portland.or.us/
Planning/SpringwaterOMSI.htm

12 Sumpter Valley Interpretive Trail

Endpoints: Malheur National Forest
Mileage: 0.2
Surface: dirt

Location: Grant
Contact: Ivan Mulder
Trail Manager
Malheur National Forest
139 N.E. Dayton Street
John Day, OR 97845-1202
(503) 575–1731

13 Woods Line Trail

Endpoints: Beatty, Fremont National Forest (Sycan)
Mileage: 47
Surface: asphalt, gravel, wood chips

Location: Klamath
Contact: Angela Roufs
Collier State Park
4600 Highway 97-N
Chiloquin, OR 97624
(541) 783–2471

PENNSYLVANIA

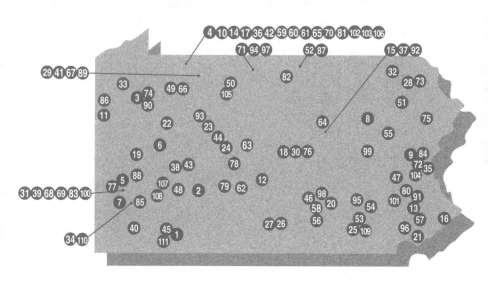

1 Allegheny Highlands Trail (part of Great Allegheny Passage)

Endpoints: Garrett, Fort Hill
Mileage: 24
Surface: crushed stone

Location: Somerset
Contact: Hank Parke
President
Somerset County Rails to Trails
829 North Center Avenue
Somerset, PA 15501-1029
www.westol.com/tat/updates/
alleg.htm

2 Allegheny Portage Railroad Trace

Endpoints: Allegheny Portage
Railroad National Historic Site
Mileage: 7 (1.5 miles are
rail-trail)
Surface: ballast, grass, wood
chips

Location: Blair; Cambria
Contact: Joanne Hanley
Superintendent
Allegheny Portage Railroad
National Historic Site
116 Federal Park Road
Gallitzin, PA 16640
(814) 886–6150
www.nps.gov/alpo

3 Allegheny River Trail

Endpoints: Franklin (8th Street Bridge over Allegheny), North of Emlenton (Quaker State Plant)
Mileage: 20.2
Surface: asphalt

Location: Venango
Contact: David Howes
Allegheny Valley Trails
Association
153 6th Avenue
Clarion, PA
avta@clarion.edu
eagle.clarion.edu/~grads/avta/
www.avta-trails.org

4 Allegheny Snowmobile Trails

Endpoints: Allegheny National Forest
Mileage: 115
Surface: gravel, ballast, grass, dirt

Location: Elk; Forest; McKean; Warren
Contact: Mary Hosmer
Forester
Allegheny National Forest
P.O. Box 847
Warren, PA 16365-0847
(814) 723–5150
mhosmer/r9-allegheny@fs.fed.us

5 Arboretum Trail

Endpoints: Hulton Road, South End (Oakmont)
Mileage: 1.4
Surface: asphalt

Location: Allegheny
Contact: Kitty Vagley
Director
Garden Club
830 Fifteenth Street
Oakmont, PA 15139-1008

6 Armstrong Trail

Endpoints: Schenley, Upper Hillville
Mileage: 52.5
Surface: asphalt, crushed stone, gravel, ballast

Location: Armstrong; Clarion
Contact: Timothy Kelly
Executive Director
Allegheny Valley Land Trust
P.O. Box 777
Kittanning, PA 16201
(412) 543–4478
armtrail@alltel.net
www.trfn.clpgh.org/avlt

7 Arrowhead Trail (Montour Trail Extension)

Endpoints: Peters Township
Mileage: 3.5
Surface: asphalt, ballast

Location: Washington
Contact: Ed Fegas
Director
Peters Township
Department of Parks and
Recreation
610 East McMurray Road
McMurray, PA 15317-3420
(724) 942–5000
www.montourtrail.org

8 Back Mountain Trail

Endpoints: Luzerne, Trucksville
Mileage: 2.2
Surface: ballast

Location: Luzerne
Contact: Judith Rimple
President
Anthracite Scenic Trails
Association
96 Hildebrandt Road
Dallas, PA 18612-9806
jcbbr@aol.com

9 Bath-Allen Trail (Nor-Bath Trail)

Endpoints: Jacksonville,
Weaversville
Mileage: 5.2
Surface: asphalt

Location: Northampton

Contact: Gordon Heller
Superintendent
County of Northampton
Division of Parks and Recreation
RD #4, Greystone Building
Nazareth, PA 18064-9278
(610) 746–1975

10 Beaver Meadows Trail System

Endpoints: Allegheny National
Forest
Mileage: 5.5
Surface: dirt
Location: Forest
Contact: Mary Hosmer
Forester
Allegheny National Forest
P.O. Box 847
Warren, PA 16365-0847
(814) 723–5150

11 Beaver to Erie Canal Trail (Shenango Trail)

Endpoints: Big Bend, Kids Mill
Bridge
Mileage: 8
Surface: dirt

Location: Mercer
Contact: Mike Cummings
Resource Manager
Army Corps of Engineers
Shenango Reservoir
2442 Kelly Road
Sharpsville, PA 16150-8208
(724) 962–7746
shenango.ranger@usace.army.mil

12 Bellefonte Central Rail-Trail

Endpoints: State College (McKee Street), Mount Nittany Expressway
Mileage: 1.3
Surface: crushed stone, grass

Location: Centre
Contact: centrebike.org/railtrail.html

13 Betzwood Rail Trail

Endpoints: Valley Forge National Historic Park
Mileage: 2
Surface: asphalt, crushed stone, grass, dirt

Location: Montgomery
Contact: John Wood
Chief of Open Space Planning
Montgomery County Planning Commission
P.O. Box 311 Courthouse
Norristown, PA 19404-0311
(610) 278–3736

14 Big Side Loop of Hickory Trail

Endpoints: Allegheny National Forest
Mileage: 11.2
Surface: dirt

Location: Forest
Contact: Mary Hosmer
Forester
Allegheny National Forest
P.O. Box 847
Warren, PA 16365-0847
(814) 723–5150
mhosmer/r9-allegheny@fs.fed.us

15 Black Forest Trail

Endpoints: Black Forest
Mileage: 30
Surface: ballast

Location: Lycoming
Contact: Jim Hyland
Recreation Forester
Tiadaghton Forest Fire Fighters Association
c/o Bureau of Forestry
423 East Central Avenue
South Williamsport, PA 17702

16 Bristol Spurline Park

Endpoints: Bristol
Mileage: 2.5
Surface: asphalt

Location: Bucks
Contact: Marie Fields
Borough of Bristol
250 Pond Street
Bristol, PA 19007-4937
(215) 788–3828

17 Brush Hollow Cross-Country Ski Trail

Endpoints: Allegheny National Forest
Mileage: 7.7
Surface: gravel, ballast, dirt

Location: Elk
Contact: Mary Hosmer
Forester
Allegheny National Forest
P.O. Box 847
Warren, PA 16365-0847
(814) 723–5150
mhosmer/r9-allegheny@fs.fed.us

18 Brush Hollow Trail

Endpoints: Bald Eagle State Forest
Mileage: 1.3
Surface: crushed stone, dirt

Location: Union
Contact: Amy Griffith
District Forester
Bald Eagle State Forest
P.O. Box 147
Laurelton, PA 17835
(570) 922–3344
www.dcnr.state.pa.us

19 Butler-Freeport Community Trail

Endpoints: Freeport; Butler
Mileage: 21
Surface: crushed stone, ballast

Location: Armstrong, Butler
Contact: Ron Bennettz
President
Butler-Freeport Community
Trail Council
P.O. Box 533
Saxonburg, PA 16056-0533

20 Capital Area Greenbelt

Endpoints: Loop around Harrisburg
Mileage: 20 (2 are rail-trail)
Surface: wood chips, asphalt, grass, stone

Location: Dauphin County
Contact: Norman Laccase
Capital Area Greenbelt
Association
2415 Patton Road
Harrisburg, PA 17112

21 Chester Valley Trail

Endpoints: Downingtown, Norristown
Mileage: 1.4
Surface: asphalt

Location: Chester
Contact: Chester County Parks and Recreation Department
601 Westtown Road, Suite 160
West Chester, PA 19380-0990
(610) 344–6415
www.montcopa.org/parks/chester
valleytrail.htm

22 Clarion Highlands Trail (Sandy Creek Trail section)

Endpoints: Belmar Village (west side of Allegheny River), Van (Route 322)
Mileage: 8.6
Surface: asphalt

Location: Venango
Contact: David Howes
Allegheny Valley Trails
Association
153 6th Avenue
Clarion, PA
avta@clarion.edu
eagle.clarion.edu/~grads/avta/
SCT.html

23 Clarion/Little Toby Creek Trail

Endpoints: Ridgway, Brockway
Mileage: 18
Surface: crushed stone, cinder

Location: Clearfield; Elk; Jefferson
Contact: Dave Lauricella
Secretary
Tri-County Rails-to-Trails
Association
P.O. Box 115
Ridgway, PA 15853
lauricde@ncentral.com

24 Clearfield-Grampian Trail

Endpoints: Clearfield, Grampian
Mileage: 10.2
Surface: crushed stone, ballast, dirt

Location: Clearfield;
Curwensville; Grampion
Contact: Benny Irwin
Secretary
Clearfield County Rails to Trails
Association
310 East Cherry Street
Clearfield, PA 16830

25 Conewago Trail

Endpoints: Elizabethtown, Lebanon Valley Rail-Trail at Lebanon county line
Mileage: 5
Surface: dirt, cinder

Location: Lancaster
Contact: John Gerencser
Recreation Coordinator
Lancaster County Parks and
Recreation
1050 Rockford Road
Lancaster, PA 17602-4624
(717) 299–8215
www.co.lancaster.pa.us/
parks.htm

26 Cumberland County Biker/Hiker Trail

Endpoints: Pine Grove Furnace State Park, Mt. Creek Campground
Mileage: 5.5
Surface: crushed stone

Location: Cumberland
Contact: William Rosevear
Park Manager
Pine Grove Furnace State Park
1100 Pine Grove Road
Gardeners, PA 17324-9802
(717) 486-7174

27 Cumberland Valley Rail-Trail

Endpoints: Newville, Shippensburg
Mileage: 10.8
Surface: ballast, dirt

Location: Cumberland
Contact: Jerry Angulo
Cumberland Valley Rails-to-Trails Council
P.O. Box 531
Shippensburg, PA 17257
ajangulo@innernet.net

28 D&H Rail-Trail

Endpoints: Simpson Viaduct at Route 171, north through Lanesboro–N.Y. State border
Mileage: 38
Surface: ballast, cinder

Location: Lackawanna; Susquehanna; Wayne
Contact: Lynn Conrad
Executive Director
Rail-Trail Council of Northeast Pennsylvania
P.O. Box 123
R 334 Main Street
Forest City, PA 18421-0123
tccrail@epix.net
www.nepa-rail-trails.org

29 Deerlick Cross-Country Ski Trail

Endpoints: Allegheny National Forest
Mileage: 9
Surface: ballast, grass, dirt

Location: Warren
Contact: Jeff Stevenson
District Ranger
Allegheny National Forest
Sheffield Ranger District
Route 6
Sheffield, PA 16347
(814) 968–3232

30 Duncan Trail

Endpoints: Bald Eagle State Forest
Mileage: 1.8
Surface: crushed stone, dirt

Location: Union
Contact: Amy Griffith
District Forester
Bald Eagle State Forest
P.O. Box 147
Laurelton, PA 17835
(570) 922–3344

31 Eliza Furnace Trail

Endpoints: Pittsburgh
Mileage: 2.43
Surface: asphalt, crushed stone

Location: Allegheny
Contact: Hannah Elrich
Office of the Mayor
414 Grant Street
Pittsburgh, PA 15219
(412) 255–2626

32 Endless Mountains Riding Trail

Endpoints: Alford, Montrose
Mileage: 14
Surface: ballast, crushed stone, gravel, dirt, cinder

Location: Susquehanna
Contact: Thomas Wooden
Center for Anti-Slavery Studies
2 Maple Street
Montrose, PA 18801
(570) 278–0277
cass@emsc.net

33 Ernst Bike Trail

Endpoints: Meadville, Watson Run
Mileage: 5
Surface: asphalt

Location: Crawford
Contact: John Wallach
French Creek Recreation Trails, Inc.
747 Terrace Street
Meadville, PA 16335
jwallach@manchs.org
www.dcnr.state.pa.us/rails/ernstbt.html

34 Five Star Trail

Endpoints: Greensburg, Youngwood
Mileage: 7.5
Surface: asphalt, crushed stone

Location: Westmoreland
Contact: Robert McKinley
Trail Manager
Regional Trail Corporation
101 N. Water Street
P.O. Box 95
West Newton, PA 15089-1535
(412) 872–5586

yrt@westol.com
www.5startrail.org
www.youghrivertrail.org

35 Forks Township Recreation Trail

Endpoints: Forks Township, Palmer Township
Mileage: 7
Surface: asphalt, gravel

Location: Northampton
Contact: Robert Fretz
Road Supervisor
Forks Township Recreation Board
1606 Sullivan Trail
Easton, PA 18040
(610) 252–0785

36 Gamelands Trail

Endpoints: Allegheny National Forest
Mileage: 2.3
Surface: dirt

Location: Warren
Contact: Mary Hosmer
Forester
Allegheny National Forest
P.O. Box 847
Warren, PA 16365-0847
(814) 723–5150
mhosmer/r9-allegheny@fs.fed.us

37 George B. Will Trail

Endpoints: Tiadaghton State Forest
Mileage: 5
Surface: ballast, grass

Location: Lycoming
Contact: Jim Hyland
Recreation Forester
Tiadaghton Forest Fire Fighters Association
Bureau of Forestry
423 East Central Avenue
South Williamsport, PA 17702
(570) 327–3450
www.dcnr.state.pa.us

38 Ghost Town Trail

Endpoints: Nanty Glo, Dilltown
Mileage: 16
Surface: crushed stone

Location: Cambria; Indiana
Contact: Mike Kzerncheck
Indiana County Parks
Blue Spruce Park Road
Indiana, PA 15701-9802
(724) 463–8636
http://cpcug.org/user/warholic/ghost.html

39 Great Shamokin Path

Endpoints: Yatesboro, Numine
Mileage: 4.5
Surface: gravel, grass

Location: Armstrong
Contact: Pam Meade
President
Cowanshannock Creek
Watershed Association
P.O. Box 307
Rural Valley, PA 16249-0307
www.dcnr.state.pa.us/rails/
greatsp.html

40 Greene River Trail

Endpoints: Greene Cove Marina,
Rice's Landing
Mileage: 4
Surface: crushed stone

Location: Greene
Contact: Jake Blaker
Greene County Parks and
Recreation
107 Fairgrounds Road
Waynesburg, PA 15370
(724) 852–5323
www.county.greenepa.net/index2.
html

41 Heart's Content Cross-Country Ski Trail

Endpoints: Allegheny National
Forest
Mileage: 7.7
Surface: grass, dirt

Location: Warren
Contact: Jeff Stevenson
District Ranger
Allegheny National Forest
Sheffield Ranger District
Route 6
Sheffield, PA 16347
(814) 968–3232

42 Hickory Creek Trail

Endpoints: Allegheny National
Forest
Mileage: 11.5
Surface: dirt

Location: Forest
Contact: Mary Hosmer
Forester
Allegheny National Forest
P.O. Box 847
Warren, PA 16365-0847
(814) 723–5150
mshosmer/r9-allegheny@fs.fed.us

43 Hoodlebug Trail

Endpoints: Indiana, Homer City
Mileage: 6
Surface: asphalt

Location: Indiana
Contact: Ed Patterson
Parks Director
Indiana County Parks
1128 Blue Spruce Road
Indiana, PA 15701-9802
(724) 463–8636
indparks@stargate.net
www.indianacountyparks.org/
parks/ht/ht.html

44 Houtzdale Line Rail-Trail (East)

Endpoints: Osceola Mills, West
Moshannon
Mileage: 4.5
Surface: ballast

Location: Clearfield
Contact: Clearfield County Rails
to Trails Association
310 East Cherry Street
Clearfield, PA 16830

45 Indian Creek Valley Hiking and Biking Trail

Endpoints: Indian Head,
Champion
Mileage: 5
Surface: crushed stone, grass

Location: Fayette
Contact: Megan Hess-Kalp
Secretary/Treasurer
Salt Lick Township
147 Municipal Building Road
P.O. Box 403
Melcroft, PA 15462-0403
(724) 455–2866

saltlick@hhs.net
www.dcnr.state.pa.us/rails/
indiancvt.html

46 Iron Horse Trail

Endpoints: Big Spring State
Park, New Germantown
Mileage: 10
Surface: crushed stone, ballast,
dirt

Location: Perry
Contact: Bob Beleski
Forester
Pennsylvania Department of
Conservation and Natural
Resources
Bureau of Forestry
RD 1, Box 42 A
Blain, PA 17006
(717) 536–3191

47 Ironton Rail-Trail

Endpoints: Whitehall, North
Whitehall
Mileage: 9
Surface: crushed stone, dirt

Location: Lehigh
Contact: Scott Cope
Pennsylvania Department of
Conservation and Natural
Resources
P.O. Box 8475
Harrisburg, PA 17105–8475
(717) 772–3319
sccope@state.pa.us

48 Jim Mayer Riverwalk

Endpoints: Johnstown
Mileage: 1.8
Surface: crushed stone

Location: Cambria
Contact: Lisa Dailey
Cambria County Tourist Council
111 Market Street
Johnstown, PA 15902-2901
(814) 536–7993

49 Kellettville to Nebraska Trace Trail

Endpoints: Kellettville
Campground, Nebraska
Recreation Area
Mileage: 12.2
Surface: grass, dirt

Location: Forest
Contact: Rodney Daum
Park Ranger
U.S. Army Corps of Engineers
1 Tionesta Lake
Tionesta, PA 16353-9613
(814) 755–3512

50 Kinzua Bridge Trail

Endpoints: Kinzua Bridge State
Park
Mileage: 2.5
Surface: wood chips, dirt

Location: McKean
Contact: Trail Manager

Kinzua Bridge State Park
c/o Bendigo State Park
P.O. Box A
Johnsonburg, PA 15845-0016
(814) 965–2646

51 Lackawanna River Heritage Trail

Endpoints: Pittston, Scranton,
and Carbondale
Mileage: 40
Surface: crushed stone, gravel

Location: Lackawanna; Luzerne;
Susquehanna; Wayne
Contact: Bernie McGurl
Executive Director
Lackawanna River Heritage Trail
P.O. Box 368
Scranton, PA 18501
(717) 282–6640
1rea@epix.net

52 Lamb's Creek Hike and Bike Trail

Endpoints: Mansfield, Lamb's
Creek Recreation Area
Mileage: 3.7
Surface: asphalt

Location: Tioga
Contact: Richard Koeppel
Park Manager
Tioga-Hammond Lakes
R.R. #1, Box 65
Tioga, PA 16946-9733
(570) 835–5281

53 Lancaster Junction Trail

Endpoints: Lancaster Junction, Landisville
Mileage: 2.5
Surface: dirt, cinder

Location: Lancaster
Contact: John Gerencser
Recreation Coordinator
Lancaster County Parks and
Recreation
1050 Rockford Road
Lancaster, PA 17602-4624
(717) 299–8215
www.xo.lancaster.pa.us/parks.htm

54 Lebanon Valley Rail-Trail

Endpoints: Conewago Trail at
Lancaster county line, Mt. Gretna
(Route 72) via Colebrook
Mileage: 9
Surface: dirt, cinder

Location: Lancaster
Contact: John Wengert
President
Lebanon Valley Rails-to-Trails
Association
630 Old Mt. Gretna Road
Lebanon, PA 17042
john_wengert@deanfoods.com
www.lvrailtrail.com

55 Lehigh Gorge State Park Trail

Endpoints: Jim Thorpe, White
Haven
Mileage: 26
Surface: crushed stone, ballast

Location: Carbon; Luzerne
Contact: Kevin Fazzini
Park Manager
Lehigh Gorge State Park
R.R. 1, Box 81
White Haven, PA 18661-9712
(570) 443–0400
www.dcnr.state.pa.us

56 LeTort Spring Run Nature Trail

Endpoints: Carlisle, South
Middleton
Mileage: 1.4
Surface: ballast, grass

Location: Cumberland
Contact: Rian Fischbach
Executive Director
LeTort Regional Authority
415 Franklin Street
Carlisle, PA 17013-1859
(717) 245–0508
blfisch@epix.net

57 Lititz-Warwick Trailway

Endpoints: Lititz, Warwick
Mileage: 1.4
Surface: asphalt

Location: Chester
Contact: Dan Zimmerman
Warwick Township
P.O. Box 308
Lititz, PA 17543
(717) 626–8900
dzimmerman@warwicktown
ship.org

58 Little Buffalo State Park Trail

Endpoints: Shoeff's Mill to western boundary of park
Mileage: 2.5
Surface: dirt, gravel

Location: Perry
Contact: Little Buffalo State Park
RD2 Box 256A
Newport, PA 17074
(717) 567–9255
www.dcnr.state.pa.us

59 Little Drummer Historic Pathway

Endpoints: Allegheny National Forest
Mileage: 3.1
Surface: grass, dirt

Location: Elk
Contact: Mary Hosmer

Forester
Allegheny National Forest
P.O. Box 847
Warren, PA 16365-0847
(814) 723–5150
mshosmer/r9-allegheny@fs.fed.us

60 Little Side Loop of Hickory Trail

Endpoints: Allegheny National Forest
Mileage: 3.9
Surface: dirt

Location: Forest
Contact: Mary Hosmer
Forester
Allegheny National Forest
P.O. Box 847
Warren, PA 16365-0847
(814) 723–5150
mshosmer/r9-allegheny@fs.fed.us

61 Loleta Hiking Trail

Endpoints: Allegheny National Forest
Mileage: 3
Location: Forest
Contact: Mary Hosmer
Forester
Allegheny National Forest
P.O. Box 847
Warren, PA 16365-0847
(814) 723–5150
mshosmer/r9-allegheny@fs.fed.us

62 Lower Trail

Endpoints: Alexandria, Williamsburg
Mileage: 11
Surface: crushed stone, ballast

Other use: Wagon
Location: Blair; Huntingdon
Contact: Jennifer Barefoot
President
Central Pennsylvania Rails-to-
Trails
P.O. Box 592
Hollidaysburg, PA 16648-0592

63 LR 651

Endpoints: Osceola Mills, West
Moshannon
Mileage: 4.5
Surface: ballast

Location: Clearfield
Contact: Clearfield County Rails
to Trails Association
310 East Cherry Street
Clearfield, PA 16830-2319

64 Lycoming Creek Bikeway

Endpoints: Williamsport,
Loyalsock
Mileage: 3.3
Surface: asphalt

Location: Lycoming
Contact: Mark Murawski
Transportation Planner
Lycoming County Planning

48 West Third Street
Williamsport, PA 17701-6536
(570) 320–2130

65 Marienville ATV/Bike Trail

Endpoints: Allegheny National
Forest
Mileage: 36.7
Surface: crushed stone, gravel,
grass, dirt

Other use: ATV
Location: Forest
Contact: Mary Hosmer
Forester
Allegheny National Forest
P.O. Box 847
Warren, PA 16365-0847
(814) 723–5150
mhosmer/r9-allegheny@fs.fed.us

66 Mill Creek Loop Trail

Endpoints: Allegheny National
Forest
Mileage: 5.6
Surface: grass, dirt

Location: Elk
Contact: Allegheny National
Forest
Marienville Ranger District
HC 2, Box 130
Marienville, PA 16239
(814) 927–6628

67 Minister Creek Trail

Endpoints: Allegheny National Forest
Mileage: 6.6
Surface: grass, dirt

Location: Forest; Warren
Contact: Jeff Stevenson
District Ranger
Allegheny National Forest
Sheffield Ranger District
Route 6
Sheffield, PA 16347
(814) 968–3232

68 Montour Trail—Cecil

Endpoints: Venice, Hendersonville
Mileage: 5.7
Surface: crushed stone

Location: Washington
Contact: Peter Kohnke
President
Montour Trail Council
P.O. Box 11866
Pittsburgh, PA 15228-0866
(724) 514–2887
pkohnke@libcom.com
www.atatrail.org

69 Montour Trail— Coraopolis to Bethel Park

Endpoints: Coraopolis, Bethel Park
Mileage: 26
Surface: crushed stone

Location: Allegheny
Contact: Peter Kohnke
President
Montour Trail Council
P.O. Box 11866
Pittsburgh, PA 15228-0866
(724) 514–2887
pkohnke@libcom.com
www.atatrail.org

70 North Country National Scenic Trail

Endpoints: State Game Lands #24, New York state line
Mileage: 96.3 (several sections)
Surface: ballast, grass, dirt

Location: Elk; Forest; McKean; Warren
Contact: Mary Hosmer
Forester
Allegheny National Forest
P.O. Box 847
Warren, PA 16365-0847
(814) 723–5150
mshosmer/r9-allegheny@fs.fed.us

71 North Link Trail

Endpoints: Susquehannock State Forest
Mileage: 9.3
Surface: dirt

Location: Potter
Contact: David Schiller
District Forester
Susquehannock State Forest
3150 East Second Street
P.O. Box 673
Coudersport, PA 16915-0673
(814) 274–600
fd15.coudersport@a1.dcnr.state.pa.us

72 Northampton–Bath Recreation Trail

Endpoints: Northampton, Bath
Mileage: 7.3
Surface: gravel, ballast

Location: Northampton
Contact: www.dcnr.state.pa.us/rails

73 O&W Trail

Endpoints: Simpson, Buckingham, Hancock Townships
Mileage: 13
Surface: gravel, dirt

Location: Wayne

Contact: Lynn Conrad
Executive Director
Rail-Trail Council of Northeast Pennsylvania
P.O. Box 123
Forest City, PA 18421-0123
(570) 785–7245
tccrail@ePix.Net
www.nepa-rail-trails.org

74 Oil Creek State Park Trail

Endpoints: Petroleum Centre, Crawford county line south of Titusville
Mileage: 9.7
Surface: asphalt

Location: Venango
Contact: Marcia Baker
Park Manager
Oil Creek State Park
R.R. 1, Box 207
Oil City, PA 16301-9733
(814) 676–5915
www.dcnr.state.pa.us
eagle.clarion.edu/~grads/avta

75 Old Railroad Trail

Endpoints: Big Pocono State Park, Crescent Lake
Mileage: 8.4
Surface: ballast

Location: Monroe
Contact: Ronald Dixon
Park Manager

Big Pocono State Park
c/o Tobyhanna State Park
P.O. Box 387
Tobyhanna, PA 18466-0387
(717) 894–8336
www.dcnr.state.pa.us

76 Old Tram Trail

Endpoints: Bald Eagle State Forest
Mileage: 1.2
Surface: crushed stone, dirt

Location: Union
Contact: Amy Griffith
District Forester
Bald Eagle State Park
P.O. Box 147
Laurelton, PA 17835
(570) 922–3344

77 Panhandle Trail (Allegheny County)

Endpoints: Washington County line near McDonald, Walker's Mill (near Carnegie)
Mileage: 6.85
Surface: crushed stone

Location: Allegheny
Contact: Ned Williams
President
Panhandle Trail Association
415 E. Maiden Street
Washington, PA 15301
ned@washtool.com
www.panhandletrail.org

78 Penns Creek Path (Mid State Trail)

Endpoints: Poe Paddy State Park
Mileage: 2.9
Surface: ballast

Location: Centre; Mifflin
Contact: Thomas Thwaites
President
Mid State Trail Association
P.O. Box 167
Boalsburg, PA 16827-0167

79 Pennsylvania Mainline Canal

Endpoints: Alexandria, Huntingdon county line
Mileage: 5
Surface: crushed stone

Location: Huntingdon
Contact: Richard Stahl
Planning Director, Huntingdon County Planning Commission
Courthouse
Huntingdon, PA 16652
(814) 643–5091

80 Perkiomen Trail (Northern Section)

Endpoints: Perkiomenville (Green Lane Park), Green Lane (Route 29 and Hopperville Road)
Mileage: 5
Surface: asphalt

Location: Montgomery
Contact: Michael Marino
Chairman
Montgomery County
Commissioners
P.O. Box 311
Norristown, PA 19404
(610) 278–3000
www.montcopa.org/parks/
perkiomentrail/

81 Pigeon Run Falls Trail

Endpoints: Allegheny National
Forest
Mileage: 5.9
Surface: dirt

Location: Forest
Contact: Mary Hosmer
Forester
Allegheny National Forest
P.O. Box 847
Warren, PA 16365-0847
(814) 723–5150
mshosmer/r9-allegheny@fs.fed.us

82 Pine Creek Trail

Endpoints: Wellsboro, Ansonia
Mileage: 41
Surface: ballast

Location: Lycoming; Tioga
Contact: District Forester
Bureau of Forestry

Department of Conservation and
Natural Resources
One Nessmuk Lane
Route 287 South
Wellsboro, PA 16901
(570) 724–2868
regesterr@pader.gov

83 Pittsburgh Riverwalk at Station Square

Endpoints: Pittsburgh
Mileage: 1.5
Surface: asphalt

Location: Allegheny
Contact: Hannah Elrich
Office of the Mayor
414 City-County Building
Room 512
Pittsburgh, PA 15219
(412) 255–4768

84 Plainfield Township Recreation Trail

Endpoints: Wind Gap,
Stockertown
Mileage: 6.7
Surface: gravel

Location: Northampton
Contact: Jenny Koehler
Treasurer
Plainfield Township
6292 Sullivan Trail
Nazareth, PA 18064-9334
(610) 759–6944

85 PW&S Railroad Hiking-Biking Trail

Endpoints: Forbes State Forest, Lynn Run State Park
Mileage: 36
Surface: gravel, dirt

Location: Somerset; Westmoreland
Contact: Ed Calahan
Assistant District Forester
Forbes Forest District 4
Laughlintown, PA 15655
(724) 238–1200

86 Pymatuning State Park Trail

Endpoints: Pymatuning State Park
Mileage: 2.9
Surface: ballast

Location: Crawford
Contact: Dennis Mihoci
Park Manager
Pymatuning State Park
2660 Williamsfield Road
Jamestown, PA 16134-0425
(724) 932–3141
Pymatuning.sp@a1.dcnr.state.pa.us

87 Railroad Grade Trail

Endpoints: Ives Run Recreation Area
Mileage: 2.6
Surface: ballast

Location: Tioga
Contact: Terry Anderson
Trails Coordinator
U.S. Army Corps of Engineers
RD 1, Box 65
Tioga, PA 16946-9733
(570) 835–5281

88 Roaring Run Trail

Endpoints: Kiskiminetas
Mileage: 3.7
Surface: crushed stone

Location: Armstrong
Contact: Don Stevenson
President
Roaring Run Watershed Association
P.O. Box 333
Apollo, PA 15613
(724) 727–7360
don_stevenson@hotmail.com
www.roaring.run.org

89 Rocky Gap ATV/Bike Trail

Endpoints: Allegheny National Forest
Mileage: 15.5
Surface: grass, dirt

Other use: ATV

Location: Warren
Contact: Jeff Stevenson
District Ranger
Allegheny National Forest
Sheffield Ranger District
Route 6
Sheffield, PA 16347
(814) 968–3232

90 Samuel Justus Recreation Trail

Endpoints: Franklin (8th Street Bridge over Allegheny), Oil City (W. 1st Street near Clarion University)
Mileage: 5.3
Surface: asphalt

Location: Venango
Contact: Frank Pankratz
Cranberry Township
P.O. Box 378
Seneca, PA 16346-0378
(814) 676–8812
eagle.clarion.edu/~grads/avta

91 Schuylkill River Trail

Endpoints: Philadelphia, Valley Forge, and Oaks (Perkiomen Trail Connection)
Mileage: 14.5
Surface: asphalt

Location: Montgomery; Philadelphia
Contact: John Wood

Chief of Open Space Planning
Montgomery County Planning Commission
P.O. Box 311 Courthouse
Norristown, PA 19404-0311
(610) 278–3736
j.wood@montcopa.org
www.montcopa.org/parks

92 Sentiero Di Shay Trail

Endpoints: Tiadaghton State Forest
Mileage: 13
Surface: ballast, grass

Location: Lycoming
Contact: Tiadaghton Forest Fire Fighters Association
c/o Bureau of Forestry
423 East Central Avenue
South Williamsport, PA 17702
(570) 327–3450
www.dcnr.state.pa.us

93 Snowshoe Trail

Endpoints: Clarence (Snowshoe), Winburne
Mileage: 19
Surface: ballast

Location: Centre; Clearfield
Contact: Erin Freer
Program Specialist
Headwaters Charitable Trust
478 Jeffers
Du Bois, PA 15801
(814) 375–1372
Headwatr@PENN.com

94 South Link Trail (Susquehannock Trail System)

Endpoints: Susquehannock State Forest
Mileage: 6
Surface: dirt

Location: Potter
Contact: David Schiller
District Forester
Susquehannock State Forest
P.O. Box 673
Coudersport, PA 16915-0673
(814) 274–7459

95 Stony Valley Railroad Grade

Endpoints: Ellendale Forge, Lebanon Reservoir
Mileage: 22
Surface: cinder, dirt

Other use: Hunting
Location: Dauphin; Lebanon; Schuylkill
Contact: Roland Bergner
Chief
Federal-State Coordination Division
Pennsylvania Game Commission
2001 Elmerton Avenue
Harrisburg, PA 17110-9797
(717) 787–9612

96 Struble Trail

Endpoints: Downingtown
Mileage: 2.5
Surface: crushed stone

Location: Chester
Contact: Chester County Parks and Recreation Department
601 Westtown Road, Suite 160
P.O. Box 2747
West Chester, PA 19380-0990
(610) 344–6415
www.chesco.org/ccparks.html

97 Susquehannock Trail System

Endpoints: Susquehannock State Forest
Mileage: 89 (30 are rail-trail)
Surface: dirt

Location: Clinton; Potter
Contact: David Schiller
District Forester
Susquehannock State Forest
P.O. Box 673
Coudersport, PA 16915-0673
(814) 274–7459

98 Swatara Multi-Use Trail

Endpoints: Lickdale, Suedberg
Mileage: 9
Surface: dirt

Location: Lebanon; Schuylkill
Contact: Pennsylvania

Department of Conservation and
Natural Resources
Swatara State Park
c/o Memorial Lake State Park
R.R. 1, Box 7045
Grantville, PA 17028-9682
(717) 865–6470
memorial.sp@a1.dcnr.state.pa.us
www.dcnr.state.pa.us

99 Switchback Railroad Trail

Endpoints: Summit Hill, Jim
Thorpe
Mileage: 18
Surface: crushed stone, ballast

Location: Carbon
Contact: Mauch Chunk Lake Park
625 Lentz Trail Road
Jim Thorpe, PA 18229
(570) 325–3669
www.dcnr.state.pa.us

100 Three Rivers Heritage Trail

Endpoints: Pittsburgh
Mileage: 12
Surface: asphalt, crushed stone

Location: Allegheny
Contact: John Stephen
Friends of the Riverfront
P.O. Box 42434
Pittsburgh, PA 15203-0434
jsdi@andrew.comm.edu
www.atatrail.org

101 Thun Trail

Endpoints: Reading, Gibraltar
Mileage: 4
Surface: ballast

Location: Berks
Contact: Dixie Swenson
Executive Director
Schuylkill River Greenway
Association
140 College Drive
Pottstown, PA 19464
(610) 372–3916
info@schuylkillriver.org
www.schuylkillriver.org

102 Tidioute Riverside RecTrek Trail

Endpoints: Allegheny National
Forest
Mileage: 4.5
Surface: ballast

Location: Warren
Contact: Mary Hosmer
Forester
Allegheny National Forest
P.O. Box 847
Warren, PA 16365-0847
(814) 723–5150
mshosmer/r9-allegheny@fs.fed.us

103 Tom Run Loop Trail

Endpoints: Allegheny National Forest
Mileage: 3.6
Surface: dirt

Location: Warren
Contact: Mary Hosmer
Forester
Allegheny National Forest
P.O. Box 847
Warren, PA 16365-0847
(814) 723–5150
mhosmer/r9-allegheny@fs.fed.us

104 Towpath Bike Trail (National Trails Towpath Bike Trail)

Endpoints: Bethlehem, Palmer Township (Easton)
Mileage: 7.8
Surface: asphalt

Location: Northampton
Contact: Ted Sales
Chairman
Palmer Township Board of
Supervisors
3 Weller Place, P.O. Box 3039
Palmer, PA 18043-3039
(610) 253–7191
www.dcnr.state.pa.us/rails/
towpathbt.html

105 Twin Lakes Trail

Endpoints: Allegheny National Forest
Mileage: 14.7
Surface: grass, dirt

Location: Elk; Warren
Contact: Leon Blashock
District Ranger
Allegheny National Forest
Ridgway Ranger District
RD 1, Box 28A
Ridgway, PA 15853
(814) 776–6172

106 Warren–North Warren Bike Trail

Endpoints: Warren, North Warren
Mileage: 2
Surface: asphalt

Location: Warren
Contact: Dan Glotz
Warren County Planning
Commission
207 West Fifth Avenue
Warren, PA 16365
(814) 726–3861

107 West Penn Trail (Conemaugh River Lake Section)

Endpoints: Bow Ridge Tunnel, Westinghouse Plant near Blairsville
Mileage: 3.3
Surface: crushed stone

Location: Indiana, Westmoreland
Contact: Conemaugh Valley Conservancy
1334 Franklin Street
Johnstown, PA 15905
jqka@twd.net
www.conemaughvalleyconservancy.org/westpenntrail

108 West Penn Trail (Saltsburg Section)

Endpoints: Saltsburg (water plant), Elders Run
Mileage: 4.5
Surface: crushed stone

Location: Westmoreland
Contact: Conemaugh Valley Conservancy
1334 Franklin Street
Johnstown, PA 15905
jqka@twd.net
www.conemaughvalleyconservancy.org/westpenntrail

109 York County Heritage Rail-Trail

Endpoints: New Freedom, York
Mileage: 21
Surface: crushed stone

Location: York
Contact: Gwen Loose
York County Trail Authority
P.O. Box 335
Seven Valleys, PA 17360
(717) 892–7934
www.yorkcountytrails.org

110 Youghiogheny River Trail—North

Endpoints: Connellsville, McKeesport
Mileage: 43
Surface: crushed stone, ballast

Location: Allegheny; Fayette; Westmoreland
Contact: Robert McKinley
Trail Manager
Regional Trail Council
101 N. Water Street
P.O. Box 95
West Newton, PA 15089-1535
yrt@nb.net
www.youghrivertrail.com

111 Youghiogheny River Trail—South

Endpoints: Confluence, Connellsville
Mileage: 28
Surface: crushed stone

Location: Fayette
Contact: Robert McKinley
Trail Manager
Regional Trail Corporation
101 N. Water Street
P.O. Box 95
West Newton, PA 15089-1535
(724) 872–5586
yrt@westol.com
www.youghrivertrail.org

RHODE ISLAND

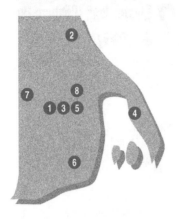

Location: Providence
Contact: Lisa Lawless
Rhode Island Department of
Environmental Management
83 Park Street
Providence, RI 02903-1037
(401) 222–6800

3 Coventry Greenway

Endpoints: Coventry, West
Warwick Border
Mileage: 2.5
Surface: asphalt, ballast

Location: Kent
Contact: Guy Lefebvre
Director of Parks and Recreation
Parks and Recreation Department
1670 Flat River Road
Coventry, RI 02816
(401) 822–9107
www.new-england-rail-trails.org

1 Arkwright Riverwalk

Endpoints: Coventry
Mileage: 1.5
Surface: wood chips, dirt

Location: Kent
Contact: Jeffrey Kos
Chairperson
Pawtuxet River Authority
P.O. Box 336
West Warwick, RI 02893-0336
(401) 828–5650

2 Blackstone River Bikeway

Endpoints: Lonsdale, Quinnville
Mileage: 5.5
Surface: asphalt

4 East Bay Bicycle Path

Endpoints: Bristol, Providence
Mileage: 14.5
Surface: asphalt

Location: Bristol
Contact: Kevin O'Malley
Regional Manager
Colt State Park
Bristol, RI 02809
(401) 253–7482
www.riparks.com

5 Phenix-Harris Riverwalk

Endpoints: West Warwick
Mileage: 1
Surface: dirt

Location: Kent
Contact: Jeffrey Kos
Chairperson
Pawtuxet River Authority
P.O. Box 336
West Warwick, RI 02893
(401) 828–5650

6 South County Bike Path

Endpoints: Kingston Station to
Rodman Street (South Kingston)
Mileage: 4.3
Surface: asphalt

Location: Washington
Contact: Steve Devine
Supervising Planner
Rhode Island Department of
Transportation

Two Capitol Hill
Providence, RI 02903
(401) 222–2023, ext. 4063

7 Trestle Trail (Charter Oak Greenway)

Endpoints: Coventry Center,
Connecticut state line
Mileage: 10
Surface: gravel, ballast, dirt

Location: Kent
Contact: Bob Sutton
Chief of Planning and
Development
Rhode Island Department of
Environmental Management
235 Promenade Street
Providence, RI 02908
(401) 222–2776
www.new-england-rail-trails.org

8 Washington Secondary

Endpoints: Cranston
Mileage: 4.5
Surface: asphalt

Location: Providence
Contact: Steve Devine
Supervising Planner
Rhode Island Department of
Transportation
Two Capitol Hill
Providence, RI, 02903
(401) 222–2023, ext. 4063

SOUTH CAROLINA

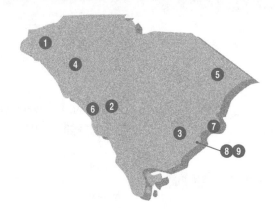

1 Blue Ridge Railroad Historical Trail

Endpoints: Stumphouse Tunnel, Walhalla
Mileage: 5
Surface: wood chips, dirt

Location: Oconee
Contact: Hurley Badders
Executive Director
Pendleton Historic and
Recreational Commission
P.O. Box 565
Pendleton, SC 29670-0565
(803) 646–3782

2 Cathedral Aisle Trail

Endpoints: Aiken
Mileage: 1
Surface: dirt

Location: Aiken
Contact: Gary Burger
Forest Manager
Hitchcock Foundation
P.O. Box 1702
Aiken, SC 29802-1702
(803) 648–8085

3 Edisto Nature Trail

Endpoints: Colleton
Mileage: 1.5
Surface: grass, dirt

Location: Jacksonboro
Contact: Westuaco Corporation
Public Affairs
P.O. 1950
Summerville, SC 29484
(843) 871–5000

4 Greenwood Mill Village and Railroad Heritage Trail

Endpoints: South Main Street, Florida Avenue (Greenwood)

Mileage: 2.5
Surface: asphalt

Location: Greenwood
Contact: Joel Cleland
President
Greater Greenwood Parks and
Trails Foundation
123 West Laurel Avenue
Greenwood, SC 29649
(864) 388-8261
jcleland@lander.edu

5 Marion Hike and Bike Trail

Endpoints: Marion
Mileage: 0.25
Surface: asphalt, dirt

Location: Marion
Contact: Ronny Pridgen
Recreation Director
City of Marion Parks and
Recreation Department
P.O. Box 1190
Marion, SC 29571-1190
(843) 423-5410

6 North Augusta Greeneway

Endpoints: North Augusta
Mileage: 5.2
Surface: asphalt, gravel

Location: Aiken

Contact: Robert Brooks
Director
North Augusta Parks and
Recreation
P.O. Box 6400
North Augusta, SC 29841-0400
(803) 441-4300
bbrooks@mail.n-augusta.sc.us
www.northaugusta.net

7 Swamp Fox National Recreation Trail

Endpoints: Francis Marion
National Forest, Awendaw-
Withenbee
Mileage: 27
Surface: dirt

Location: Berkeley; Charleston
Contact: Cheron Rhodes
Recreation Forester
Francis Marion National Forest
P.O. Box 788
McClellanville, SC 29458-0788
(803) 887-3257

8 West Ashley Bikeway

Endpoints: Charleston
Mileage: 2
Surface: asphalt

Location: Charleston
Contact: Amanda Barton
Charleston Department of Parks
823 Meeting Street
Charleston, SC 29403-3108
(843) 724-7321

9 West Ashley Greenway

Endpoints: Charleston
Mileage: 8.5
Surface: crushed stone, grass, dirt

Location: Charleston
Contact: Dave Eason
Recreation Services
Superintendent
City of Charleston Recreation
Department
823 Meeting Street
Charleston, SC 29403
(843) 724-7327
easond@ci.charleston.sc.us

SOUTH DAKOTA

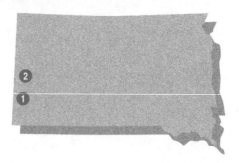

1 George S. Mickelson Trail

Endpoints: Deadwood, Edgemont
Mileage: 114
Surface: crushed stone, gravel

Location: Custer; Fall River; Lawrence; Pennington
Contact: Scott Carbonneau
Trails Program Specialist
South Dakota Department of Game, Fish, and Parks
Division of Parks and Recreation
523 East Capitol Avenue
Pierre, SD 57501-3182
(605) 773–6671
scott.carbonneau@state.sd.us

2 Spearfish Recreational Trail

Endpoints: Spearfish
Mileage: 2.8
Surface: concrete

Location: Lawrence
Contact: Keith Hepper
City of Spearfish
625 Fifth Street
Spearfish, SD 57783-2311
(605) 642–1333
keithh@spearfish.sd.us

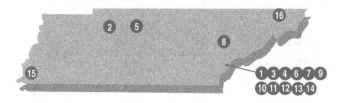

1 Bald River Trail

Endpoints: Bald River Falls, Bald River Road (Cherokee National Forest)
Mileage: 5.6
Surface: dirt

Location: Monroe
Contact: Larry Fleming
District Ranger
Cherokee National Forest
Tellico Ranger District
250 Ranger Station Road
Tellico Plains, TN 37385-5804
(423) 253–2520
www.chattanooga.net/hiking/
citicolor.htm

2 Betsy Ligon Park & Walking Trail

Endpoints: Erin (Front Street)
Mileage: 2
Surface: asphalt, dirt

Location: Houston
Contact: Linda Bratchi
Recorder
Erin City Hall

P.O. Box 270
Erin, TN 37061-0270
(931) 289–4108

3 Conasauga River Trail

Endpoints: Cherokee National Forest
Mileage: 11.75
Surface: dirt

Location: Monroe
Contact: Larry Fleming
District Ranger
Cherokee National Forest
Tellico Ranger District
250 Ranger Station Road
Tellico Plains, TN 37385-5804
(423) 253–2520

4 Crowder Branch Trail

Endpoints: Cherokee National Forest
Mileage: 2.6
Surface: dirt

Location: Monroe
Contact: Larry Fleming
District Ranger

Cherokee National Forest
Tellico Ranger District
250 Ranger Station Road
Tellico Plains, TN 37385-5804
(423) 253–2520

5 Cumberland River Bicentennial Trail

Endpoints: Ashland City, Sycamore Recreation Area
Mileage: 6.5
Surface: asphalt, gravel, ballast

Location: Cheatham
Contact: Kathleen Williams
Director
Tennessee Parks and Greenways
Foundation
2704 12th Avenue S.
Nashville, TN 37204-2506
(615) 386–3171
www.cheathamchamber.org/trail

6 Grassy Branch Trail

Endpoints: Cherokee National Forest
Mileage: 3.2
Surface: dirt

Location: Monroe
Contact: Larry Fleming
District Ranger
Cherokee National Forest
Tellico Ranger District
250 Ranger Station Road
Tellico Plains, TN 37385-5804
(423) 253–2520

7 Hemlock Trail

Endpoints: Cherokee National Forest
Mileage: 3
Surface: dirt

Contact: Larry Fleming
District Ranger
Cherokee National Forest
Tellico Ranger District
250 Ranger Station Road
Tellico Plains, TN 37385-5804
(423) 253–2520

8 Holston River Greenway (Holston River Park)

Endpoints: Knoxville (Holston Hills Road)
Mileage: 1.1
Surface: asphalt

Location: Knox
Contact: Sam Anderson
Director
Parks and Recreation Department
Knoxville, TN 37901
(615) 215–2090
www.ci.knoxville.tn.us/kat/web%
20pages/Schedule/GreenwayInfo.
asp

9 Laurel Branch Trail

Endpoints: Cherokee National Forest
Mileage: 3
Surface: dirt

Location: Monroe
Contact: Larry Fleming
District Ranger
Cherokee National Forest
Tellico Ranger District
250 Ranger Station Road
Tellico Plains, TN 37385-5804
(423) 253–2520

10 Long Branch Trail

Endpoints: Cherokee National
Forest
Mileage: 2.7
Surface: dirt

Location: Monroe
Contact: Larry Fleming
District Ranger
Cherokee National Forest
Tellico Ranger District
250 Ranger Station Road
Tellico Plains, TN 37385-5804
(423) 253–2520

11 McNabb Creek Trail

Endpoints: Cherokee National
Forest
Mileage: 3.9
Surface: ballast

Location: Monroe
Contact: Larry Fleming
District Ranger
Cherokee National Forest
Tellico Ranger District
250 Ranger Station Road
Tellico Plains, TN 37385-5804
(423) 253–2520

12 North Fork Citico Trail

Endpoints: Cherokee National
Forest
Mileage: 5
Surface: ballast

Location: Monroe
Contact: Larry Fleming
District Ranger
Cherokee National Forest
Tellico Ranger District
250 Ranger Station Road
Tellico Plains, TN 37385-5804
(423) 253–2520

13 South Fork Citico Trail

Endpoints: Cherokee National
Forest
Mileage: 8.1
Surface: dirt

Location: Monroe
Contact: Larry Fleming
District Ranger
Cherokee National Forest
Tellico Ranger District
250 Ranger Station Road
Tellico Plains, TN 37385-5804
(423) 253-2520

14 Tellico Plains Rail-Trail

Endpoints: Tellico Plains
Mileage: 0.8
Surface: asphalt

Location: Monroe
Contact: Sam Stamey
Mayor
City Hall
201 Southard Street
Tellico Plains, TN 37385-5125
(423) 253–2333
wn.cityhall.com

15 V&E Greenline

Endpoints: Memphis (Vollintine-Evergreen neighborhood)
Mileage: 1.7
Surface: grass, dirt, ballast

Location: Shelby
Contact: Michael Kirby
Treasurer
Vollintine–Evergreen Community Park
1680 Jackson Avenue
Memphis, TN 38107
mkirby@ionictech.com
www.vegreenline.org

16 Wes Davis Greenway

Endpoints: Anderson Street, Melrose Street (Bristol)
Mileage: 0.8
Surface: asphalt

Location: Sullivan
Contact: Kevin Hamed
Director
Bristol Department of Leisure Services
(423) 764–4023

TEXAS

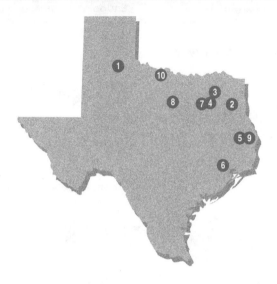

1 Caprock Canyons State Park Trailway

Endpoints: Estelline, South Plains
Mileage: 64.2
Surface: ballast

Location: Briscoe; Floyd; Hall
Contact: Geoffrey Hulse
Park Manager
Caprock Canyons State Park and
Canyonlands Trailway Complex
Texas Parks and Wildlife
Department
P.O. Box 204
Quitaque, TX 79255-0204
(806) 455–1332

2 Cargill Long Park Trail

Endpoints: Longview
Mileage: 2.5
Surface: asphalt

Location: Gregg
Contact: Terry Owens
Manager
Longview Parks and Recreation
P.O. Box 1952
Longview, TX 75606-1952
(903) 237–1391
tgowens@internetwork.net

3 Chaparral Trail

Endpoints: Farmersville, Ladonia
Mileage: 29
Surface: crushed stone

Location: Collin; Fannin; Hunt
Contact: Joe Barton
Constable
P.O. Box 367
Farmersville, TX 75442-0367
(972) 424–1460
JoeBarton@worldnet.att.net

4 Denton Branch Rail-Trail (Trinity Trail System)

Endpoints: Downtown Denton
(Hickory and Railroad Streets),
Corinth (Burt Street)
Mileage: 8
Surface: crushed stone

Location: Denton
Contact: www.cityofdenton.com/
pages/parksrailtrail.cfm

5 Four-C Hiking Trail

Endpoints: Davy Crockett
National Forest
Mileage: 20
Surface: ballast, dirt

Location: Houston
Contact: Duane Strock
Landscape Architect
Davy Crockett National Forest
701 North First Street
Lufkin, TX 75901-3057
(409) 639–8529

6 Harrisburg and Sunset Rail-Trails

Endpoints: Drennan to Marsden,
Avenue H to Hidalgo Park
(Houston)
Mileage: 5.29
Surface: asphalt

Location: Harris
Contact: Lilibeth Andre
Bicycle-Pedestrian Coordinator
Houston Bikeway Program
lilibeth.andre@cityofhouston.net
www.houstonbikeways.org

7 Katy Trail

Endpoints: Dallas
Mileage: 2.3
Surface: concrete

Location: Dallas
Contact: Darryl Baker
Dallas Parks and Recreation
New City Hall
Room 6F South
Dallas, TX 75201
(214) 670–4282

8 Lake Mineral Wells State Trailway

Endpoints: Mineral Wells,
Weatherford
Mileage: 20
Surface: asphalt, crushed stone

Location: Palo Pinto; Parker
Contact: Lee Ellis
Assistant Superintendant
Texas Parks and Wildlife
R.R. 4, Box 39C
Mineral Wells, TX 76967
(940) 328–1171

9 Sawmill Hiking Trail

Endpoints: Angelina National
Forest
Mileage: 5.5
Surface: dirt

Location: Jasper
Contact: Catherine Albers
Resource Forester
Angelina National Forest
Angelina Ranger District
Lufkin, TX 75904
(409) 639–8620

10 Wichita River Trail

Endpoints: Lucy Park, Texas
240/Eastside Drive (Wichita Falls)
Mileage: 4
Surface: concrete

Location: Wichita
Contact: Wichita Falls Parks and
Recreation Department
Memorial Auditorium
1300 7th Street, Room 107
Wichita Falls, TX 76031
(940) 761–7490
www.cwftx.net/PARKS%20&%
20RECREATION.htm

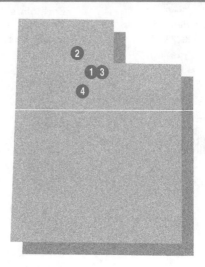

1 Historic Union Pacific Rail Trail

Endpoints: Echo Reservoir, Park City
Mileage: 28
Surface: asphalt, crushed stone

Location: Summit; Wasatch
Contact: Troy Duffin
Mountain Trails Foundation
P.O. Box 754
Park City, UT 84060
(435) 649–6839

2 Little Mountain Rail Trail

Endpoints: Plain City, Little Mountain Junction
Mileage: 10
Surface: gravel

Location: Box Elder; Weber
Contact: Stan Hadden
Trails Coordinator
Weber County Trails
2510 Washington Boulevard, 1M
Ogden, UT 84401-3113
(801) 399–8682
rivkpr1@uswest.com
www.weberpathways.org

3 Olympic Parkway

Endpoints: Park City
Mileage: 1
Surface: asphalt
Location: Summit
Contact: Jennifer Harrington
Senior Landscape Architect
Park City Municipal Corporation
P.O. Box 1480
445 Marsac Avenue
Park City, UT 84060-1480
(801) 645–5016

4 Provo Jordan River Parkway Trail

Endpoints: Provo, Provo Canyon
Mileage: 43
Surface: asphalt

Location: Utah
Contact: Clyde Naylor
Engineer
Utah County
2855 South State
Provo, UT 84606-6502
(801) 370–8600

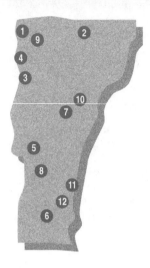

2 Beebe Spur Rail-Trail

Endpoints: Newport (Prouty Drive), Derby (Beebe Plain Road/Canadian Border)
Mileage: 4
Surface: gravel

Location: Orleans
Contact: Bonnie Waninger
Special Projects Planner
Northwest Regional Planning Commission
140 South Main Street
St. Albans, VT 05478-1850
(802) 524–5958
nrpcvt@together.net

1 Alburg Recreational Rail-Trail

Endpoints: Alburg Village (Alburg Industrial Park at Route 2 and Industrial Park Road), East Alburg (at Route 78)
Mileage: 3.5
Surface: ballast, cinder

Location: Grand Isle
Contact: Charles Vile
Forestry District Manager North
Vermont Department of Forests, Parks & Recreation
111 West Street
Essex Junction, VT 05452-4615
(802) 879–6565
cvile@anressex.anr.state.vt.us

3 Burlington Waterfront Bikeway

Endpoints: Burlington (Oakledge Park at Flynn Avenue), Winooski River
Mileage: 7.6
Surface: asphalt

Location: Chittenden
Contact: Robert Whalen
Superintendent
Burlington Department of Parks and Recreation
1 LaValley Lane
Burlington, VT 05401-2779
(802) 865–7247
www.new-england-rail-trails.org

4 Causeway Park Rail-Trail

Endpoints: Colchester (Airport Road), tip of causeway south of South Hero
Mileage: 3.2
Surface: gravel

Location: Chittenden
Contact: Colchester Parks and Recreation Department
P.O. Box 55
Colchester, VT 05446
(802) 655–0811

5 Delaware and Hudson Rail-Trail

Endpoints: West Rupert, Castleton
Mileage: 19.2 (two sections)
Surface: ballast

Location: Bennington; Rutland
Contact: Gary Salmon
Trails Coordinator
Department of Forests, Parks and Recreation
317 Sanitorium Road, West Wing
Pittsford, VT 05763-9802
(802) 483–2733
gsalmon@anrpitts.anr.state.vt.us

6 East Branch Trail

Endpoints: Searsburg (Route 71/Somerset Road), Somerset (Somerset Road and Somerset Reservoir)

Mileage: 8
Surface: gravel

Location: Windham, Bennington
Contact: John Ragonese
Recreation Planner
New England Power Company
33 West Lebanon Road
P.O. Box 528
Lebanon, NH 03784-1917
(603) 448–2200

7 Graniteville Trails

Endpoints: Websterville, Graniteville
Mileage: 1.4
Surface: asphalt, ballast

Location: Washington
Contact: Cail Rogers
Town Manager
Town of Berrytown
Municipal Building
Websterville, VT 05678
(802) 479–9331

8 Lye Brook Trail

Endpoints: Manchester (Lye Brook Road at Route 7), Stratton (Winhall River)
Mileage: 4.6
Surface: gravel

Location: Bennington; Windham
Contact: Robert Pramuk

Recreation Forester
Green Mountain National Forest
231 North Main Street
Rutland, VT 05701-2412
(802) 747–6700

9 Missisquoi Valley Rail-Trail

Endpoints: St. Albans (Routes 7 and 105), Richford (Route 105)
Mileage: 26.4
Surface: crushed stone, asphalt

Other use: Dog sled
Location: Franklin
Contact: Bonnie Waninger
Special Projects Planner
Northwest Regional Planning
Commission
140 S. Main Street
St. Albans, VT 05478-1850
(802) 524–5958
nrpcvt@together.net

10 Montpelier and Wells River Trail

Endpoints: Groton (Ricker Pond State Park, Route 232), Marshfield (Route 2)
Mileage: 14.5
Surface: gravel, ballast, dirt, sand

Location: Caledonia; Washington
Contact: David Willard
Trails Coordinator
Vermont Agency of Natural
Resources
Department of Forests, Parks and
Recreation

184 Portland Street
St. Johnsbury, VT 05819-2099
(802) 751–0110

11 Toonerville Trail

Endpoints: Springfield (Route 11/Clinton Street), Connecticut River Bridge (Route 11 and Route 5)
Mileage: 3
Surface: asphalt

Location: Windsor
Contact: Bettina McCrady
Springfield Trails and Greenways
Committee
108 Summer Street
Springfield, VT 05156-3539

12 West River Trail (Railroad Bed Trail)

Endpoints: South Londonderry, Townshend
Mileage: 14 (two sections)
Surface: gravel, ballast

Location: Windham
Contact: Rick White
Trails Coordinator
Vermont Agency of Natural
Resources
Department of Forests, Parks
and Recreation
100 Mineral Street, Suite 304
Springfield, VT 05156
(802) 885–8824
rick.white@anr.state.vt.us

VIRGINIA

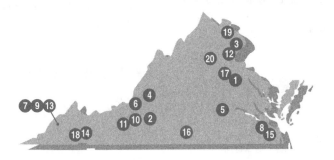

1 Ashland Trolley Line

Endpoints: Gwathmey Church Road and Trolley Line
Mileage: 1
Surface: gravel

Location: Hanover
Contact: Hanover County Parks and Recreation Department
(804) 365–4695
www.co.hanover.va.us/parksrec/default.htm#discover

2 Blackwater Creek Natural Area Bikeway

Endpoints: Lynchburg
Mileage: 18
Surface: asphalt, gravel

Location: Lynchburg
Contact: Andy Reeder
Parks Manager

City of Lynchburg Parks and Recreation Division
301 Grove Street
Lynchburg, VA 24501
(804) 847–1640
reedeah@ci.lynchburg.va.us

3 Bluemont Junction Trail

Endpoints: Bluemont Park, Ballston
Mileage: 1.3
Surface: asphalt

Location: Arlington
Contact: Ritch Viola
Arlington County Department of Public Works
2100 Clarendon Boulevard
Suite 717
Arlington, VA 22201-5445
(703) 358–3699
www.co.arlington.va.us/dpw/planning/bike

4 Chessie Nature Trail

Endpoints: Lexington, Buena Vista
Mileage: 7.5
Surface: crushed stone, gravel, grass, dirt, cinder, sand

Location: Rockbridge
Contact: Louise Dooley
Assistant Vice President
VMI Foundation
P.O. Box 932
Lexington, VA 24450-0932
(540) 464-7221

5 Chester Linear Park

Endpoints: Chester
Mileage: 1
Surface: crushed stone

Location: Chesterfield
Contact: Mike Golden
Director
Chesterfield Parks and Recreation
Box 40
Chesterfield, VA 23832
(804) 748-1623

6 Craig Valley Scenic Trail

Endpoints: Eagle Rock, Horton
Mileage: 15 (in two sections)
Surface: dirt, crushed stone

Location: Botetourt; Craig

Contact: Jerry Jacobsen
Recreation Forester
U.S. Forest Service
P.O. Box 246
New Castle, VA 24127-0246
(540) 864-5195
jljacobsen@fs.fed.us

7 Devils Fork Loop Trail

Endpoints: Dungannon, George Washington National Forest
Mileage: 5.1
Surface: dirt

Location: Scott
Contact: John Stallard
Recreation Forester
USDA Forest Service/Clinch Ranger District
9416 Darden Drive
Wise, VA 24293
(540) 328-2931
www.fsfed.us\gwjnf

8 Elizabeth River Trail (Atlantic City Spur)

Endpoints: Redgate Avenue, near Fort Norfolk (Norfolk)
Mileage: 1
Surface: crushed stone

Location: Norfolk City
Contact: Jennifer White
City of Norfolk Department of Planning
508 City Hall Building
Norfolk, VA 23510
(757) 664-4769
jswhite@city.norfolk.va.us

www.baygateways.net/visiting/
gateways.cfm?id=16

9 Guest River Gorge Trail

Endpoints: Coeburn, Jefferson
National Forest
Mileage: 5.5
Surface: crushed stone

Location: Scott; Wise
Contact: Jim McIntyre
Clinch Ranger District
Jefferson National Forest
9416 Darden Drive
Wise, VA 24293-5900
(540) 328–2931

10 Hanging Rock Battlefield Trail

Endpoints: Hanging Rock, Salem
(Kessler Mill Road)
Mileage: 1.7
Surface: cinder

Location: Roanoke
Contact: David Robbins
Hanging Rock Battlefield and
Railway Preservation
620 High Street
Salem, VA 24153-2830
www.greenways.org/hangrock.
html

11 Huckleberry Trail

Endpoints: Blacksburg,
Christiansburg
Mileage: 6
Surface: asphalt

Location: Montgomery
Contact: Joe Powers
Planning Director
Montgomery County Planning
Department
County Courthouse
P.O. Box 6126
Christiansburg, VA 24068
(540) 382–5750
www.mfrl.org/compages/
huckleberry

12 Lake Accotink Trail

Endpoints: Springfield (Lake
Accotink Park)
Mileage: 6
Surface: crushed stone, gravel

Location: Fairfax
Contact: Tawny Hammond
Park Manager
Fairfax County Park Authority
Lake Accotink Park
7500 Accotink Park Road
Springfield, VA 22150
(703) 569–3464

13 Little Stony National Recreation Trail

Endpoints: Dungannon, George Washington National Forest
Mileage: 2.8
Surface: dirt

Location: Scott
Contact: Jim McIntyre
Clinch Ranger District
Jefferson National Forest
9416 Darden Drive
Wise, VA 24293-5900
(540) 328–2931

14 New River Trail State Park

Endpoints: Pulaski to Galax, spur to Fries
Mileage: 57
Surface: gravel, dirt, cinder

Location: Carroll; Grayson; Pulaski; Wythe
Contact: Eric Houghland
Chief Ranger
Virginia Department of Conservation and Recreation
Division of State Parks
Route 2, Box 126F
Foster Falls, VA 24360
(540) 699–6778
www.chr.vt.edu/Colors/nrt/NRTS.
html.nrt.org

15 Park Connector Bikeway

Endpoints: Mt. Trashmore, Princess Anne Park
Mileage: 4.9
Surface: asphalt

Location: Virginia Beach
Contact: Travis Campbell
Planner
Department of Planning
Room 115, Operations Building
2405 Courthouse Road
Virginia Beach, VA 23456-9121
(757) 427–8593
tcampbel@city-virginia-beach.va.us

16 Patrick Henry Trail

Endpoints: Staunton River Battlefield
Mileage: 0.8
Surface: crushed stone

Location: Halifax
Contact: Jim Zanarihi
Chief Ranger
Staunton River Bridge Battlefield State Park
1035 Fort Hill Trail
Randolph, VA 23962
(804) 454–4312

17 Virginia Central Railway Trail

Endpoints: Salem Church Road, Gordon Road
Mileage: 1.2
Surface: asphalt

Location: Spotsylvania
Contact: Joe Lerch
Trails Coordinator
Spotsylvania Company
P.O. Box 876
Spotsylvania, VA 22553
(540) 582–7040, ext. 655
jlerch@spotsylvania.va.us

18 Virginia Creeper National Recreation Trail

Endpoints: Abingdon, White Top
Mileage: 34.1
Surface: gravel, dirt

Location: Grayson; Washington
Contact: Ginny Williams
Recreation Program Manager
Mount Rogers National
Recreation Area
George Washington and
Jefferson National Forests
3714 Highway 16
Marion, VA 24354
ginndoug@smyth.net
www.vacreepertrail.org

19 W&OD Railroad Regional Park

Endpoints: Arlington, Purcellville
Mileage: 45
Surface: asphalt, crushed stone

Location: Arlington; Fairfax;
Loudoun

Contact: Paul McCray
Park Manager
Northern Virginia Regional Park
Authority
21293 Smiths Switch Road
Ashburn, VA 20147
(703) 729–0596
wodtrail@erols.com
www.wodfriends.org

20 Warrenton Branch Greenway

Endpoints: Warrenton (Fourth
Street), Calverton
Mileage: 1.5
Surface: asphalt

Location: Fauquier
Contact: Larry Miller
Director
Fauquier County Parks and
Recreation
62 Culpeper Street
Warrenton, VA 20186-3289
(540) 347–6896
parks@crosslink.net
http://cofauguier.va.us/services/
parks/greenway

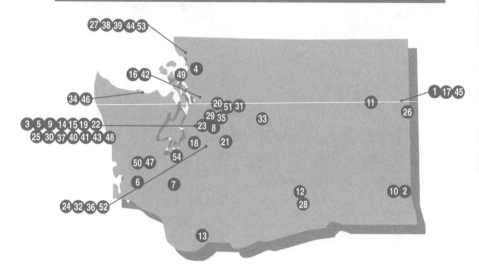

WASHINGTON

1 Benn Burr Trail

Endpoints: Spokane
Mileage: 1.1
Surface: crushed stone, gravel, dirt

Location: Spokane
Contact: Taylor Bressler
Division Manager
City of Spokane Parks
Department
N. 809 Washington Street
Spokane, WA 99201-2233
(509) 625–6655

2 Bill Chipman Palouse Trail

Endpoints: Pullman, WA,
Moscow, ID
Mileage: 7.5

Surface: asphalt

Location: Whitman; Latah
Contact: Roger Marens
Whitman County Parks
310 North Main Street
Colfax, WA 99111
(509) 397–6238
ranger@co.whitman.wa.us

3 Burke-Gilman Trail

Endpoints: Seattle, Bothell
Mileage: 18
Surface: asphalt

Location: King
Contact: Peter Lagerwey
Bicycle/Pedestrian Coordinator
Seattle Engineering Department
708 Municipal Building
600 Fourth Avenue
Seattle, WA 98104-1879
(206) 684–5108
pete.lagerwey@ci.seattle.wa.us
www.ci.seattle.wa.us/seattle/td/
bikeprog/bg-trail.html

4 Cascade Trail

Endpoints: Sedro-Woolley,
Concrete (Senior Center on
Highway 20)
Mileage: 22.3
Surface: crushed stone

Location: Skagit
Contact: Peter Mayer
Operations Manager
Skagit County Parks, Recreation
and Fair Department
315 South Third Street
Mount Vernon, WA 98273-3822
(360) 336–9414
peterm@co.skagit.wa.us
www.skagitparksfoundation.com/
cascadetrail.htm

5 Cedar River Trail

Endpoints: Lansburg Park,
Renton
Mileage: 19.5
Surface: asphalt, gravel, ballast

Location: King

Contact: King County
Parks and Recreation Division
201 S. Jackson Street, Suite 700
Seattle, WA 98104
(206) 296–8687
www.metrokc.gov/parks

6 Chehalis to Raymond (Raymond to Southbend Riverfront Trail)

Endpoints: Raymond, Southbend
Mileage: 3.5
Surface: asphalt

Location: Lewis; Pacific
Contact: Rebecca Chafee
City Engineer
City of Raymond
230 Second Street
Raymond, WA 98577-2420
(360) 942–3451

7 Chehalis Western Trail (Woodard Bay Trail)

Endpoints: Woodard Bay
Natural Resource Conservation
Area, Martin Way (Lacey), Vail
Mileage: 13
Surface: asphalt

Location: Thurston
Contact: Michael Welter
Thurston County Parks and
Recreation
2617-A Court, S.W.
Olympia, WA 98502
(360) 786–5595
welterm@co.thurston.wa.us
www.thurston-parks.org

8 City of Snoqualmie Centennial Trail

Endpoints: Snoqualmie
Mileage: 0.5
Surface: asphalt

Location: King
Contact: Jeff Mumma
Superintendent of Parks
City of Snoqualmie
P.O. Box 987
Snoqualmie, WA 98065-0987
(206) 888–5337
jeff@ci.snoqualmie.wa.us
www.ci.snoqualmie.wa.us

9 Coal Creek Park Trail

Endpoints: Coal Creek Park
Mileage: 3
Surface: ballast, grass, dirt

Location: King
Contact: King County
Parks and Recreation Division
201 S. Jackson Street, Suite 700
Seattle, WA 98104
www.metrokc.gov/parks

10 Colfax Trail

Endpoints: Colfax
Mileage: 3
Surface: dirt

Location: Whitman
Contact: Tim Myers

Superintendent of Parks
Whitman County Parks and
Recreation
310 N. Main
Colfax, WA 99111-1850
(509) 397–6238

11 Columbia Plateau Trail State Park

Endpoints: Fish Lake, Martin
Road
Mileage: 23
Surface: asphalt, crushed stone

Location: Lincoln; Spokane
Contact: Bill Byrne
Area Manager
Washington State Parks
10152 State Route 127
Pomeroy, WA 99347
(509) 549–3551
www.parks.wa.gov/develop.asp

12 Cowiche Canyon Trail

Endpoints: Yakima
Mileage: 2.9
Surface: gravel, dirt

Location: Yakima
Contact: Ray Paolella
President
Cowiche Canyon Conservancy
P.O. Box 877
Yakima, WA 98907-0877
(509) 577–9585

13 Dry Creek Trail

Endpoints: Gifford Pinchot National Forest
Mileage: 4
Surface: dirt

Location: Skamania
Contact: Jim Slagle
Trails Coordinator
Gifford Pinchot National Forest
6926 E. Fourth Plain Boulevard
P.O. Box 8944
Vancouver, WA 98661-7254
(360) 750–5011

14 Duwamish Bikeway

Endpoints: Seattle
Mileage: 4.5
Surface: asphalt

Location: King
Contact: Peter Lagerwey
Bicycle/Pedestrian Coordinator
Seattle Engineering Department
708 Municipal Building
600 Fourth Avenue
Seattle, WA 98104-1879
(206) 684–5108
pete.lagerwey@ci.seattle.wa.us

15 Elliot Bay Trail

Endpoints: Broad Street and
W. Marina Place
Mileage: 3.3
Surface: asphalt

Location: King
Contact: City of Seattle
Transportation, Bicycle and
Pedestrian Program
700 Fifth Street
Suite 3900
Seattle, WA 98104–5043
(206) 684–7583

16 Everett-Shoreline Interurban

Endpoints: Everett, Mt. Lake
Terrace
Mileage: 8.5
Surface: asphalt, gravel

Location: Snohomish
Contact: Marc Krandel
Trail Manager
Snohomish County Parks and
Recreation Department
3000 Rockefeller Avenue, MS 303
Everett, WA 98201-4060
(206) 339–1208
planning@premier1.net

17 Fish Lake Trail

Endpoints: Fish Lake, Cheney
Mileage: 7
Surface: asphalt

Location: Spokane
Contact: Robert Hudson
City of Cheney Parks and
Recreation
520 4th Street
Cheney, WA 99004
(509) 235–7295

18 Foothills Trail

Endpoints: Buckley, Orting
Mileage: 8
Surface: asphalt, ballast

Location: Pierce
Contact: Ernest Bay
President
Foothills Rails-to-Trails Coalition
P.O. Box 192
Puyallup, WA 98371-0021
bugtrail@aol.com
www.piercecountytrails.org

19 Green to Cedar River Trail (Lake Wilderness Trail)

Endpoints: Maple Valley, Lake
Wilderness
Mileage: 4

Surface: ballast

Location: King
Contact: King County
Parks and Recreation Director
201 S. Jackson Street, Suite 700
Seattle, WA 98104
(206) 296–8687
www.metrokc.gov/parks

20 Iron Goat Trail

Endpoints: Mt. Baker
Snoqualmie National Forest
Mileage: 6
Surface: crushed stone, ballast

Location: King
Contact: Ian Ritchie
Archaeologist
Mt. Baker Snoqualmie National
Forest
Skykomish Ranger District
P.O. Box 305
Skykomish, WA 98288-0305
(206) 677–2412
www.bcc.ctc.edu/cpsha/
irongoat/default.htm

21 Iron Horse State Park

Endpoints: North Bend, Vantage
Mileage: 82
Surface: gravel, ballast

Other use: Dogsledding; llamas
Location: King; Kittitas

Contact: Keith Wersland
Park Ranger Iron Horse State
Parks
P.O. Box 26
Easton, WA 98925-0026
(509) 656–2586

22 Issaquah Creek Trail

Endpoints: High Point, Issaquah
Mileage: 2
Surface: ballast

Location: King
Contact: King County
Parks and Recreation Director
201 S. Jackson Street, Suite 700
Seattle, WA 98104
(206) 296–8687
www.metrokc.gov/parks

23 Issaquah Trail

Endpoints: Issaquah
Mileage: 2
Surface: concrete

Location: King
Contact: Margaret McCleod
Issaquah Parks and Recreation
Department
P.O. Box 1307
Issaquah, WA 98027
(425) 837–3322
margm@ci.issaquah.wa.us

24 Iverson Railroad Grade Trail

Endpoints: Tiger Mountain State
Forest

Mileage: 2
Surface: dirt

Location: King
Contact: Jim Matthews
Recreation Forester
Tiger Mountain State Forest
P.O. Box 68
Enumclaw, WA 98022-0068
(360) 825–1631

25 King County Interurban Trail

Endpoints: Tuckwila, Pacific
Mileage: 14
Surface: asphalt

Location: King
Contact: Tom Eksten
Trails Coordinator
King County Office
of Open Space
2040 Eighty-fourth Avenue S.E.
Mercer Island, WA 98040-2222
(206) 296–7808
www.metrokc.gov/parks/trails/
trails/integr.

26 Liberty Lake Stateline Trail

Endpoints: Spokane River
Centennial Trail at Spokane
Bridge Road and Appleway,
Appleway and Simpson Road
(Liberty Lake)
Mileage: 1.8
Surface: asphalt

Location: Spokane
Contact: Pat Harper
Spokane County
1026 W. Broadway Avenue
Spokane, WA 99260
(509) 477–3600
pharper@spokanecounty.org

27 Lower Padden Creek Trail

Endpoints: Bellingham
Mileage: 1
Surface: crushed stone

Location: Whatcom
Contact: Leslie Bryson
Design and Development
Manager
Bellingham Parks and
Recreation Department
3424 Meridian
Bellingham, WA 98225-1764
(360) 676–6985

28 Lower Yakima Valley Pathway

Endpoints: Grandview,
Sunnyside
Mileage: 6.4
Surface: asphalt

Location: Yakima
Contact: Dave Veley
Assistant Director
Yakima County Parks
1000 Ahtanum Road
Union Gap, WA 98903-1202
(509) 574–2430

29 Middle Fork Snoqualmie River Trail

Endpoints: Mt. Baker–
Snoqualmie National Forest
Mileage: 14.5
Surface: dirt, gravel

Location: King
Contact: William S. Sobieralski
Wilderness and Trails Program
Coordinator
U.S. Forest Service
Snoqualmie Ranger District
42404 S.E. North Bend Way
North Bend, WA 98045-9545
(425) 744–3563, ext. 239
bsobieralski@fs.fed.us

30 Myrtle Edwards Park Trail

Endpoints: Seattle
Mileage: 1.25
Surface: asphalt

Location: King
Contact: Peter Lagerwey
Bicycle/Pedestrian Coordinator
Seattle Transportation
Municipal Building, Room 410
600 Fourth Avenue
Seattle, WA 98104-1879
(206) 684–5108
pete.lagerwey@ci.seattle.wa.us
www.ci.seattle.wa.us/parks/
parkspaces/medwards.htm

31 Necklace Valley Trail

Endpoints: Skykomish
Mileage: 8
Surface: dirt

Location: King
Contact: Tom Davis
Trail Specialist
Snoqualmie National Forest
Skykomish Ranger District
P.O. Box 305
Skykomish, WA 98288-0305
(206) 677–2414

32 Northwest Timber Trail

Endpoints: North Bend
Mileage: 2.5
Surface: gravel, dirt

Location: King
Contact: Shirley Shuttle
Washington State Department of
Natural Resources
P.O. Box 68
Enumclaw, WA 98022
(360) 825–1631

33 Pacific Crest National Scenic Trail

Endpoints: Stevens Pass, Yodelin
Mileage: 36
Surface: dirt

Location: Chelan
Contact: Roger Ross
Trails/Wilderness Coordinator

U.S. Forest Service
22976 Highway 207
Leavenworth, WA 98826
(509) 763–3103

34 Port Angeles Waterfront Trail

Endpoints: Port Angeles (Old
Rayonier Mill), Port Angeles (end
of Ediz Hook)
Mileage: 8
Surface: asphalt

Location: Clallam
Contact: John Hicks
Recreation Manager
City of Port Angeles
Parks and Recreation
321 East Fifth Street
Port Angeles, WA 98362-3206
(360) 417–4552

35 Pratt River Trail

Endpoints: Mt. Baker–
Snoqualmie National Forest
Mileage: 7.5
Surface: ballast

Location: King
Contact: William Sobieralski
Wilderness and Trails Program
Coordinator
U.S. Forest Service
Snoqualmie Ranger District
(425) 744–3563, ext. 239
bsobieralski@fs.fed.us

36 Preston Railroad Trail

Endpoints: Tiger Mountain State Forest
Mileage: 32
Surface: crushed stone, gravel, dirt

Location: King
Contact: Jim Matthews
Recreation Forester
Tiger Mountain State Forest
P.O. Box 68
Enumclaw, WA 98022-0068
(360) 825–1631

37 Preston-Snoqualmie Trail

Endpoints: Preston, Snoqualmie
Mileage: 6.5
Surface: asphalt

Location: King
Contact: King County
Parks and Recreation Director
201 S. Jackson Street, Suite 700
Seattle, WA 98104
(206) 296–8687
www.metrokc.gov/parks

38 Railroad Trail

Endpoints: Bellingham, Memorial Park
Mileage: 4
Surface: crushed stone

Location: Whatcom
Contact: Leslie Bryson
Design and Development Manager
Bellingham Parks and Recreation Department
3424 Meridian
Bellingham, WA 98225-1764
(360) 676–6985

39 Scudder Pond Trail

Endpoints: Bellingham
Mileage: 0.5
Surface: crushed stone

Location: Whatcom
Contact: Leslie Bryson
Design and Development Manager
Bellingham Parks and Recreation Department
3424 Meridian
Bellingham, WA 98225-1764
(360) 676–6985

40 Seattle Waterfront Pathway

Endpoints: Seattle
Mileage: 0.8
Surface: asphalt

Location: King
Contact: Peter Lagerwey
Bicycle/Pedestrian Coordinator
Seattle Transportation
Seattle Municipal Building

600 Fourth Avenue, Room 410
Seattle, WA 98104-1879
(206) 684–5108
pete.lagerwey@ci.seattle.wa.us

41 Ship Canal Trail

Endpoints: Seattle
Mileage: 2
Surface: asphalt

Location: King
Contact: Peter Lagerwey
Bicycle/Pedestrian Coordinator
Seattle Transportation
600 Fourth Avenue, Room 410
Seattle, WA 98104-1879
(206) 684-5108
pete.lagerwey@ci.seattle.wa.us

42 Snohomish County Centennial Trail

Endpoints: Arlington,
Snohomish/King county line
Mileage: 17
Surface: asphalt, dirt

Location: Snohomish
Contact: Mark Krandel
Park Planning Supervisor
Snohomish County Parks and
Recreation Department
9623 32nd Street S.E.
Everett, WA 98201-4060
(425) 388–6621
krandel@co.snohomish.wa.us
www.co.snohomish.wa.us/parks

43 Snoqualmie Valley Trail

Endpoints: Carnation,
Snoqualmie Falls
Mileage: 27.9
Surface: ballast

Location: King
Contact: King County
Parks and Recreation Director
201 S. Jackson Street, Suite 700
Seattle, WA 98104
(206) 296–8687
www.metrokc.gov/parks

44 South Bay Trail

Endpoints: Bellingham
Mileage: 4
Surface: asphalt, crushed stone,
concrete

Location: Whatcom
Contact: Leslie Bryson
Design and Development
Manager
Bellingham Parks and
Recreation Department
3424 Meridian
Bellingham, WA 98225-1764
(360) 676–6985

45 Spokane River Centennial Trail

Endpoints: Idaho state line, Nine Mile Falls
Mileage: 39
Surface: asphalt

Location: Spokane
Contact: Charlie Karb
Park Ranger 2
Riverside State Park
North 4427 A.L. White Parkway
Spokane, WA 99205
(509) 456–3964
www.spokanecentennialtrail.org

46 Spruce Railroad Trail (Lake Crescent Trail)

Endpoints: Olympic National Park
Mileage: 4
Surface: gravel, dirt

Location: Clallam
Contact: Polly Angelakis
Supervisor, Visitor Center
Olympic National Park
600 East Park Avenue
Port Angeles, WA 98362
(360) 452–0330
www.nps.gov/olym

47 Sylvia Creek Forestry Trail

Endpoints: Montesano
Mileage: 2.3

Surface: asphalt, dirt

Location: Gray's Harbor
Contact: Dan Kincaid
Park Manager
Lake Sylvia State Park
P.O. Box 701
Montesano, WA 98563
(360) 249–3621

48 Terminal 91 Bike Path (Elliot Bay Bike Trail)

Endpoints: Seattle
Mileage: 1
Surface: asphalt

Location: King
Contact: Bill Health
Property Manager
Port of Seattle
P.O. Box 1209
Seattle, WA 98111-1209
(206) 728–3379

49 Tommy Thompson Parkway

Endpoints: Anacortes
Mileage: 1
Surface: asphalt

Location: Skagit
Contact: Gary Robinson
Parks and Recreation Director
City of Anacortes
P.O. Box 547
Anacortes, WA 98221-0547
(360) 293–1918
gary@cityofanacortes.org

50 Two Mile Trail

Endpoints: Montesano
Mileage: 2
Surface: gravel, dirt

Location: Gray's Harbor
Contact: Dan Kincaid
Park Manager
Lake Sylvia State Park
P.O. Box 701
Montesano, WA 98563
(360) 249–3621

51 Wallace Falls Railway Trail

Endpoints: Wallace Falls State Park
Mileage: 2.5
Surface: grass, dirt

Location: Snohomish
Contact: Susan Evans
Park Ranger
Washington State Parks and
Recreation Commission
P.O. Box 230
Gold Bar, WA 98251-0230
(360) 793–0420

52 West Tiger Railroad Grade

Endpoints: West Tiger State Forest
Mileage: 4
Surface: ballast, dirt

Location: King
Contact: Jim Matthews
Recreation Forester
Tiger Mountain State Forest
P.O. Box 68
Enumclaw, WA 98022-0068
(360) 825–1631

53 Whatcom County and Bellingham Interurban Trail

Endpoints: Bellingham, Larrabee State Park
Mileage: 7
Surface: crushed stone

Location: Whatcom
Contact: Roger DeSpain
Director
Whatcom County Parks and
Recreation Board
3373 Mount Baker Highway
Bellingham, WA 98226-9522
(360) 733–2900

54 Yelm-Tenino Trail

Endpoints: Yelm, Rainier
Mileage: 7
Surface: asphalt

Location: Thurston
Contact: Michael Welter
Thurston County Parks and
Recreation
2617-A 12th Court S.W.
Olympia, WA 98502
(360) 786–5595
welterm@co.thurston.wa.us
www.thurston-parks.org

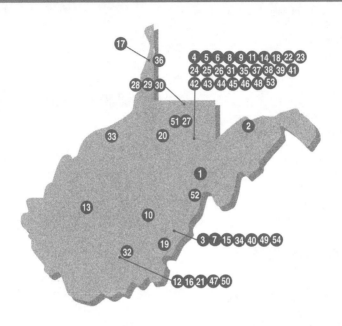

1 Allegheny Highlands Trail

Endpoints: Elkins, Parsons
Mileage: 21
Surface: asphalt, sand

Location: Randolph; Tucker
Contact: Karen Carper
President
Highland Trails Foundation
P.O. Box 2862
Elkins, WV 26241-2862
www.highlandstrail.org

2 Barnum Trail

Endpoints: Barnum, Hampshire
Mileage: 4
Surface: gravel, ballast

Location: Mineral
Contact: Rex Riffle
Director of County Properties
Mineral County Parks and
Recreation Commission
150 Armstrong Street
Keyser, WV 26726-3500
(304) 788–5732

3 Bear Pen Ridge Trail

Endpoints: Tea Creek Recreation Area
Mileage: 3.5
Surface: grass, dirt

Location: Pocahontas
Contact: Tim Henry
Assistant Ranger
Marlinton Ranger District
Tea Creek Recreation Area
P.O. Box 210
Marlinton, WV 24954-0210
(304) 799–4334

4 Big Stonecoal Trail

Endpoints: Monongahela National Forest
Mileage: 4.4
Surface: dirt

Location: Tucker
Contact: Carol Rucker
Assistant Ranger
Monongahela National Forest
Cheat Ranger District
P.O. Box 368
Parsons, WV 26287-0368
(304) 478–3251

5 Black Ridge Trail

Endponts: Monongahela National Forest
Mileage: 5
Surface: dirt

Location: Tucker
Contact: Carol Rucker
Assistant Ranger
Monongahela National Forest
Cheat Ranger District
P.O. Box 368
Parsons, WV 26287-0368
(304) 478–3251

6 Blackwater Canyon Trail

Endpoints: Monongahela National Forest
Mileage: 10.2
Surface: gravel, dirt

Location: Tucker
Contact: Judith Rodd
Friends of Blackwater
51 Elizabeth Street
Charlestown, WV 25311
(304) 345–7663
info@saveblackwater.org
www.saveblackwater.org/
recreational.htm

7 Boundary Trail

Endpoints: Tea Creek Recreation Area
Mileage: 3.8
Surface: grass, dirt

Location: Pocahontas
Contact: Tim Henry
Assistant Ranger
Marlinton Ranger District
Tea Creek Recreation Area
P.O. Box 210
Marlinton, WV 24954-0210
(304) 799–4334

8 Clover Trail

Endpoints: Monongahela National Forest
Mileage: 2
Surface: dirt

Location: Tucker
Contact: Carol Rucker
Assistant Ranger
Monongahela National Forest
Cheat Ranger District
P.O. Box 368
Parsons, WV 26287-0368
(304) 478–3251

9 County Line Trail

Endpoints: Monongahela National Forest
Mileage: 11.2
Surface: dirt

Location: Tucker
Contact: Carol Rucker
Assistant Ranger
Monongahela National Forest
Cheat Ranger District
P.O. Box 368
Parsons, WV 26287-0368
(304) 478–3251

10 Cranberry/Tri-Rivers Rail Trail

Endpoints: Richwood, Allingdale
Mileage: 26
Surface: crushed stone

Location: Nicholas; Webster
Contact: Bruce Donaldson
Rail-Trail Chairman
Richwood Area Chamber of Commerce
One East Main Street
Richwood, WV 26261-0796
(304) 846–6790
ktylerstirling@richwoodwv.com
www.wvrtc.org

11 Davis Trail (Engine Run Trail)

Endpoints: Monongahela National Forest
Mileage: 2.3
Surface: dirt

Location: Tucker
Contact: Carol Rucker
Assistant Ranger
Monongahela National Forest
Cheat Ranger District
P.O. Box 368
Parsons, WV 26287-0368
(304) 478–3251
www.wvrtc.org

12 Dunloup Creek Trail (Thurmond-Minden Connector)

Endpoints: New River Gorge National River
Mileage: 0.5
Surface: gravel, dirt

Location: Fayette
Contact: Cal Hite
Superintendent
New River Gorge National River

P.O. Box 246
Glen Jean, WV 25846-0246
(304) 465–0508
neri_interpretation@nps.gov
www.wvrtc.org

13 The Elk River Trail

Endpoints: Coonskin Park
Mileage: 1
Surface: gravel

Location: Kanawha
Contact: Tom Raker
Director
Kanawha County Parks and
Recreation Commission
2000 Coonskin Drive
Charleston, WV 25311-1087
(304) 341–8000
www.wvrtc.org

14 Flatrock Run Trail

Endpoints: Monongahela
National Forest
Mileage: 5.1
Surface: dirt

Location: Tucker
Contact: Carol Rucker
Assistant Ranger
Monongahela National Forest
Cheat Ranger District
P.O. Box 368
Parsons, WV 26287-0368
(304) 478–3251

15 Gauley Mountain Trail

Endpoints: Tea Creek Recreation
Area
Mileage: 5.2
Surface: gravel, dirt

Location: Pocahontas
Contact: Tim Henry
Assistant Ranger
Marlinton Ranger District
Tea Creek Recreation Area
P.O. Box 210
Marlinton, WV 24954-0210
(304) 799–4334

16 Glade Creek Trail

Endpoints: New River Gorge
National River
Mileage: 5.6
Surface: gravel, dirt

Location: Raleigh
Contact: Cal Hite
Superintendent
New River Gorge National River
P.O. Box 246
Glen Jean, WV 25846-0246
(304) 465–0508
neri_interpretation@nps.gov
www.wvrtc.org

17 Greater Wheeling Trail

Endpoints: Wheeling
Mileage: 8.5
Surface: asphalt

Location: Ohio
Contact: Tom Murphy
Planning Administrator
Department of Development
City-County Building
1500 Chapline Street
Wheeling, WV 26003-3553
(304) 234-3701
dod@hgo.net
www.cityofwheeling.com

18 Green Mountain Trail

Endpoints: Monongahela
National Forest
Mileage: 4
Surface: dirt

Location: Tucker
Contact: Carol Rucker
Assistant Ranger
Monongahela National Forest
Cheat Ranger District
P.O. Box 368
Parsons, WV 26287-0368
(304) 478-3251

19 Greenbrier River Trail

Endpoints: North Caldwell, Cass
Mileage: 75
Surface: gravel, ballast

Location: Greenbrier;
Pocahontas

Contact: Pocahontas County
Convention and Visitors Center
P.O. Box 275
Marlinton, WV 24954
(800) 336-7009

20 Harrison County Parks & Recreation Bike and Hike Trail

Endpoints: North View
Mileage: 7
Surface: gravel, grass, cinder

Location: Harrison
Contact: Michael Book
Director
Harrison County Parks and
Recreation Commission
Harrison County Courthouse
Room 238
Clarksburg, WV 26301-2980
(304) 624-8619
www.wvrtc.org

21 Kaymoor Trail

Endpoints: New River Gorge
National River
Mileage: 1.8
Surface: gravel, dirt

Location: Fayette
Contact: Cal Hite
Superintendent
New River Gorge National River
P.O. Box 246
Glen Jean, WV 25846-0246
(304) 465-0508

neri_interpretation@nps.gov
www.wvrtc.org

22 Laurel Fork River Trail—South

Endpoints: Monongahela
National Forest
Mileage: 9.6
Surface: dirt

Location: Tucker
Contact: Carol Rucker
Assistant Ranger
Monongahela National Forest
Cheat Ranger District
P.O. Box 368
Parsons, WV 26287-0368
(304) 478–3251

23 Laurelly Branch

Endpoints: Monongahela
National Forest
Mileage: 3.4
Surface: dirt

Location: Tucker
Contact: Carol Rucker
Assistant Ranger
Monongahela National Forest
Cheat Ranger District
P.O. Box 368
Parsons, WV 26287-0368
(304) 478–3251

24 Limerock Trail

Endpoints: Monongahela
National Forest
Mileage: 4.1
Surface: dirt

Location: Tucker
Contact: Carol Rucker
Assistant Ranger
Monongahela National Forest
Cheat Ranger District
P.O. Box 368
Parsons, WV 26287-0368
(304) 478–3251

25 Little (Black) Fork Trail

Endpoints: Monongahela
National Forest
Mileage: 3.5
Surface: dirt

Location: Tucker
Contact: Carol Rucker
Assistant Ranger
Monongahela National Forest
Cheat Ranger District
P.O. Box 368
Parsons, WV 26287-0368
(304) 478–3251

26 Lumberjack Trail

Endpoints: Monongahela National Forest
Mileage: 3.3
Surface: dirt

Location: Tucker
Contact: Carol Rucker
Assistant Ranger
Monongahela National Forest
Cheat Ranger District
P.O. Box 368
Parsons, WV 26287-0368
(304) 478–3251

27 Marion County Trail (MCTRAIL)

Endpoints: Prikets Fort State Park, Fairmont
Mileage: 2
Surface: gravel, cinder

Location: Marion
Contact: Marion County Parks and Recreation Commission
P.O. Box 1258
Fairmont, WV 26555-1258
(304) 363–7037
mcparc@access.mountain.net
www.wvtrc.org

28 Mon River Rail Trail System (Caperton Trail)

Endpoints: Morgantown City Limits, Star City Limits
Mileage: 6
Surface: asphalt, crushed stone

Location: Monongalia
Contact: Ella Belling
Mon River Trails Conservancy
P.O. Box 4157
Star City, WV 26504
(304) 293–2941, ext. 2414
montrail@montrails.org
www.montrails.org

29 Mon River Rail Trail System (Deckers Creek Trail)

Endpoints: Morgantown (Hazel Ruby McQuain Park), Reedsville
Mileage: 19
Surface: asphalt, crushed stone

Location: Monongalia; Preston
Contact: Mon River Trails Conservancy
P.O. Box 4157
Star City, WV 26504
(304) 293–2941, ext. 2414
montrail@montrails.org
www.montrails.org

30 Mon River Rail Trail System (Mon River Trail South)

Endpoints: Morgantown City Limits, Pricketts Fort State Park
Mileage: 17.7
Surface: crushed stone

Location: Marion; Monongalia
Contact: Mon River Trails Conservancy
P.O. Box 4157
Star City, WV 26504
(304) 293–2941, ext. 2414
montrail@montrails.org
www.montrails.org

31 Moore Run Trail

Endpoints: Monongahela National Forest
Mileage: 4.1
Surface: dirt

Location: Tucker
Contact: Carol Rucker
Assistant Ranger
Monongahela National Forest
Cheat Ranger District
P.O. Box 368
Parsons, WV 26287-0368
(304) 478–3251

32 Narrow Gauge Trail

Endpoints: Babcock State Park, Old Sewell Road
Mileage: 2.5
Surface: crushed stone, dirt

Location: Fayette
Contact: Richard Morris
Superintendent
Babcock State Park
HC-35, Box 150
Clifftop, WV 25831-9000
(304) 438–3004
www.wvtrc.org

33 North Bend State Park Rail-Trail

Endpoints: Parkersburg, Walker
Mileage: 72
Surface: crushed stone, gravel, dirt

Other use: Horse-drawn carriage
Location: Doddridge; Harrison; Ritchie; Wood
Contact: Scott Fortney
Supervisor
North Bend State Park Rails to Trails
P.O. Box 221
Cairo, WV 26337
(304) 643–2931
www.wvweb.com/www/travel_recreation/state_parks/north_bend_rail/north_bend_rail.htm

34 North Face Trail

Endpoints: Tea Creek Recreation Area
Mileage: 3.1
Surface: grass, dirt

Location: Pocahontas
Contact: Tim Henry

Assistant Ranger
Marlinton Ranger District
Tea Creek Recreation Area
P.O. Box 210
Marlinton, WV 24954-0210
(304) 799–4334

35 Otter Creek Trail

Endpoints: Monongahela
National Forest
Mileage: 11.4
Surface: dirt

Location: Tucker
Contact: Carol Rucker
Assistant Ranger
Monongahela National Forest
Cheat Ranger District
P.O. Box 368
Parsons, WV 26287-0368
(304) 478–3251

36 Panhandle Trail (WV Section)

Endpoints: Colliers, WV, WV/PA
state line
Mileage: 4.4
Surface: crushed stone

Location: Brooke; Hancock;
Washington
Contact: David Cline
Panhandle Trail Association
269 South 12th Street
Weirton, WV 26062
dcline@weir.net
www.panhandletrail.org

37 Possession Camp Trail

Endpoints: Monongahela
National Forest
Mileage: 3.3
Surface: dirt

Location: Tucker
Contact: Carol Rucker
Assistant Ranger
Monongahela National Forest
Cheat Ranger District
P.O. Box 368
Parsons, WV 26287-0368
(304) 478-3251

38 Railroad Grade Trail

Endpoints: Elkins, Davis
Mileage: 4
Surface: dirt

Location: Randolph; Tucker
Contact: Carol Rucker
Assistant Ranger
Cheat Ranger District
P.O. Box 368
Parsons, WV 26287-0368
(304) 478–3251

39 Red Creek Trail

Endpoints: Monongahela
National Forest
Mileage: 6.1
Surface: dirt

Location: Tucker
Contact: Carol Rucker
Assistant Ranger
Monongahela National Forest
Cheat Ranger District
P.O. Box 368
Parsons, WV 26287-0368
(304) 478–3251

40 Red Run Trail

Endpoints: Tea Creek Recreation Area
Mileage: 2.5
Surface: grass, dirt

Location: Pocahontas
Contact: Tim Henry
Assistant Ranger
Marlinton Ranger District
Tea Creek Recreation Area
P.O. Box 210
Marlinton, WV 24954-0210
(304) 799–4334

41 Rocky Point Trail

Endpoints: Monongahela National Forest
Mileage: 1.8
Surface: dirt

Location: Tucker
Contact: Carol Rucker
Assistant Ranger
Monongahela National Forest
Cheat Ranger District
P.O. Box 368
Parsons, WV 26287-0368
(304) 478–3251

42 Rohbaugh Plains Trail

Endpoints: Monongahela National Forest
Mileage: 3.5
Surface: dirt

Location: Tucker
Contact: Carol Rucker
Assistant Ranger
Monongahela National Forest
Cheat Ranger District
P.O. Box 368
Parsons, WV 26287-0368
(304) 478–3251

43 Rough Run Trail

Endpoints: Monongahela National Forest
Mileage: 3
Surface: dirt

Location: Tucker
Contact: Carol Rucker
Assistant Ranger
Monongahela National Forest
Cheat Ranger District
P.O. Box 368
Parsons, WV 26287-0368
(304) 478–3251

44 Senaca Creek Trail

Endpoints: Monongahela National Forest
Mileage: 5
Surface: dirt

Location: Tucker
Contact: Carol Rucker
Assistant Ranger
Monongahela National Forest
Cheat Ranger District
P.O. Box 368
Parsons, WV 26287-0368
(304) 478–3251

45 Shingletree Trail

Endpoints: Monongahela
National Forest
Mileage: 1.4
Surface: dirt

Location: Tucker
Contact: Carol Rucker
Assistant Ranger
Monongahela National Forest
Cheat Ranger District
P.O. Box 368
Parsons, WV 26287-0368
(304) 478–3251

46 South Prong Trail

Endpoints: Monongahela
National Forest
Mileage: 5.9
Surface: dirt

Location: Tucker
Contact: Carol Rucker
Assistant Ranger
Monongahela National Forest
Cheat Ranger District
P.O. Box 368
Parsons, WV 26287-0368
(304) 478–3251

47 Southside Junction– Brooklyn Trail

Endpoints: New River Gorge
National River
Mileage: 6.4
Surface: gravel, dirt

Location: Fayette
Contact: Cal Hite
Superintendent
New River Gorge National River
P.O. Box 246
Glen Jean, WV 25846-0246
(304) 465–0508
neri_interpretation@nps.gov
www.wvrtc.org

48 Stone Camp Run Trail

Endpoints: Monongahela
National Forest
Mileage: 1.5
Surface: dirt

Location: Tucker
Contact: Carol Rucker
Assistant Ranger
Monongahela National Forest
Cheat Ranger District
P.O. Box 368
Parsons, WV 26287-0368
(304) 478–3251

49 Tea Creek Trail

Endpoints: Tea Creek Recreation Area
Mileage: 7
Surface: grass, dirt

Location: Pocahontas
Contact: Tim Henry
Assistant Ranger
Marlinton Ranger District
Tea Creek Recreation Area
P.O. Box 210
Marlinton, WV 24954-0210
(304) 799–4334

50 Thurmond-Minden Trail

Endpoints: New River Gorge National River
Mileage: 3.2
Surface: gravel, dirt

Location: Fayette
Contact: Cal Hite
Superintendent
New River Gorge National River
P.O. Box 246
Glen Jean, WV 25846-0246
(304) 465–0508
neri_interpretation@nps.gov

51 West Fork Rail-Trail

Endpoints: Fairmont, Shinnston
Mileage: 16
Surface: crushed stone, cinder

Location: Harrison; Marion
Contact: Marion County Parks and Recreation Commission
P.O. Box 1258
Fairmont, WV 26555-1258
(304) 363–7037
mcparc@access.mountain.net
www.wvrtc.org

52 West Fork Trail

Endpoints: Durbin, Glady
Mileage: 24
Surface: crushed stone, ballast

Location: Pocahontas; Randolph
Contact: Gary Willison
Assistant District Ranger
Monongahela National Forest
Greenbrier Ranger District
P.O. Box 67
Bartow, WV 24920-0067
(304) 456–3335

53 Whitemeadow Ridge Trail

Endpoints: Monongahela
National Forest
Mileage: 4.6
Surface: dirt

Location: Tucker
Contact: Carol Rucker
Assistant Ranger
Monongahela National Forest
Cheat Ranger District
P.O. Box 368
Parsons, WV 26287-0368
(304) 478–3251

54 Williams River Trail

Endpoints: Tea Creek Recreation
Area
Mileage: 2.5
Surface: gravel, dirt

Location: Pocahontas
Contact: Tim Henry
Assistant Ranger
Marlinton Ranger District
Tea Creek Recreation Area
P.O. Box 210
Marlinton, WV 24954-0210
(304) 799–4334
Trailnet88@aol.com

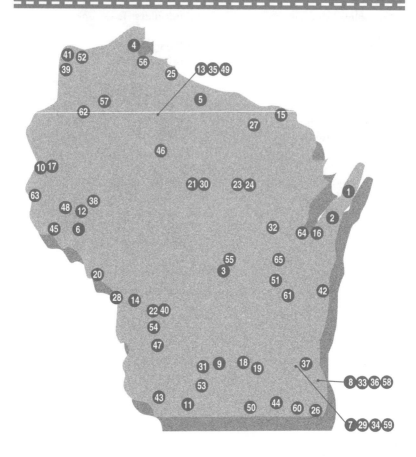

1 Ahnapee State Park Trail

Endpoints: Village of Casco in Kewaunee County, downtown Sturgeon Bay in Door County
Mileage: 27.7
Surface: crushed stone

Location: Door; Kewaunee

Contact: Jean Romback-Bartels
Park Manager
Ahnapee State Park Trail
c/o Potawatomi State Park
3740 Park Drive
Sturgeon Bay, WI 54235-9091
(920) 746–2890
www.ahnapeetrail.org

2 Algoma to Casco Junction

Endpoints: Algoma, Casco junction

Mileage: 12.4
Surface: crushed stone

  (wheelchair)

Location: Kewaunee
Contact: Jean Romback-Bartels
Park Manager
Ahnapee State Park Trail
c/o Potawatomi State Park
3740 Park Drive
Sturgeon Bay, WI 54235-9091
(920) 746–2890

3 Bannerman Trail

Endpoints: Red Granite, 5 miles
south of Wautoma
Mileage: 7
Surface: grass, dirt

Location: Waushara
Contact: Scott Schuman
Parks Superintendent
Waushara County Parks
Wautoma, WI 54982
(262) 787–7037

4 Bayfield County Snowmobile Trail

Endpoints: Washburn, Hayward
Mileage: 65
Surface: ballast

Location: Bayfield; Sawyer
Contact: Patricia Thornton
Snowmobile Coordinator

Bayfield County Tourism and
Recreation
P.O. Box 832
Washburn, WI 54891
(800) 472–6338
tourbc@win.bright.net
www.travelbayfieldcounty.com

5 Bearskin State Park Trail

Endpoints: Minocqua and
Heatford junction, Highway K
and Tomahawk
Mileage: 24.7
Surface: crushed stone

(wheelchair)

Location: Lincoln; Oneida
Contact: John Brandenburg
Trails Manager
Wisconsin Department of Natural
Resources
4125 Highway M
Boulder Junction, WI 54548
(715) 385–2727

6 Buffalo River State Park Trail

Endpoints: Fairchild, Mondovi
Mileage: 36.4
Surface: gravel, ballast, dirt

Other use: ATVs
Location: Buffalo; Eau Claire;
Jackson; Trempealeau
Contact: Jean Rygiel
Park and Recreation Specialist
Wisconsin Department of Natural

Resources, Western Division
1300 West Clairmont Avenue
P.O. Box 4001
Eau Claire, WI 54701-6127
(715) 839–1607
rygiej@dnr.state.wi.us

7 Bugline Trail

Endpoints: Menomonee Falls,
Merton
Mileage: 13
Surface: crushed stone

Location: Waukesha
Contact: David Burch
Senior Landscape Architect
Waukesha County Department of
Parks and Land Use
1320 Pewaukee Road, Room 230
Waukesha, WI 53188-3868
(414) 548-7790
dburch@groupwise.co.
www.waukeshacounty.gov/parks/
bugline.htm

8 Burlington Trail

Endpoints: Burlington, Rochester
Mileage: 4
Surface: crushed stone, gravel

Location: Racine
Contact: Tom Statz
Park Planning and Program
Director
Racine County Public Works
Department

14200 Washington Avenue
Sturtevant, WI 53177-1253
(414) 886–8440

9 Capital City Trail (Southwest Trail)

Endpoints: Madison, Fitchburg
Mileage: 3.9
Surface: asphalt, crushed stone

Location: Dane
Contact: Ken Lepine
Director
Dane County Parks
4318 Robertson Road
Madison, WI 53714-3123
(608) 246–3896
www.co.dane.wi.us/parks

10 Cattail Trail

Endpoints: Almena, Amery
Mileage: 17.8
Surface: gravel, ballast, dirt

Other use: ATV
Location: Barron; Polk
Contact: Sue Mathews
Manager
Polk County Information Center
710 Highway 35 South
St. Croix Falls, WI 54024
(800) 222–7655

11 Cheese Country Recreation Trail

Endpoints: Mineral Point, Monroe
Mileage: 47
Surface: crushed stone

Other use: ATVs
Location: Green; Iowa; Lafayette
Contact: Mike Doyle
Trail Coordinator
Tri-County Trail Commission
Courthouse Green County
Monroe, WI 53530
(608) 328–9430
www.state.wi.us/agencies/
tourism.html

12 Chippewa River State Trail

Endpoints: Eau Claire, Caryville
Mileage: 20
Surface: asphalt, crushed stone

Location: Eau Claire; Dunn
Contact: Jean Rygiel
Park and Recreation Specialist
Wisconsin Department of Natural
Resources, Western Division
1300 West Clairmont Avenue
P.O. Box 4001
Eau Claire, WI 54701-6127
(715) 839–1607
rygiej@dnr.state.wi.us

13 Clover Creek Trail

Endpoints: Chequamegon
National Forest
Mileage: 15.8
Surface: grass, dirt

Other use: ATVs
Location: Price
Contact: Victor Peterson
Forestry Technician
Chequamegon National Forest
1170 Fourth Avenue South
Park Falls, WI 54552-1921
(715) 762–2461

14 Elroy-Sparta State Park Trail

Endpoints: Elroy, Sparta
Mileage: 32
Surface: crushed stone

Location: Juneau; Monroe
Contact: Lenore Schroeder
Sub-Team Supervisor
Wisconsin Department of Natural
Resources
c/o Wildcat Mountain State Park
P.O. Box 99
Ontario, WI 54651
(608) 337–4775

15 Florence County Snowmobile Trail

Endpoints: Nicolet National Forest
Mileage: 130
Surface: gravel, dirt

Location: Florence
Contact: Jeffrey Herrett
Assistant District Ranger
Nicolet National Forest
USFS, Florence Ranger District
HC 1, Box 83
Florence, WI 54121-9764
(715) 528–4464

16 Fox River Trail

Endpoints: Colliers, Greenleaf
Mileage: 13.5
Surface: asphalt, crushed stone, grass

Location: Brown
Contact: Mike McFarlane
Brown County Park Department
305 East Walnut Street
Green Bay, WI 54301-5027
(920) 448–4465
McFarlene_MG@co.brown.wi.us

17 Gandy Dancer Trail

Endpoints: St. Croix Falls, Superior
Mileage: 97
Surface: crushed stone, ballast

Other use: ATVs
Location: Burnett; Douglas; Polk
Contact: Debbie Peterson
Director
Polk County Parks Department
100 Polk County Plaza, Suite 10
Balsam Lake, WI 54810
(715) 485–9272

18 Glacial Drumlin State Park Trail

Endpoints: Cottage Grove, Waukesha
Mileage: 51.6
Surface: asphalt, crushed stone

Location: Dane; Jefferson; Waukesha
Contact: Brian Hefty
Glacial Drumlin State Park
W329 N846 Co. C
Delafield, WI 53018
(262) 646–3025

19 Glacial River Trail

Endpoints: Fort Atkinson, Koshkonong
Mileage: 6.5
Surface: asphalt, crushed stone

Location: Jefferson

Contact: Joseph Nehmer
Director
Jefferson County Parks
Department
320 South Main Street
Courthouse, Room 204
Jefferson, WI 53549-1718
(920) 674–7260
joen@co.jefferson.wi.us

20 Great River State Park Trail

Endpoints: Onalaska,
Trempealeau National Wildlife
Refuge
Mileage: 4
Surface: crushed stone

Location: Buffalo; La Crosse;
Trempealeau
Contact: Lois Isaacson
Ranger
Perrot State Park
P.O. Box 407
Trempealeau, WI 54661-0407
(608) 534–6409

21 Hiawatha Trail (Bearskin-Hiawatha State Trail)

Endpoints: Tomahawk, Sara Park
Mileage: 5.6
Surface: crushed stone

Location: Lincoln
Contact: William Wengeler
County Forestry Administrator

Lincoln County Forestry Land and
Parks
1106 East Eighth Street
Merrill, WI 54452-1100
(715) 536–0327

22 Hillsboro Trail

Endpoints: Hillsboro, Union
Center
Mileage: 4.3
Surface: crushed stone

Location: Juneau
Contact: Dale Dorow
Administrator
Juneau County Forest and Parks
Department
250 Oak Street
Mauston, WI 53948-1365
(608) 847–9390

23 Ice Age Trail—Lumber Camp Segment

Endpoints: Langlade County
Forest
Mileage: 9.2
Surface: gravel, ballast

Location: Langlade
Contact: Michael Sohasky
County Forest Administrator
Langlade County Forestry
Department
P.O. Box 460
Antigo, WI 54409-0460
(715) 627–6236

24 Ice Age Trail—Old RR Segment

Endpoints: Langlade County Forest
Mileage: 9.2
Surface: gravel, ballast

Location: Langlade
Contact: Michael Sohasky
County Forest Administrator
Langlade County Forestry
Department
1633 Neva Road
Antigo, WI 54409-0460
(715) 627–6300

25 Iron Horse Trail

Endpoints: Manitowish Frontier Campground
Mileage: 55
Surface: gravel

Other use: ATVs
Location: Iron
Contact: Tom Salzmann
Forest Administrator
Iron County Forestry Office
603 Third Avenue
Hurley, WI 54534-1012
(715) 561–2697

26 Kenosha County Bike Trail

Endpoints: Racine county line, Illinois state line
Mileage: 14.2
Surface: asphalt, crushed stone

Location: Kenosha
Contact: Ric Ladine
Director of Parks
Kenosha County Parks
P.O. Box 549
Bristol, WI 53104-0549
(414) 857–1862

27 Kimball Creek Trail

Endpoints: Nicolet National Forest
Mileage: 12
Surface: ballast

Other use: Dog sledding
Location: Forest
Contact: Bill Reardon
Forestry Technician
Nicolet National Forest
Eagle River Ranger District
P.O. Box 1809
Eagle River, WI 54521-1809
(715) 479–2827

28 La Crosse River State Park Trail

Endpoints: La Crosse; Sparta
Mileage: 23
Surface: crushed stone

Location: La Crosse; Monroe
Contact: Jim Moorhead
Park Ranger
Wildcat Mountain State Park
Work Unit
P.O. Box 99
Ontario, WI 54651-0099
(608) 337–4775

29 Lake Country Recreation Trail

Endpoints: Delafield, Waukesha
Mileage: 8
Surface: asphalt, crushed stone

Location: Waukesha
Contact: David Burch
Senior Landscape Architect
Waukesha County Department of
Parks and Land Use
1320 Pewaukee Road, Room 230
Waukesha, WI 53188-3868
(414) 548–7790
dburch@groupwise.co.
waukesha.wi.us

30 Lincoln County Snowmobile Trail

Endpoints: Tomahawk,
Lincoln/Price county line
Mileage: 15
Surface: ballast

Location: Lincoln
Contact: William Wengeler
County Forestry Administrator
Lincoln County Forestry
Land and Parks
1106 E. Eighth Street
Merrill, WI 54452-1100
(715) 536–0327

31 Military Ridge State Park Trail

Endpoints: Dodgeville, Verona
Mileage: 39.6
Surface: crushed stone

Location: Dane; Iowa
Contact: Cindy Delkamp
Manager
Wisconsin Department
of Natural Resources
c/o Blue Mounds State Park
4350 Mounds Park/P.O. Box 98
Blue Mounds, WI 53517-0098
www.military.ridge@mail01.dnr.
state.wi.us

32 Mountain-Bay State Trail (Delly Trail)

Endpoints: Duck Creek (near
Green Bay), Kelly (near Wausau)
Mileage: 83.4
Surface: crushed stone

Other use: ATV
Location: Brown; Marathon;
Shawano
Contact: Pat Vail
Shawano County Parks
Department
311 North Main Street
Shawano, WI 54166
(715) 526–6766

33 MRK Trail

Endpoints: Racine, Caledonia
Mileage: 5
Surface: crushed stone, gravel, ballast

Location: Racine
Contact: Tom Statz
Park Planning and Programming
Director
Racine County Public Works
Department
14200 Washington Avenue
Sturtevant, WI 53177-1253
(414) 886–8440

34 New Berlin Trail

Endpoints: Waukesha
(Springdale Road), West Allis
(S. 24th Street)
Mileage: 7
Surface: crushed stone

Location: Waukesha
Contact: David Burch
Senior Landscape Architect
Waukesha County Department of
Parks and Land Use
1320 Pewaukee Road, Room 230
Waukesha, WI 53188-3868
(414) 548–7790
dburch@groupwise.co.
www.waukeshacounty.gov/parks/
newberlin

35 North Flambeau Cycle Trail

Endpoints: Chequamegon
National Forest
Mileage: 23
Surface: dirt

Other use: ATVs
Location: Price
Contact: Victor Peterson
Forestry Technician
Chequamegon National Forest
1170 Fourth Avenue S.
Park Falls, WI 54552-1921
(715) 762–2461

36 North Shore Trail

Endpoints: Racine, Kenosha
county line
Mileage: 3
Surface: crushed stone, gravel

Location: Racine
Contact: Tom Statz
Park Planning and Programming
Director
Racine County Public Works
Department
14200 Washington Avenue
Sturtevant, WI 53177-1253
(414) 886–8440

37 Oakleaf Trail (old-76 bike tour)

Endpoints: Milwaukee
Mileage: 96.4
Surface: asphalt

Location: Milwaukee
Contact: Paul Hathaway
Associate Director of Parks
Milwaukee County Parks
9480 Watertown Plank Road
Wauwatosa, WI 53226-3560
(414) 257–6100
parksmke@execpc.com

38 Old Abe Trail

Endpoints: Chippewa Falls, Cornell
Mileage: 19.7
Surface: asphalt, ballast

Location: Chippewa
Contact: Jean Rygiel
Park and Recreation Specialist
Wisconsin Department of Natural
Resources, Western Division
1300 West Clairmont Avenue
P.O. Box 4001
Eau Claire, WI 54701-6127
(715) 839–1607
rygiej@dnr.state.wi.us

39 Oliver-Wrenshall Trail

Endpoints: Oliver-Wrenshall, Minnesota
Mileage: 12
Surface: grass, dirt

Other use: ATVs
Location: Carlton; Douglas
Contact: Mark Schroeder
Resource and Recreation
Manager
Douglas County Forestry
Department
P.O. Box 211
Solon Springs, WI 54873-0211
(715) 378–2219

40 Omaha Trail

Endpoints: Camp Douglas, Elroy
Mileage: 12.5
Surface: asphalt, gravel

Location: Juneau
Contact: Dale Dorow
Administrator
Juneau County Forest and Parks
Department
250 Oak Street
Mauston, WI 53948-1365
(608) 847–9390
dottsl@yahoo.com

41 Osaugie Trail

Endpoints: Superior
Mileage: 2.2
Surface: asphalt, gravel

Location: Douglas
Contact: Superior Parks and
Recreation Department
1409 Hammond Avenue
Superior, WI 54880
(715) 394–0270

42 Ozaukee Interurban Trail

Endpoints: Ozaukee/Sheboygan
county line, Brown Dear
Mileage: 30
Surface: asphalt

Location: Ozaukee
Contact: www.interurbantrail.us/
index2.htm

43 Pecatonica State Park Trail

Endpoints: Calamine, Belmont
Mileage: 10
Surface: crushed stone

Other use: ATVs, golf carts
Location: Grant; Lafayette
Contact: Mike Doyle
Trail Coordinator
Tri-County Trail Commission
Green County Courthouse
Monroe, WI 53530
(608) 328–9430

44 Pelishek Nature Trail

Endpoints: Clinton, Allens
Grove, Darien
Mileage: 7
Surface: gravel, ballast, sand

Location: Rock; Walworth
Contact: Tom Kautz
Director
County of Rock Parks and
Conservation Division
3715 Newville Road
Janesville, WI 53545-8844
(608) 757–5450
kautz@co.rock.wi.us

45 Pierce County Snowmobile Trail

Endpoints: Plum City, River Falls
Mileage: 221
Surface: ballast, grass

Location: Pierce
Contact: Scott Schoepp
Snowmobile Coordinator
Pierce County Snowmobile Trail
c/o Nugget Lake County Park
N4351 County Road HH
Plum City, WI 54761
(715) 639–5611

46 Pine Line Trail (Taylor County Snowmobile Trail)

Endpoints: Medford, Prentice
Mileage: 25.9
Surface: grass, gravel, crushed stone

Other uses: ATVs
Location: Price; Taylor
Contact: Brad Ruesch
County Forest Administrator
Taylor County Forestry Parks and Recreation
224 South Second Street
Medford, WI 54451
(715) 748–1486
BRuesch@mail.co.taylor.wi.us

47 Pine River Trail

Endpoints: Lone Rock, Richland Center
Mileage: 14.2
Surface: crushed stone

Location: Richland
Contact: Bonnie Gruber
Natural Resources Specialist
Wisconsin Department of Natural Resources
PR/1
P.O. Box 7921
Madison, WI 53707-7921
(608) 267–7459

48 Red Cedar State Trail

Endpoints: Menomonie, The Dunnville Wildlife Area
Mileage: 14.5
Surface: crushed stone

Location: Dunn; Eau Claire
Contact: James Janowak
Manager
Red Cedar State Trail
921 Brickyard Road
Menomonie, WI 54751-9100
(715) 232–1242

49 Riley Lake Snowmobile Trail

Endpoints: Chequamegon National Forest
Mileage: 23
Surface: grass, dirt

Other use: ATV
Location: Price
Contact: Victor Peterson
Forestry Technician
Chequamegon National Forest
1170 Fourth Avenue, South
Park Falls, WI 54552-1921
(715) 762–2461

50 Rock River Parkway Trail

Endpoints: Janesville, Beloit
Mileage: 1.9
Surface: crushed stone

Location: Rock
Contact: Tom Presny
Director of Parks
Janesville Leisure Services
17 North Franklin Street
Janesville, WI 53545-2917
(608) 755–3025

51 Rush Lake Trail (Greenlake, Winnebago, Ripon Trails)

Endpoints: Berlin, Ripon
Mileage: 10.3
Surface: ballast

Location: Winnebago
Contact: Robert Way
Parks Director
Winnebago County Parks
Department
625 E. County Road Y
Suite 500
Oshkosh, WI 54901-9774
(920) 232–1960
rway@co.winnebago.wi.us

52 Saunders Grade Recreation Trail

Endpoints: Superior, Douglas
Mileage: 8.4
Surface: ballast

Location: Douglas
Contact: Mark Schroeder
Resource and Recreation
Manager
Douglas County Forestry
Department
P.O. Box 211
Solon Springs, WI 54873-0211
(715) 378–2219

53 Sugar River State Park Trail

Endpoints: New Glarus,
Brodhead
Mileage: 23.5
Surface: crushed stone

Location: Green
Contact: Steve Colden
Park Manager
Sugar River State Park Trail
W5446 City Highway NN
P.O. Box 805
New Glarus, WI 53574
(608) 527–2335
coldes@dnr.state.wi.us

54 The 400 State Trail

Endpoints: Elroy, Reedsburg
Mileage: 22.3
Surface: crushed stone

Location: Juneau; Sauk
Contact: Jim Moorhead
Park Ranger
Wildcat Mountain State Park
Work Unit
P.O. Box 99
Ontario, WI 54651-0099
(608) 337–4775

55 Tomorrow River State Trail

Endpoints: Plover, Amherst junction
Mileage: 15
Surface: crushed stone

Location: Portage
Contact: Gary Speckmann
Portage County Park Commission
1462 Strongs Avenue
Stevens Point, WI 54481-3501
(715) 346–1433
www.dnr.state.wi.us/org/land/parks/specific

56 Tri-County Corridor

Endpoints: Ashland, Superior
Mileage: 61.8
Surface: crushed stone, ballast

Other use: ATVs, hunting
Location: Ashland; Bayfield; Douglas
Contact: Richard Mackey
Executive Director

Tri-County Recreational Corridor
Commission
Ashland, WI 54806
(800) 472–6338

57 Tuscobia State Trail

Endpoints: Park Falls, Rice Lake
Mileage: 74
Surface: gravel, ballast, grass

Other use: ATV
Location: Barron; Price; Sawyer; Washburn
Contact: Raymond Larsen
Superintendent
Tuscobia State Park Trail
10220 North State Road 27
Hayward, WI 54843-9505
(715) 634–6513

58 Waterford-Wind Lake Trail

Endpoints: Waterford, Wind Lake
Mileage: 5
Surface: crushed stone, gravel

Location: Racine
Contact: Tom Statz
Park Planning and Programming Director
Racine County Public Works Department
14200 Washington Avenue
Sturtevant, WI 53177-1253
(414) 886–8440

59 Waukesha Bike Trails

Endpoints: Madison, Waukesha
Mileage: 60
Surface: asphalt, crushed stone

Location: Dana; Jefferson; Waukesha
Contact: David Kopp
City Planner
Waukesha City Planning
Room 200
201 Delafield Street
City Hall
Waukesha, WI 53188-3690
(414) 524–3752

60 White River State Trail

Endpoints: Elkhorn, Lyons
Mileage: 9
Surface: crushed stone

Location: Walworth
Contact: Walworth County
Department of Public Works
W4097 County Road N.N.
Elkhorn, WI 53121
www.dnr.state.wi.us/org/land/
parks/specific/whiteriver/
index.htm

61 Wild Goose State Trail

Endpoints: Clyman Junction, Fond du Lac
Mileage: 34
Surface: asphalt, crushed stone

Location: Dodge; Fond du Lac
Contact: Sam Tobias
Director
Fond du Lac County Planning
and Parks Department
160 South Macy Street
Fond du Lac, WI 54935-4241
(920) 929–3135
joanne.nitz@co.fond-du-lac.wt.us
www.dodgecountywi.com

62 Wild Rivers State Trail

Endpoints: Rice Lake, Superior
Mileage: 90
Surface: ballast

Location: Barron; Douglas; Washburn
Contact: Terry Jordan
Northern Regional Trails
Coordinator
Wisconsin Department of Natural
Resources—Northern Region
810 West Maple
Spooner, WI 54801
(715) 635–4121
jordat@mail01.dnr.state.wi.us

63 Wildwood Trail

Endpoints: Woodville South
through Eau Galle, Spring Valley
(St. Croix county line)
Mileage: 7.6
Surface: gravel, dirt, cinder

Location: St. Croix
Contact: Sue Nelson
County Clerk
Government Center
1101 Carmichael Road
Hudson, WI 54016
(715) 386–4600
suen@co.saint-croix.wi.us
www.co.saint-croix.wi.us/
departments/countypark/wild

64 WIOUWASH Trail—North

Endpoints: Aniwa, New London
Mileage: 20
Surface: crushed stone

Location: Outagamie; Shawano;
Waupaca
Contact: Gary Hanson
Regional Trails Coordinator
Wisconsin Department of Natural
Resources
1125 N. Military Avenue
Green Bay, WI 54303-4413
(920) 492–5823
hansog@dnr.state.wi.us

65 WIOUWASH Trail—South

Endpoints: Hortonville, Oshkosh
Mileage: 23
Surface: crushed stone

Location: Outagamie;
Winnebago
Contact: Christopher Brandt
Director
Outagamie County Parks
1375 E. Broadway Drive
Plamann Park
Appleton, WI 54915
(414) 832–4790
cbrandt48@aol.com

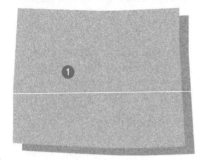

1 Wyoming Heritage Trail

Endpoints: Riverton, Shoshoni
Mileage: 22
Surface: asphalt, ballast

Other use: ATVs
Location: Fremont
Contact: Lewis Diehn
Fremont County Recreation
Board
213 East Lincoln
Riverton, WY 82501

Appendix: State Trail Planners

Alabama
Jon Strickland
Recreation Programs Manager
Department of Economic and
Community Affairs
401 Adams Avenue, Suite 580
P.O. Box 5690
Montgomery, AL 36103-5690
(334) 242–5483
jons@adeca.state.al.us

Alaska
Kim Kruse
Trails Administrator
Alaska State Parks
Division of Parks and Outdoor
Recreation
3601 C Street, Suite 1280
Anchorage, AK 99503-5921
(907) 269–8704
ronc@dnr.state.ak.us

Arizona
Eric Smith
State Trails Coordinator
Arizona State Parks
1300 West Washington
Phoenix, AZ 85007
(602) 542–7116
esmith@pr.state.az.us

Arkansas
Steve Weston
Transportation Study Coordinator
Arkansas Highway and
Transportation Department
P.O. Box 2261
Little Rock, AR 72203-2261
(501) 569–2020
steve.weston@ahd.state.ar.us

California
Odel King, Jr.
Manager
Department of Parks and
Recreation
Local Assistance Section
1416 Ninth Street, Room 918
P.O. Box 942896
Sacramento, CA 94296-0001
(916) 653–8758
oking@parks.ca.gov

Colorado
Stuart Macdonald
State Trails Coordinator
Colorado Division of Parks and
Outdoor Recreation
1313 Sherman Street, Room 618
Denver, CO 80203-2240
(303) 866–3203
mactrail@aol.com

Connecticut
Leslie Lewis
Environmental Analyst
Department of Environmental
Protection
State of Connecticut
79 Elm Street. 6th Floor
Hartford, CT 06106
(860) 424–3081
leslie.lewis@po.state.ct.us

Delaware
Susan Moerschel
Manager
Division of Parks and Recreation
89 King's Highway
Dover, DE 19903-1401
(302) 739–5285
smoerschel@state.de.us

District of Columbia
Theodore Pochter
Chief, Planning and Design
Department of Recreation and
Parks, Policy and Planning Division
3149 Sixteenth Street, N.W.
4th Floor
Washington, DC 20010-3302
(202) 673–7692
tedp@dcpr.dcgov.org

Florida
Alexandra Weiss
Community Assistance Consultant
Office of Greenways and Trails
3900 Commonwealth Boulevard
Tallahassee, FL 32303-4113
alexandra_weiss@dep.state.fl.us

Georgia
Alicia Soriano
Trails Coordinator, Planning
Department of Natural Resources
205 Butler Street S.E., Suite 1352
Atlanta, GA 30334-4910
(404) 656–6530
alicias@mail.dnr.state.ga.us

Hawaii
Curt Cottrell
Program Manager
Department of Land and Natural
Resources
1151 Punchbowl Street
Kalanimoku Building
Honolulu, HI 96813
(808) 587–0062

Idaho
Brian Miller
State Trails Coordinator
Idaho Department of Parks and
Recreation
5657 Warm Springs Avenue

P.O. Box 83720
Boise, ID 83720-0065
(208) 334–4180
bmiller@idpr.state.id.us

Illinois
Todd Hill
Bicycle and Pedestrian Program
Manager
Division of Highways, Department
of Transportation
2300 South Dirksen Parkway
Room 330
Springfield, IL 62764-0002
(217) 782–2148
hilltw@nt.dot.state.il.us

Richard Westfall
Supervisor, Trails and Greenways
Section
Department of Natural Resources
1 Natural Resources Way
Springfield, IL 62702-1271
(217) 782–3715
dwestfall@dnrmail.state.il.us

Indiana
Bob Bronson
Chief/Outdoor Recreation Planning
State and Community Outdoor
Recreational Planning Department
of National Resources
402 West Washington Street,
Room W271
Indianapolis, IN 46204-2212
(317) 232–4070
bbronson@dnr.state.in.us

Iowa
Steve Bowman
Trails Coordinator
Iowa Department of Transportation,
Office of Systems Planning
800 Lincoln Way
Ames, IA 50010-6993

(515) 239–1337
steve.bowman@dot.state.ia.us

Kansas
Gerald Hover
Director of State Parks
Kansas State Parks
512 S.E. Twenty-fifth Avenue
Pratt, KS 67124-8174
(316) 672–5911
JerryRH@wp.state.ks.us

Kentucky
Buddy Renaker
State Trail Coordinator
Department of Local Government,
Division of Financial Services
1024 Capital Center Drive
Suite 340
Frankfurt, KY 40601-8204
(502) 573–2382
buddy.renaker@mail.state.ky.us

Louisiana
Matthew Rovira
Director of Programs
Governor's Office of Community
Programs
P.O. Box 94004
Baton Rouge, LA 70804-9004
(225) 342–0332
matt.rovira@doa.state.la.us

Maine
Mike Gallagher
Grants and Community Recreation
Division
Maine Bureau of Parks and Land
Department of Conservation
State House Station #22
Augusta, ME 04333-001
(207) 287–2163
mike.gallagher@state.me.us

Maryland
Terry Maxwell
Recreation Trail Coordinator
Maryland State Highway
Administration
Office of Environmental Design
707 N. Calvert Street
Mailstop C-303
P.O. Box 717
Baltimore, MD 21203-0717
(410) 545–8640
tmaxwell@sha.state.md.us

Massachusetts
Gary Briere
Recreation Bureau Chief
Division of Forests and Parks,
Department of Environmental
Management
251 Causeway Street
600
Boston, MA 02114-2119
(508) 792–7716
gary.briere@state.ma.us

Michigan
Jim Radabaugh
State Trails Coordinator
Department of Natural Resources,
Forest Management Division
Stevens T. Mason Building
P.O. Box 30452
Lansing, MI 48909-7952
(517) 373–1275
radabauj@michigan.gov

Minnesota
Tim Mitchell
Grants Specialist
Minnesota Department of Natural
Resources, Trails and Waterways
Division
500 Lafayette Avenue
St. Paul, MN 55126
(651) 297–1718
tim.mitchell@dnr.state.mn.us

Mississippi
Robert Boxx
Recreational Trails Program
Administrator
Department of Wildlife, Fisheries,
and Parks
1505 Eastover Drive
Jackson, MS 39211-6374
(601) 432–2225
tommyb@mdfwp.state.ms.us

Missouri
Chris Buckland
Grants Administrator
Department of Natural Resources,
Division of State Parks
P.O. Box 176, 1659 Elm Street
Jefferson City, MO 65102-0176
(573) 751–8462
nrbuckland@mail.dnr.state.mo.us

Montana
Bob Walker
Trails Program Coordinator
Montana Department of Fish,
Wildlife, and Parks
1420 East Sixth Avenue
P.O. Box 200701
Helena, MT 59620-0701
(406) 444–4585
bwalker@mt.gov

Nebraska
Duane Westerhoff
State Trail Coordinator
Nebraska Games and Parks
Commission
2201 N. 33rd Street
Lincoln, NE 68503-1417
(402) 471–5511
dwester@ngpc.state.ne.us

Nevada
Brad Eckert
Recreational Trails Program
Manager
Nevada Division of State Parks
1300 S. Curry Street
Carson City, NV 89706-0818
(775) 687–3845
rectrails@parks.state.nv.us

New Hampshire
Paul Gray
Chief, Bureau of Trails
Division of Parks and Recreation
172 Pembroke Road
P.O. Box 1856
Concord, NH 03302-1856
(603) 271–3254
pgray@dred.state.nh.us

New Jersey
Larry Miller
Trails Coordinator
New Jersey Department of
Environmental Protection and
Energy Division of Parks and
Forestry
22 South Clinton Street, CN 404
P.O. Box 404
Trenton, NJ 08625-0404
(609) 984–1014
larry.miller@dep.state.nj.us

New Mexico
Sandra Massengill
Planner/Director
State Parks Division, EMNRD
Pinon Building, 2nd Floor
1220 South Saint Francis Drive
P.O. Box 1147
Santa Fe, NM 87505-1147
(505) 476–3392
smassengill@state.nm.us

New York
Robert Reinhardt
Director of Planning
Parks, Recreation, and Historic
Preservation
Empire State Plaza, Building #1
Albany, NY 12238
(518) 474–0415
robert.reinhardt@oprhp.state.ny.us

North Carolina
Darrell McBane
State Trails Coordinator
Division of Parks and Recreation
12700 Bayleaf Church Road
P.O. Box 27687
Raleigh, NC 27614-9633
(919) 846–9995
darrell_mcbane@ncmail.net

North Dakota
Dan Schelske
Recreation Planner
Parks and Recreation Department
1835 East Bismarck Expressway
Bismarck, ND 58504-6708
(701) 328–5369
dschelske@state.nd.us

Ohio
William Daehler
Research Administrator
Department of Natural Resources,
Division of Real Estate and Land
Management
1952 Belcher Drive C-4
Columbus, OH 43224-1386
(614) 265–6402
bill.daehler@dnr.state.oh.us

Oklahoma
Susan Henry
Planning Coordinator
Oklahoma Tourism and Recreation
Department
Planning and Development Division
15 North Robinson, Suite 100
Oklahoma City, OK 73102
(405) 521–2904
shenry@otrd.state.ok.us

Oregon
Susan Loughran
State Trail Coordinator
Oregon Parks and Recreation
Department
1115 Commercial Street N.E.
Suite 1
Salem, OR 97310-1000
(503) 378–6378
susan.loughran@state.or.us

Pennsylvania
Scott Cope
Pennsylvania Department of
Conservation and Natural
Resources
P.O. Box 8475
Harrisburg, PA 17105-8475
(717) 772–3319
sccope@state.pa.us

Rhode Island
Richard Tierney
Trails Program Specialist
Rhode Island Department of
Environmental Management
235 Promenade Street
Providence, RI 02908
(401) 222–2776
rtierney@dem.state.ri.us

South Carolina
Wendy Coplen
Trail Coordinator
South Carolina Department of
Parks, Recreation, and Tourism,
State Trails Program
1205 Pendleton Street, Room 246
Columbia, SC 29201-3731
(803) 734–0130
wcoplen@scprt.com

South Dakota
Scott Carbonneau
Trails Program Specialist
South Dakota Department of
Game, Fish, and Parks
Division of Parks and Recreation
523 E. Capitol Avenue
Pierre, SD 57501-3182
(605) 773–6671
scott.carbonneau@state.sd.us

Tennessee
Kay Vance
Greenways and Trails Coordinator
Department of Environmental
Conservation, Recreation and
Education Services
401 Church Street
L & C Tower, 10th Floor
Nashville, TN 37243
(615) 532–0755
kvance@mail.state.tn.us

Texas
Andrew Goldbloom
Greenways Program Administrator
Texas Parks and Wildlife Division
4200 Smith School Road
Austin, TX 78744-3291
(512) 389–4737

Utah
John Knudson
Trails Program Coordinator
Utah Division of Parks and
Recreation
1594 West North Temple, Suite 116
Box 14001
Salt Lake City, UT 84116-3156
(801) 538–7344
nrdpr.jknudson@state.ut.us

Vermont
Sherry Smecker
Recreation and Trails Administrative
Assistant
Department of Forests, Parks, and
Recreation
103 S. Main Street, 10 South
Waterbury, VT 05671-0604
(802) 241–3690
ssmecker@fpr.aner.state.vt.us

Virginia
Jerry Cassidy
Grant Administrator
Department of Conservation and
Recreation
203 Governor Street, Suite 326
Richmond, VA 23219
(804) 786–3218
jcassidy@dcr.state.va.us

Washington
Greg Lovelady
Recreation Resource Planner
Interagency Committee for
Outdoor Recreation
1111 Washington Street S.E.
P.O. Box 40917
Olympia, WA 98504-0917
(360) 902–3008
GregL@iac.wa.gov

West Virginia
Bill Robinson
Grants Administrator
West Virginia Department of
Transportation
1900 Kanawha Boulevard East
Building 5, Room 863
Charleston, WV 25305
(304) 558–3165
wrobinson@dot.state.wv.us

Wisconsin
Larry Freidig
Manager
Motorized Recreation Grant
Programs
Bureau of Community Assistance
P.O. Box 7921
Madison, WI 53707
(608) 266–5897
freidl@dnr.state.wi.us

Wyoming
Kim Raap
Trails Program Manager
Wyoming Division of State Parks
Herschler Building, First N.E.
122 W. Twenty-fifth Street
Cheyenne, WY 82002
(307) 777–7550
kraap@state.wy.us

Puerto Rico
Cesar de Jesus
Trails Coordinator
Department of Recreation and
Sports
Fomento Cooperative
Box 3207
San Juan, Puerto Rico 00902-3207
(787) 725–2396

RAILS
- to -
TRAILS
CONSERVANCY

Welcome to an American adventure...

Rails-to-Trails Conservancy (RTC) was created in 1986 to preserve former railroad corridors and recycle them into public trails. Imagine... a nationwide network of trails connecting our city centers to the countryside and countless communities to each other... a network linking neighborhoods to workplaces and congested areas to open spaces... a system serving transportation needs and meeting the demand for close-to-home recreation.

This is not a dream, but a vision shared by Rails-to-Trails Conservancy and its members across the country and throughout the world. When Rails-to-Trails Conservancy opened its door, with the goal of making this vision a reality, there were a mere few thousand miles of rail-trails. Today, there are nearly 13,000 open miles on more than 1,200 rail-trails.

Throughout the years RTC has:

* provided countless hours of assistance to community groups, local governments and regional park authorities,
* defended trail-friendly policies, such as "railbanking," in front of the Congress and the Supreme Court,
* advocated on the local, state and national level for trail funding,
* secured miles and miles of corridors for trail conversion,
* produced numerous resources and meetings for trail professionals, and
* been *the* leader of the rail-trail movement.

Rails-to-Trails Conservancy is a nonprofit charitable organization that depends on the generous contributions from individuals and organizations to help achieve our purpose. It is our members' support — through membership contributions and additional gifts — that provides the resources we need to continue our work to enhance our society with a nationwide network of trails and greenways. We cannot accomplish this without you.

It's easy to support the rail-trail movement. Simply…

✳ Be a member of Rails-to-Trails Conservancy — today, tomorrow and next year. Your RTC member benefits include our quarterly magazine, special discounts and the satisfaction of knowing you're leaving a legacy of trails linking yesterday with the future.

✳ Extend your generosity beyond your membership and give additional contributions to RTC throughout the year. These — and all your contributions — are extremely important in providing the critical resources needed for our core trail building programs.

✳ Purchase RTC merchandise — including rail-trail guidebooks, T-shirts, bike jerseys and more — from our online store at www.railtrails.org, where every purchase helps support our work.

✳ Make a planned gift or bequest to RTC. This is a great way to ensure the future of rail-trails.

To join Rails-to-Trails Conservancy,
further your support or request more information,
visit RTC Membership on our Web site at www.railtrails.org
or call 866-202-9788.

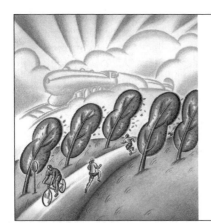

The purpose of
Rails-to-Trails Conservancy

To enrich America's communities
and countryside by creating a
nationwide network of public
trails from former rail lines and
connecting corridors.

Your Rails-to-Trails Conservancy Member Benefits

Thank you for supporting Rails-to-Trails Conservancy (RTC). As a member of RTC, you will receive several benefits designed to help you enjoy your time on and off the trail.

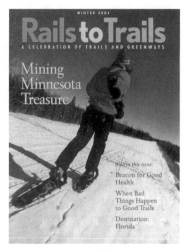

- ✳ FOUR ISSUES, a one year subscription, of *Rails to Trails*, RTC's full-color magazine celebrating trails and greenways
- ✳ DISCOUNTS on rail-trail guidebooks, clothing and gift items
- ✳ 10% DISCOUNT on GORE™ BikeWear apparel featuring GORE-TEX® and WINDSTOPPER® fabrics (and 25% of your purchase price is contributed to RTC!)
- ✳ OPPORTUNITY to carry the RTC credit card and help support rail-trails every time you shop

Yet, the most important benefit of a Rails-to-Trails Conservancy membership is satisfaction — the satisfaction of knowing that your dollars are helping to create a network of trails throughout the country. Member support has helped put more than 12,000 rail-trail miles on the ground. Each of your dollars helps us help the rail-trail community, secure the future of rail-trails and enhance America's communities and countryside.

Only a Rails-to-Trails Conservancy member can get that special feeling of satisfaction...and every time you're on a rail-trail it will make the journey even more enjoyable.

To join, contribute or renew your membership, send a check payable to RTC to the address below. To charge your membership gift, order books or merchandise or to get more information, call us at 1-866-202-9788 or visit www.railtrails.org.

Happy trails!

Please visit our Web site, www.railtrails.org for the latest member benefits.
Rails-to-Trails Conservancy is a charitable organization, which means your contributions are tax-deductible.